THE
LAST LANDSCAPE

This book came about because William H. Whyte was born in the Brandywine Valley of Pennsylvania, which he declares "the most beautiful countryside in America." Viewing its imminent despoliation in the fifties, he wondered how, practically, the valley and places like it could be saved. After publication of THE ORGANIZATION MAN, IS ANYBODY LISTENING? and THE EXPLODING METROPOLIS, he decided to spend full time finding answers.

He became a prime mover in the action he writes about. His pioneering work on easements led to the passage of major open space statutes in many states. He drafted the innovative conservation program enacted in Connecticut. Working with Laurance S. Rockefeller and the American Conservation Association, he produced the highly influential book, CLUSTER DEVELOPMENT. He was a member of President Johnson's Task Force on Natural Beauty, and authored the proposal later enacted by Congress as the Urban Beautification Program. Out of his experience comes the basic optimism expressed in this book.

THE
LAST LANDSCAPE

>>>

William H. Whyte

ANCHOR BOOKS

DOUBLEDAY & COMPANY, INC.

GARDEN CITY, NEW YORK

1970

The Last Landscape was originally
published in a hardbound edition by
Doubleday & Company, Inc. in 1968.

Anchor Books edition: 1970

Contents

>>>

THE
LAST LANDSCAPE

1. Introduction

>>>

This book is about the way our metropolitan areas look and
the way they might look. Its thesis is that they are going to
look much better, that they are going to be much better
places to live in, and that one of the reasons they are is that
a lot more people are going to be living in them.

Many thoughtful observers believe the opposite is true.
They hold that not only is the landscape of our cities and
suburbs a hideous mess, as indeed much of it is, but that it
is bound to become much worse. The saturation point has
been reached, they say, and unless growth and population
trends are redirected, our metropolitan areas will become
fouler yet. Some think they are beyond redemption already
and that the only real hope is to start afresh, somewhere
else, with new towns and cities.

But there is a good side to the mess. We needed it. It is
disciplining us to do out of necessity what we refused to do
by choice. We have been the most prodigal of people
with land, and for years we wasted it with impunity. There

was so much of it, and no matter how much we fouled it, there was always more over the next hill, or so it seemed.

For all our romantic veneration of the frontier tradition, however, we were steadily moving closer together. Well before 1900, most Americans were living in cities, and the great growth of the metropolitan areas that we think is so recent was well under way. Much more growth was yet to come, but by the twenties the trolley lines and commuter railroads had pushed the outer edge of suburbia almost as far as it is today.

In filling out the metropolis, however, we treated land as though we were in fact on the frontier. With the great postwar expansion of suburbia in the forties and fifties, we carried this to the point of caricature. We were using five acres to do the work of one, and the result was not only bad economics but bad aesthetics. People began to feel that if things looked this awful, something had gone wrong. At last we were having our noses rubbed in it.

The less of our landscape there is to save, the better our chances of saving it. It is a shame we have to lose so much land to learn the lesson, but desecration does seem a prerequisite for action. People have to be outraged. Most of the new land-use legislation and the pioneering programs did not come about as the result of foresighted, thoughtful analysis. They came about because people got mad over something they could see. Some of the most significant legislation can be traced to a small local outrage—a line of trees being chopped down for a highway, a meadow being asphalted for a parking area.

The quality of the environment was becoming a gut issue, and politicians sensed it well. The result was a wave of public programs. Starting in 1961 with New York State's open-space bond issue of $75 million, voters began approving bond issues and additional taxes for the saving of open space. They approved them by large pluralities, city people especially.

During this period there was a significant shift of emphasis in Washington toward the needs of city people. The report of the Outdoor Recreation Resources Review

Commission marked a notable turn in this respect. When Congress established the Commission in 1958 it expected a traditional approach to recreation, with the emphasis on the big open spaces and national parks; as a matter of fact, it specifically excluded city areas from the study. The Commission looked at them just the same. It had to. The simple, close-to-home activities, it discovered, are by far and away the most important to Americans. The place to meet this need, said chairman Laurance S. Rockefeller, is where most Americans live—in the cities and suburbs.

Congress was coming around to this way of thinking. In 1961 a modest grant program for urban open spaces had been proposed by Senator Harrison Williams; for a number of extraneous reasons (including an over-violent attack on it by Senator Everett Dirksen) the proposal wound up as part of the 1961 Housing Act. Several years later Congress set up the Land and Water Conservation Fund that had been recommended by ORRRC. These new programs and those of the states did not earmark as much grant money for cities as cities would have liked, but far more was being sent their way than had ever been sent before. More yet came with President Johnson's "natural beauty" programs. Terminology to the contrary, these dealt more with man-made beauty than nature and were directed primarily at the urban areas.

Almost as important as the money programs were a succession of state acts broadening the public's control powers over land use. Measures that would have seemed wildly socialistic only a decade or so before were being approved by state legislators with remarkably little controversy, and often by unanimous vote. Many of these statutes are still sleepers and local governments are only now beginning to realize what has been handed them. But the powers are considerable and the first court tests have been favorable. Communities can, among other things, use the right of eminent domain to acquire not only land outright but rights in private land; in the form of easements, they can buy away from landowners the right to build along roadsides or stream banks; or they can buy for the public the right to fish along the stream, communities can also buy land and then sell it or lease it back to people who will use it the way the community wants them to. There are techniques for buying open space on the installment plan, and for fouling up speculators' plans. In terms of need, let it be said, nowhere near enough money has yet been provided, and certainly more legislation is needed. But let us count some blessings. With the tools at hand, there is a tremendous amount we can do to make the metropolis more amenable, and we can do it now.

Others have a more apocalyptic vision. Some say that we are on the threshold of a "post-industrial society"—i.e. it's a whole new ball game now—and that entirely new forms of living must be devised. They see a breakthrough in environmental planning with teams of specialists applying systems analysis and computer technology to create the city of the future. A number of people have already begun jumping the gun, and in the recent upsurge of futurology have been devoting great energy and imagination to anticipating what forms these cities will take. Even the popular magazines are now full of pictures of megacities, stilt cities, linear cities, and such.

Some are to be located far, far away from any place. A government-aided research project has just been launched for the planning of an "Experimental City" to be located somewhere in Minnesota or the Great Plains. Dr. Athelstan Spilhaus, the prime mover of the project, visualizes a self-contained city with a population limit of 250,000 people. The city would test a host of technological advances. Many of its functions would be put underground and possibly a transparent dome two miles in diameter might be constructed. Dr. Spilhaus, who thinks present cities are something of a lost cause, believes that Experimental City can be the progenitor of many such settlements.

These visions are not like those of the science-fiction writers, whose mordant utopias have a nasty way of crossing up the people who devise them. They are clearly meant to be beneficent. The forms of them differ: some stick up into the sky, much like Le Corbusier's "Radiant City" of the twenties; some are domes; others are horizontal, consisting of a single eight- or ten-tiered building stretching miles and miles across the landscape. But they are all alike in one fundamental respect. The slate on which they are drawn has been wiped absolutely clean. In the perspective renderings of them, there is no trace of what once was. The old cities appear to have vanished, and in the great sea of greenness in which the new ones are seen, even the traces of today's suburbia are extinguished.

Far out as these visions may seem, they are only a projection of current planning orthodoxies, and the same decentralist, clean-slate urge they manifest is to be found in many of the metropolitan plans that are now being drafted for the year 2000 (the third millennium—what an emboldening ring it has!). As a first step, planners draw detailed projections as to the number of people to be housed in the year 2000, what their incomes will be, their work week, pleasure hours and so on. Their graphs are surprisingly precise. Some even extend to the year 2020.

Whatever prophecy is in this book is for the short term. It is difficult enough to look ten years ahead, and for the life of me I do not see how anyone can hope to say with any exactitude how people are going to be living some thirty-five years hence. Computer technology may make it more fun to try but it is not going to give us the gift of prophecy previously withheld.

What is being fed into the machines is a set of rather questionable assumptions. What comes out is an extrapolation of the trends of the last twenty years—surging population, increasing affluence, and more leisure. Maybe these will continue. Maybe they will not. The very unanimity and assurance with which these projections are made should be enough to make one quite nervous. As I will suggest in a later chapter, by trying to meet the problems of surging prosperity, we may have let ourselves in for a gigantic cross-up.

But planners are a sanguine lot. They have taken literally Daniel Burnham's admonition to make no little plans, and like him they believe that a noble design once set on paper will have the capacity to bring about its reality. These fatuous maxims have been beggared by reality time and again, but faith in the grand design is stronger than ever.

To arrive at it, the planners hypothesize a number of alternatives. The first will be termed "unplanned growth" or "semi-planned growth" or "planned sprawl." Actually, this will be the most challenging alternative to work with, since there is a fair chance something like it will come about. It is anathema to planners, however, some of whom would as soon go to hell with a comprehensive plan as heaven without one. They go on to sketch the grand designs, such as rings of satellite cities, radial corridors, or wedges. After the pros and cons of each are matched against the others, the optimum is chosen. Whatever its geometrics, it will call for a sweeping rearrangement of the region with its growth dispersed into self-contained new cities, each separated from the other by huge expanses of open space.

Designs can indeed help shape growth, but only when the designs and growth are going in the same direction. Most of the year 2000 plans are essentially centrifugal— that is, they would push everything outward away from the city, decentralize its functions, and reduce densities by spreading the population over a much greater land area. I think the evidence is staring us in the face that the basic growth trends are in the other direction; that they are toward greater centralization and toward higher rather than lower density.

There will be no brief here for letting the free market decide how we are going to grow, but where people and institutions are putting their money is a phenomenon worthy of respect, and planning which goes against the grain usually comes a cropper. The English, who have far more stringent land controls than we do, have been doing their best to constrain London, but the beast keeps growing. Most thinking Frenchmen agree that Paris is much too big in relation to the rest of the country, and Paris keeps growing. The Russians have been doing everything they can to curb Moscow, and it keeps on growing.

Maybe there is a reason. This kind of growth is not so unplanned. It is the result of a multitude of planning decisions by individuals and groups, and not some blind, lemminglike urge. Consider, for example, the great office building boom that has taken place in our cities. After the war it was widely prophesied that there would be a wholesale exodus of managerial people from the city as businesses resettled in campuses out in the country. Business proceeded to concentrate more managerial and service people in the city than ever before—and in the most crowded, highest-priced part of it. Each year alarmed observers warned that the saturation point had now been reached and that for sanity's sake it had to stop. The load on the streets, on the trains, on restaurants, and on people's nerves was surely becoming intolerable. But more and more buildings went up, with big old buildings being torn down to put up bigger new buildings. It was crazy, perhaps, but somehow it seemed to work out.

At the same time, of course, metropolitan areas have been pushing outward along the periphery, and they will probably continue to. But there is a built-in limit to lateral extension, and I don't think that our metropolitan areas are going to congeal into one undifferentiated mess. They certainly do not have to. A metropolitan area can take care of a great many more people by only a very slight expansion of its radius. Once it is a certain size—say fifty miles across—a slight enlargement of the periphery will vastly increase the acreage, with each additional mile outward adding almost a fifth again as much area.

But outward expansion can be an extremely costly way to handle growth. If the trend to low density sprawl were to continue, the result would be what New York's Regional Plan Association calls Spread City—"not a true city because it lacks centers, nor a suburb because it is not a satellite of any city, nor is it truly rural because it is loosely covered with houses and urban facilities." This pattern scatters the places where people work as well as the homes they live in; it makes them utterly dependent on cars and unnecessarily lengthens the trip they have to make.

When commercial and job facilities are so scattered, the kind of concentration that makes possible a high level of urban services is ruled out. The facilities are all over the place, and you have to drive from one to get to the other. Each one serves a single function—a discount center here, a string of steak ranches there—and they are rarely massed so that the parts make a whole. The same thing applies to culture centers, museums, and libraries that have been going up. They are not being located in high-traffic areas; as the Regional Plan Association says, "Cheap land and monumentality of buildings seem to be the major criteria."

On the face it would appear that we are in for more of the same kind of scatteration; drive out along almost any fringe area and you can see the same wasteful pattern being repeated. Yet there are signs of a counter trend to centralization. By this I do not mean a return to one center, the old core center of the business district, but the growth of a number of centers, some of them based on older communities, some of them new.

So far, the new centers have been a largely unplanned phenomena. A good example is the huge complex of facilities that has been going up around the Valley Forge interchange outside Philadelphia. Twenty years ago it was a crossroads hamlet. Now it is filled with research laboratories, light industrial plants, shopping centers, and large scale motels. It is not an ideal center—you have to have a car to use any part of it—but it is indicative of the direction we are headed in. We are likely to see much more clustering of facilities and more emphasis on multipurpose centers. Shopping centers, for example, started as single-purpose facilities devoted almost entirely to retailing. Most of the new ones, however, embrace a large and mutually supported mixture of activities, theaters, convention facilities, recreation centers, and the like.

There is still, to be sure, a good bit of what could be

called strip growth along the highways. The string of electronic firms along Boston's circumferential Route 128 is the most notable example; similar growth is taking place along other beltways, but I think that the multipurpose center, like the one at Valley Forge, is likely to be the pattern of the future. There is, I must concede, some wishful thinking in this respect. Having just scolded planners for trying to predict too far ahead, I should be circumspect myself. But this much can be said. The move to high-density centers not only makes for a much better land-use pattern, it happens to be more economic for the commercial interests involved. Planning that seeks to strengthen this trend will be working with the grain rather than against it.

I think that the bulk of the significant growth is going to take place within our present metropolitan areas. I think we are going to see a build-up, not a fragmentation, of the core cities. There will be a filling in of the bypassed land in the gray area between the cities and suburbia and a more intensive development—a redevelopment, if you will—of suburbia itself. New towns, yes, but I will wager that the ones which work out will not be self-contained and that they will not be somewhere off in the hinterland. We are, in sum, going to operate our metropolitan areas much closer to capacity and with more people living on a given amount of land.

A prescription for disaster, some would say. The literature of planning and conservation—indeed, American literature in general—has a deep antiurban streak, and the very reason for the city concentration is viewed as its mortal defect. The terms carry their own censure—"insensate concentration," "urban overgrowth," "urbanoid"—and by epithet they take it as self-evident that people must pay a terrible price for living close together. Lately there has been much talk about experiments with rats that show that when they get crowded they get neurotic, and therefore, by implication, so must human beings. The bias is also evident in planning brochures and documentary films on the urban plight. The stock shots of bad things always show forms of concentration: telephoto shots of massed rooftops, telephoto shots of cars jammed on a freeway, shots of harried, nervous-looking people crowding sidewalks. None of this is supported with any research on actual human behavior, which is a pity, for there are some interesting questions to look into. If people do not like being crowded, why do they persist in going where they will be crowded? How much is too much?

But the questions are somewhat beside the point, and of all people we Americans probably have the least reason for fretting about them. Our densities are not high at all. They are low. In some of the slum sections of the city, to be sure, there are too many people crowded together. But overcrowding—which is too many people per room—is not the same thing as high density. The residential density in most of our cities is quite reasonable.

So is the density of the metropolitan areas around them. By European standards they are enviably underpopulated. The densest in this country are the metropolitan areas along the Boston-New York-Washington axis; the 150 counties that make up this Atlantic urban region contain 67,690 square miles and 43 million people. If this region was developed to the same average density as the western Netherlands, the number of people would be tripled. The comparison is an extreme one perhaps, but so is the difference in appearance. Our areas *look* more filled up than the ones that really are.

I am not arguing that it would be good to have many extra people, nor am I decrying the long-range importance of population control. In one of those unheralded shifts that confound analysis, Americans have lately begun having somewhat fewer babies than before and if the trend continues, the increase in population will not be as fearful as the demographers have forecast. But there still will be an increase. Even with the decline in the birth rate, enough babies have already been born to assure that there will be many millions more households for our metropolitan areas over the next twenty years.

There is no point bemoaning the fact. There is room for them. There is not too little land. There are not too many people. Together, our metropolitan areas take thirty thousand square miles—less than two percent of the total land area of the country—and within this thirty thousand square miles almost half the land is unused. Increasing density does not mean putting everyone in towers; it means making a much more intensive use of the land we have not been using, or using very well, and we would be the better were it done.

Our eyes are not a bad guide. The kind of land we find ugliest is not that which is overused but the land that is largely vacant or hardly used at all: worked out gravel pits, derelict waterfronts, obsolete freight yards, the scores of vacant lots, the rubbish-strewn areas underneath the high tension lines. (Probably the dreariest of all urban views is that of the Jersey flats, with its billboards all the more obscene for the emptiness around.) Almost as bad are the lands that are devoted to only one use, and only a fraction of the time at that. The great seas of asphalt around our shopping centers, for example, chew up enormous amounts of high-priced land, yet they are used to capacity only four days of each December.

But the very existence of this waste land means that our metropolitan areas have a great capacity for regeneration. The increased competition for land use is not a force for blight; it is a discipline for enforcing a much more economic use of land, and a more amenable one. Developers, for example, are now taking to a subdivision pattern that treats land much more sensitively and is far more attractive than the conventional pattern; they have been doing this not because planners and architects convinced them it was better—planners and architects have been trying to do that for years—but because land prices had finally gotten so high they had to adopt the new pattern to make money.

The same discipline is going to apply to open space as well as developed space. We should try to save all the big spaces we can get our hands on, but there are only so many left. From here on out we are going to have to work much more inventively with the smaller spaces, the over-looked odds and ends; we are going to have to rediscover the obsolescent rights of way that thread the metropolitan area. We must use all sorts of devices for conserving key features of the landscape that are in private hands. We must explore much more diligently the use of air rights, and of creating open spaces where none existed before. We must make the spaces more accessible to people—to their eyes most of all. To overstate the case, we will have to jam more people in and make them feel that they are not jammed.

We must seek not only space, but the effect of space —illusion, if you will. This calls for artifice, to be sure, but every good landscape has been the product of artifice. The English countryside, for example, was virtually invented by eighteenth-century landscape architects, and in applying their techniques they showed far more sophistication about reality and illusion than we show today.

We don't have to wait for the grand design. It is there already. The structure of our metropolitan areas has long since been set by nature and man, by the rivers and the hills, and the railroads and the highways. Many options remain, and the great task of planning is not to come up with another structure but to work with the strengths of the structure we have—and to discern this structure as people experience it in their everyday life. It is not an easy thing to comprehend nor to work with. There is no one clear image, but thousands of them. Grappling with these gritty realities, however, provides a far greater and more exciting challenge than the search for perfection some-where else.

Let me now sketch briefly the plan of the book. After a short look at the postwar mess and the turnabouts it led to, I take up some of the political realities of open space. One problem is that the people who are planning the way the open space of the metropolis is to be used and the people who are sitting on what is left of it are quite different parties. More divisive is the difference in local tax bases. The communities that already have fat tax revenues are the ones that get more industry and more taxes; the communities that have open space do not, and it is tax revenues, not open space, that they want.

For all the problems to be resolved, however, there is a great deal that can be done now to secure the key open spaces. I next take up the principal tools for doing this: the police power, the purchase of land, and such relatively unexploited variants as purchase and leaseback and the acquisition of easements on private property.

There is a surprisingly large gift potential. Many more landowners than one would think can be persuaded to give land, and thanks to changes in tax laws it is more to their self-interest to do so than before. To illustrate the possibilities, I will tell of a group that has set up what amounts to a door-to-door selling campaign to work on landowners. It is a presumptuous operation and a remarkably effective one. I conclude the section on saving open space by taking up the question of encroachment and how to make highway engineers and others keep their hands off the land once it is saved.

Part Two is about the planning of spaces. At this point let me interject a note about the use of the term "planners." By this I mean land-use planners, chiefly those employed by government agencies, either directly or as consultants. Since I refer to planners so often in the book, I have dispensed with repetitious qualifying phrases to the effect that they may belong to a particular school of thought. When I am criticizing planners, the reader will understand that I do not necessarily mean all planners, but simply those with whose views I differ. Good planners are the ones with whose views I agree. This does not sound well put so baldly, but one might as well be frank.

In the case of open-space planning, there are several very different schools of thought. One holds that open space is chiefly useful as a means for shaping planners' plans. This is more or less the dominant view, and I think it is a very bad one. The best illustrations are the year

2000 plans being drawn up for metropolitan areas. Some of these channel development into neat geometric patterns by laying down vast swaths of open space. But just how are these open spaces to be secured? They are not going to be secured, for they bear very little relation to the ground or to the market forces for development. Some have already come a cropper thirty-five years before their target date.

Another school of thought, so far confined to a handful of people, believes that open-space planning should take its cue from the patterns of nature itself—the water table, the flood plains, the ridges, the woods, and, above all, the streams. They have come up with some ingenious techniques for applying this approach to specific places. I think these people are right and that there is strong evidence to prove that their way works and that the other way does not. The English green belt experience is particularly relevant in this respect, and I will devote a chapter to the history of this experiment and the lessons that it has for us.

The trouble with the generalized green belt approach is that it asks for too much land and without justifying it. We will not save much open space that way. In a chapter on linkage I argue that we must concentrate on the smaller spaces, the irregular bits and pieces, and especially those that we can connect together. There are an amazing number of connective links right under our noses if we will only look for them—old aqueducts, abandoned canals, railroad rights of way, former streams the engineers have put in concrete troughs.

In Part Three, Development, I turn to the other side of the coin. When I first got into open-space work, the general idea was to get as much of it as possible and to let developers take the hindmost. But this is tackling only half the problem. Open space and development are reciprocals; if we expect to save much more open space in the future, we are going to have to be equally concerned with finding more compact ways of developing the space that has to be developed. There are some encouraging trends in this respect, notably cluster development, and we are now being treated to the odd spectacle of developers pleading with towns to let them give half of their tracts away as community open space.

After exploring the pros and cons of cluster development to date, I look at the "new town" movement. In its purest form the "new town" is supposed to be an independent, self-sufficient community out in the hinterland and it is to have all of the advantages of the metropolis and none of the disadvantages. It is an unattainable goal, and a good thing too. It would be insufferably dull. Some superb new communities are going up under the "new town" banner, notably Reston and Columbia, but they are not new towns in the pure sense and will probably end up as good places to live in.

I next explore the most interesting question these prototypes pose, which is, how do we have great big projects which do not seem like great big projects? As a side note, I will go into the way architects and planners are handling space within the new communities. There is some very imaginative work being done, but if children are any guide, there is much still to be learned; the children seem to play almost everywhere except where they were meant to.

Part Four is about the landscape. For all practical purposes this is what we see from the road, and a sorry hash have we made of it. We have an excellent chance to reclaim it; we have the latent zoning power to curb desecration by billboards, and more positively we have both authority and money to widen the scenic corridor. The billboard lobby has been the principal block to progress, but almost as serious a problem has been bureaucratic inertia. To illustrate, I will note the fate of the Section 319 funds, some hundreds of millions of dollars that Congress made available for improving roadsides but which, because of administrative sabotage, has been used almost entirely for concrete. The highway engineers now say they have religion and are talking about building a new system of

scenic roads. We should look over their shoulders very
carefully.

There are great opportunities for local action, and
thanks to several new but little-known programs the machinery is at hand for realizing them. Such programs need
not be scorned as "cosmetic"; they call more for pruning
than adding. The trouble with the landscape of the rural
fringe, to this observer, at least, is that there are *too many*
trees and shrubs—more than there were a century ago—
and as farms have been reverting to second growth the
view of the countryside is being smothered by a dank and
lugubrious mass of greenery. It needs to be uncovered.

Moving inward toward the city, the opportunities are
of a different order—the reclamation of quarries, the de-
cluttering of town entrances, the opening up of urban
waterfronts. But in the city as in suburbia, the big task is
to get governments to think about these opportunities; to
inventory the strengths and weaknesses of the townscape
and landscape, and from eye-level view, the way people
see it. The record of most cities is miserable in this respect.

There are many things that I do not go into in this book:
mass transportation, air and water pollution, noise, the
handling of solid wastes. I do not grapple with the problem of the slums or of economic growth. I do not do justice to the immensely important and complex problems of
governmental machinery, or of the ways these problems
can be tackled in concert, which assuredly they must be.

But we need not be paralyzed by the enormity of it all.
The land-use measures that I take up are only parts, but
they are very determining parts, and the choices they
present are immediate. Whatever shape our future plans
may take, the kind of environments we are going to have
in 1985, or in 2000, will depend on the land-use decisions
that we will be making in the relatively few years ahead.
Our choices are many, but they are forced choices.

2. The Politics of Open Space

>>>

The less of our landscape there is to save, I have argued, the better our chance of saving it. I want to amplify this point by giving a brief account of how the postwar mess became so horrendous, and the action the mess finally prompted. I will follow this up with a look at some of the conflicting parties at interest, and the political dilemmas that are still to be resolved between them.

Let me start with my home county, Chester County, Pennsylvania. It is an unusually beautiful expanse of rolling countryside—to some eyes, and not just my own, the most beautiful in all the country—but its growth problems have been those of any semirural area on the edge of the metropolis. In the early 1950s, its eastern flank, only twenty miles from Philadelphia, had been suburbanized, but the great bulk of the countryside was still largely untouched. Much of the farmland was very good farmland, and it was, if anything, getting better. One of the foremost watershed associations of the country, the Brandywine

Valley Association, was proving tremendously effective in getting landowners to follow soil practices and erosion-control measures. Most of the hillside cropland was plowed in contoured strips. Farm ponds were being constructed. The banks of the innumerable brooks that laced the area were being planted with roses. Wood lots were being thinned of underbrush. Brooks that once ran muddy after every rainstorm flowed clear and sweet. Never had the valley been so well cared for or so beautiful.

But for whom was the land being saved? It was being made all the richer a prize for developers, but there was a widespread feeling that they could be made to go somewhere else. Most of the townships were zoning the open land for minimum lots of two to four acres. That would do the trick, they thought, and other measures would be unnecessary. For a while the county did join with the suburban counties around Philadelphia in a regional planning commission (from which Philadelphia was excluded) but soon withdrew because it felt its problems were much different from the others. Nor did it feel the need for any strong planning program of its own. A young planner was hired, but right-wing citizens raised a great fuss about the socialistic menace of planning. The planner was given nothing to do and shortly left.

Private conscience, rather than public action, was expected to save the land. One would be told, as in many similar areas, that the landowners simply were not the kind who would sell out. They cared much too deeply about the land; many of them were the third, fourth, or fifth generation on the land, and the "new people" who had been buying gentlemen farms would certainly not sell either. If anyone did sell, the large-lot zoning would keep the bad element away. Mass developers, people like the Levitts, were the ones to watch out for, and the zoning would surely keep them at bay.

It did. The damage was done by the locals; the farmer who sold off a few acres; the contractor who bought it and put up a string of cinder-block ranchers; the couple who opened a frozen-custard stand by the old covered bridge; the local officials who had the bridge torn down and a concrete one put up to carry the extra traffic created by the people in the cinder-block ranchers.

The defilement was for a pittance. Characteristically, the farmer would sell much too early for his own good, when land prices were just beginning their real move. Worse yet, by selling his frontage land, he would seal off the rest to later, better, and more remunerative development.

The citizens who had put through two-acre zoning had been under the erroneous impression that plots of this size would more or less dictate expensive houses. In the first stages of an area's desecration, however, land prices are not yet high enough to enforce such a correlation. Two acres may be a lot of land for a $12,000 rancher, but the two acres do not cost much, and they provide a good field for septic tanks. There is an immediate local market for $12,000 ranchers, and that is what goes up.

It does not take much of this sort of partial development to irretrievably determine the future character of an area. Opportunities for a more amenable treatment of the land will have been pre-empted by the scatteration of second-rate developments. Add the frozen-custard stand, an automobile junkyard, and soon the place will look completely filled up—long before the real invasion gets under way.

It would have been better if the mass developers had come. If they had had a crack at one part of the area, they could have concentrated the same number of houses in a fraction of the space. In Bucks County, Pennsylvania, for example, the new Levittown took care of 75,000 people on a tract in the southern part of the county. The layout was not notably compressed—about three detached houses to the acre—but it put 4000 people on each square mile developed and this was far more sparing of land than the usual pattern. Thanks to the concentration, there was something left of the rest of Bucks County to save.

But in most rural areas, scattered development is what took place, and once begun it started an inexorable sequence of events. Local governments soon found that scattered development is extraordinarily costly to service, and to take care of the extra load they had to raise taxes. This in turn prompted landowners to sell off more lots.

All this time the main body of developers and new people moving out from the city was getting closer. Somewhat in advance of them, moving at the rate of about half a mile or a mile a year, was a sort of greed line, and once touched by it an owner's fealty to the land was put to sore trial. The majority of landowners did resist it; some turned down extraordinary offers. Unfortunately, however, only a handful have to fall from grace to spoil things for others. One landowner, for example, might decide to sell a piece of meadowland for a drive-in theater. This would be intolerable to the abutting landowner, and his property would go on the market. Then the next one.

So on it went. Much of the open space that remained, furthermore, was being stockpiled by speculators for re-sale at a later date. They may have leased it in the interim to a farmer, but often they simply left the land idle. Soon it would revert to a dense growth of saplings and weeds and poison ivy. Some inhabitants would be reassured by this resurgence of nature but to the practiced eye it would be a sure tip-off the area was doomed. Thus does the speculator leave his tracks.

By the mid-fifties developments were going up all over the place. There still was no pattern. Developers leap-frogged over vacant land that was too stiffly zoned for their liking or too stiffly priced. Pressure for variances mounted. Zoning squabbles of unparalleled ferocity broke out in many of the townships.

Outrage followed outrage. A severe outbreak of hepatitis was traced to the septic tanks of a new subdivision. Several townships were refused further service by the septic tank emptiers of the area: There was no place left for them to dump the wastes. Over the bitter protests of landowners, the Philadelphia Electric Company put up a string of transmission line towers through the most historic and beautiful stretch of the Brandywine—reminding conservatives that while they might quail at the idea of using eminent domain for open space, utilities had no such qualms. Nor did the highway engineers, who decided to run a freeway through the last unspoiled creek valley to the east. Men with power saws came to destroy trees so that old roads could be widened.

But outrages are educational. People were jolted to action—too few, perhaps, and often too late, but enough to make a difference. The fifties had been a time of ruination, but by the mid-sixties a countermovement had set in, and it has been picking up momentum. There is now a county planning commission. The county is cooperating with the state in setting up a system of small dams and recreation areas. Its Water Resources Authority is co-sponsoring an experimental program to test various land preservation devices along the east branch of the Brandy-wine. The growth problems are tougher than ever, but the county is probably better able to cope with them than it was ten or fifteen years ago when the pressures were far less intense.

The same pattern of outrage and response can be found along the edges of virtually every metropolitan area. Some local governments are doing a much better job than others, but in almost all of them, people have the feeling that they may be dealing with a last chance.

Will it be muffed? We now have the tools for seeing to it that the next round of growth is a lot better than what went before, and we are beginning to hammer out regional mechanisms for applying them. But formidable problems remain, one being that the people who are doing the planning of how the land of the region ought to be used and the people who own or control what is left of the open land are quite different people. They may join in bespeaking the need for "balanced growth" but when it gets down to cases, balance means lots of development to some people, little or none of it to others. There are accommodations to be made, but to make them we need to understand the parties at interest and the issues that divide them.

At the antidevelopment extreme are the simon-pure conservationists. These people have a deep, almost passionate commitment to nature—and to nature as it is, unimproved, undefiled, inviolate. The general run of conservationists are less adamant, and will not always be upset when they hear that a dam is to be built or a forest area opened up with roads. They assume that man is a part of nature, too, and that it is all right for him to use nature's resources as long as he uses them wisely.

This view is too sweetly reasonable for the simon pures. To them "wise use" is a contradiction in terms, a convenient euphemism for the lumbermen, mining companies, developers, and other exploiters and destroyers. The simon pures think our resources have already been used much too much; that these resources are in perilously short supply and that the solution is not more use but less people.

In any confrontation between man and nature, it is nature's side they take. They are against public works development; they are frequently against development of public recreation facilities as well. This would destroy the very values that people should seek, they believe, and they are unabashedly elitist as to whose values should come first. The wilderness experience may be ennobling, but not for the many.

The simon-pure conservationists used to concern themselves mainly with wilderness preservation, and through the good offices of the Sierra Club, they have served this cause vigorously and well. Now they are taking an increasing part in the battle for nature within the metropolis, the further growth of which they view as utterly malignant. Considering their small numbers, they have been enormously effective. Among other things, they helped foil the plans of the Port Authority of New York to build a jetport in the great swamp area of New Jersey's Morris County; in alliance with residents of the area they had the swamp acquired as an ecological area of unique importance. It has now been declared a national wildlife refuge. When Consolidated Edison proposed a pumped storage reservoir at Storm King Mountain on the Hudson, they launched such an effective legal and political campaign as to put a stop to the project for some three years.

By being splendidly unreasonable the simon-pure conservationists have saved many fine areas which should have been saved and which would not have been saved without good old-fashioned zealotry. Furthermore, by taking an uncompromising position at the far end of the conservation-development spectrum, they have helped more moderate conservationists move the middle of the road closer to their position. The fact that the simon pures can be counted on to raise hell over most new highway or public works projects can have a chastening effect on administrators and engineers and make them think more about resource values and concessions before the battle lines have hardened.

But the wilderness ethos can go just so far in a metropolitan area. How many last stands can one lose? The conflicts are going to be coming much thicker and faster and by being so unrelentingly hostile to works of man, the simon pures are boxing themselves out of an effective role. They can't talk alternatives. They may say they're not against growth, that all they want is to protect the particular resource that is threatened by a particular project, but the truth is that they are incapable of seeing any site as suitable for development.

If they have been successful in stopping a project in one place, it will not be long before they come to similar apprehensions over any alternative place that might be under consideration. No matter how humdrum it may look to the eye of the Philistine, they will see unique flora, the habitat of an endangered species of wildlife, a rare and important geological formation—in short, one more utterly irreplaceable resource and a test case so crucial as to admit of no compromise.

Such a dispute almost split the Sierra Club asunder. Several years ago the Pacific Gas and Electric Company, an historic antagonist, chose a stretch of beautiful dune land as a site for an atomic reactor. The directors of the

Sierra Club thought this would be a desecration, but they also felt that they ought to do something more constructive than merely fight it. They persuaded P.G.&E. to look for another site. Eventually P.G.&E. found one in a canyon some miles to the north. When the Club's directors voted approval of the canyon site, subject to certain safeguards, the utility reciprocated by announcing the dune site would be made available for a state park.

For both sides, it seemed a reasonably good accommodation. But some Club members began to have misgivings. They decided to take a second look at the canyon. When further study convinced them that it too was unique, they took the unprecedented step of calling for a referendum of the membership to reverse the directors' action. They maintained that not only did the specifics of the situation warrant the reversal, but that principle did too. It was not conservationists' business, they charged, to endorse development sites or to trade "one area off in the hopes of ransoming another." When it came to a vote, the membership sustained the board. The dispute cut deep, however, and the kind of forced choice it presented is going to bother conservationists with increasing frequency.

Another small but pivotal group is the gentry. These are the people who own the gentlemen farms, the remodeled grist mills, and estates beyond the fringe of suburbia. They are not an hereditary gentry, like their English counterparts, and if they are landed it is recently so. Meet a group of these tweedy countrymen before the fireplace on a winter's evening and you would swear they had been tied to the soil for generations. You will soon find, however, that most of them came from somewhere else, and not so long ago at that. They are of all kinds: a retired naval or foreign service couple; a general and his wife who have taken up horticulture; a businessman who raises Aberdeen Angus, or on the West Coast, has become a rancher; professional people who want a farm as a weekend retreat from the city. There will be at least one white-haired lady of vast energy, not the kind who wear tennis shoes, but who are bridge sharks and winners of battles. There will be several writers and artists, and in the exurbias, such as Bucks County in Pennsylvania, a leavening of theater and television people as well.

Because the various gentries seem so atypical it is easy to overlook their collective importance. They are indeed fringe groups, and rather fluid ones; since the newcomers tend to be in the older age groups, the turnover of personnel is fairly high. Each gentry is convinced that it is absolutely unique and its members will tell you, with a mixture of pride and parody, that they have accomplished great things because of an accidental, and wildly improbable combination of doers and screwballs. But there is an underlying consistency, year in and year out, and for all the singularities, the gentry of any one area act much the same as the gentry of the others.

What links them together is a feeling for the countryside, and if their conversion to the land is recent, their feeling is no less strong for that. They are surprisingly knowledgeable about soils, trees, kinds of grasses, the idiosyncrasies of the local weather, and are generally the leading activists in the watershed associations and conservation groups of the area. They are also keenly interested in its history and usually know more about it than the long-time residents. If there is an old building threatened by a highway, they are the ones who will discover that its 1910 façade masks an old structure of great architectural and historical significance, and they will organize the drive for its preservation, with the white-haired lady at the lead.

They want to save open space, and since they own the best of it they are a key factor for effective regional action. They do not, however, necessarily think regional. What they do may have the effect of providing amenity for the city and its people, but they certainly are not motivated by this concern. They want to protect the land *from* the city, and from some of its people. They do not, for one thing, welcome the idea of parks. Exclusionary bias has something to do with this, but it is not the domi-

nating concern it is for suburbanites. The gentry's bias is
essentially aesthetic. They love the "natural" landscape
and they don't think park development enhances it at all,
at least, not the kind of park development they've seen.
They don't mind parks off in woods so much; the vision
that disturbs them is the open countryside manicured with
conventional landscaping and rusticated buildings and picnic areas. They also worry a great deal about the bad
habits of the picnickers and Sunday drivers they have already encountered.

Yet the gentry are a great source of gifts of land—particularly for natural areas, bird sanctuaries, woodland preserves, and they will give land for more active recreation
if they think this will help preserve the balance of the
area. Few park officials, however, understand the gentry's
motivations. This is unfortunate, for park acquisition plans
drafted with more flexibility and sensitivity could prompt
reciprocal gestures from the landowners. Not many plans
are, and this is one of the reasons they so frequently run
into fierce resistance.

Farmers are less prompted by aesthetic concerns. If the
area is a prime agricultural one, however—a thriving milk
shed, for example—the leading farmers tend to share the
gentry's attitude about the land, albeit for different reasons. They are mindful of the money they might eventually reap by selling out to a developer, but most of them
really do want to continue farming. They have a big capital investment in their operation, and as the smaller farmers on the marginal land give up farming, the big farmers
get bigger. Better soil practices, watershed planning, and
such are an economic necessity for them, and they will
be as activist in conservation programs as the gentry—to
the great delight of the latter, who are enormously pleased
to rub elbows with real farmers.

But the farmer has a price. He is highly aggrieved over
taxes; and complains that if assessors keep raising the
valuation of his land to match its rising market price, he
will be forced to sell. He knows very well that the thought

of this horrifies conservationists and the gentry and he turns this to good advantage. If you want me to help keep the countryside, he says, you are going to have to help me get a tax break. His argument has some holes in it; he is not against the rising market value, only assessments that recognize it, and his tax-reform proposals do not include any restrictions on his selling out when it suits him. While there is a touch of aesthetic blackmail about all this, conservationists and the gentry are quite sympathetic—they *need* the farmers—and with their support, farm groups have succeeded in pushing through "preferential assessment" laws in a number of states. These laws instruct assessors to value farmers' land only at farm value, and thus encourage farmers not to think of development. The effect, as I will take up later, has not been quite as expected, but the proponents still are hopeful that much open space is going to be saved this way.

The merchants and citizens of the towns and villages beyond suburbia have a different attitude toward open space. They think there is quite enough of it in their area. The members of the village and township boards are sympathetic toward the farmers—they would not stay in office if they weren't—but what preoccupies them is the possibility of development, and they are not too choosy as to what kind. They are, in fact, pushovers for any entrepreneur who promises to increase the local tax base. They are especially keen on industrial development. In more cases than not, they are quite unrealistic in their expectations. The community may lack rail access, be miles from a freeway interchange, have no labor supply and limited water resources; no matter, the town will declare part of its acreage as industrial—often the poorest acreage—and hopefully await the plant that is going to come and solve their tax problems.

Talk of regional or state-park acquisition programs makes the locals nervous. Of all areas, they ask, why pick on theirs? They have a skimpy enough tax base, they complain, and they do not want it cut down even more.

Since state-park officials have historically sought low-price land outside the urban area, a community on the fringe will already have a good bit of its land in state ownership, and off the local tax rolls. To make matters worse, these fringe areas provide the kind of land holdings that tax-exempt religious and educational institutions seek. Some of these voluntarily give money to the town to make up for the taxes, but most do not.

States can ease matters by making payment in lieu of taxes on land they buy. There are different formulas for this, some of them quite complicated, but the general idea is to give the town an amount equivalent to the former annual tax on the property and to continue this for five or ten years. In principle, there are good arguments against this practice. The new parks add little to the service load of the community and will, in all probability, increase local revenues and tourism. The community may get a free tax ride it does not deserve, and this can create troublesome problems in dealing with other communities. Such payments in lieu of taxes, furthermore, are a drain on funds that would otherwise be available for additional acquisition.

Practically speaking, however, there is a good case for payment in lieu of taxes. The money does not add up to a great deal. The communities that need it usually have fairly low tax rates to begin with and the land involved is usually of relatively low value. What is gained in return is a sort of truce with rural people, and this can be of no small value for critical legislation.

One of the best state open-space programs was passed in part because of such an accommodation. Rural legislators wanted to be sure that the money would *not* be spent in their areas. They were promised (1) the state would try not to buy open space in any town that already had a given percentage of its land in public ownership; (2) where acquisition was unavoidable, the state would pay full taxes for ten years; (3) towns could have grant money for buying their own open space but they would not have to apply for it. Thus assured that the open-space money would be directed toward other constituencies, the legislators supported the program.

Payment in lieu of taxes, however, does not eliminate locals' antagonism to park acquisition. The payments would be based on the previous value of the open space, and the locals like to think of the much higher taxes they might get if the land were developed. Furthermore, they say, the park will not really be for them. It will be for city people. They will tell stories about other places being overrun by busloads every weekend.

Conservationists and park people tell them they should take the larger view. They will argue that not only the local economy but the whole local environment will be greatly enhanced by the park. Surrounding land values will go up. A better class of industrial enterprise will be attracted to the area. They will also argue that if the parkland were developed with a conventional subdivision, the town would probably lose on the deal by paying more in services than it would get back in taxes. The locals will not be impressed. ("You conservationists," one rural leader remarked to me, "are a bunch of city people who have it and do not want us to have it.")

There is a genuine conflict of interests here and it is no good lecturing the rural people about taking the larger view, and how it will be best for everyone in the long run if development goes somewhere else. They want in and they want in now. Furthermore, they have power. Despite reapportionment, rural interests are still strongly enough represented in our state legislatures and their key committees so that regional land-use programs will not get very far if the rural interests do not believe they are getting a square deal. If past history is a guide, in any showdown they will probably end up with more than a square deal. Be that as it may, there is an accommodation to be made and it would be to the good of the metropolitan region if it were more vigorously sought.

This brings us to another key group: the people who do the thinking and planning for the metropolitan **region**.

They do it from the city. They may live in the suburbs, some may have weekend farms far out in the country. But their point of view is from the center out. The perspective is fine, and they are highly conscious of the freedom this gives them from rural and suburban bias. The loftiness with which they regularly deplore this bias, however, obscures the fact that they have some rather strong biases of their own.

The planner, for example. He thinks the rural people and the suburbanites have a selfish view of open space. But he is selfish about open space too. He wants it for his maps. The paramount function of open space, he believes, is to shape and structure the growth of the region. He also tends to believe that any open-space measures undertaken for other reasons are apt to be wrong measures. He is particularly concerned with whether the open space will be in the right place. Several times I have heard planners worry about the possibility that federal and state grants-in-aid might tempt local communities to premature action, and that they would acquire land in advance of regional land-use studies that would show what land should be acquired. (In practice, let it be noted, the point has proved fairly academic; whenever a local application for open-space grant has been referred to planning agencies for an opinion as to whether it is regionally okay, the planners usually find that it is.)

The planner, trained as a physical designer and social scientist, does not share the commitment to the resource and agricultural aspects of land that the rural interests do. Their soil-conservation districts, small water-shed dam projects, and farmland conservation programs can be of tremendous benefit for the metropolis, but since they are set up for quite different, and to the planner, parochial reasons, the connection of self-interests is not made. When rural groups press for conservation legislation at state capitols, they usually go it alone. At the legislative hearings on their measures, city people will rarely be there to testify for the measure. They will not even be there to testify against it. They have enough trouble with their own measures, and they don't see any rural people at their hearings.

The split is equally apparent in Washington. The city and metropolitan interests look on the Department of Housing and Urban Development as their primary vehicle, while the rural and resource-oriented groups look to the Department of the Interior and the Department of Agriculture. These various constituencies do some log rolling for each other, and occasionally builders and architects and city planners will cross the line and put in a word for a measure proposed for the Department of Agriculture by the farmers and soil conservationists. Considering the great overlap of interests, however, this happens with remarkable infrequency.

When the first open-space grant program was before Congress as part of the Housing Act of 1961, the only lobbying support came from the metropolitan interests. Recreation, conservation, and farm groups did not know anything about it, or were suspicious of it because it was bound up with a housing act about development. Conversely, when the Land and Water Conservation Fund Act came up, recreation and conservation organizations furnished the support; the metropolitans sat on their hands. They did the same some years later when the Department of Agriculture proposed a program of grants for converting excess farmland into recreation areas. These measures passed, but many a good one, and many a necessary appropriation, has failed because the parties at interest did not see their interest.

In many areas the metropolitans have launched ambitious educational programs for achieving what they call a "dialogue" with groups of the region, featuring clinics and workshops to sell regional planning and get citizen reaction. The agreement that marks these gatherings can be misleading. The people that turn up tend to be the true believers or those who for occupational reasons have to think regional. The critical minority who control the land on the fringe are hardly represented at all.

There is a great faith that regional planning can resolve

the various conflicts of interest. Up to a point, this is true. Even if it has no powers to speak of, a regional planning body can be a unifying influence; it can stimulate communities to adopt better and more uniform zoning ordinances; it can give them the technical assistance on municipal problems. Since such bodies are usually asked to pass upon communities' requests for state and federal grants-in-aid, they have the leverage to get them to embark on comprehensive planning efforts of their own.

But this is the easy part. When a regional planning effort moves on to the business of drawing up a master land-use plan, it begins to get divisive. It has to. In any growth plan, some communities are going to be winners and some are going to be losers. Which are going to be which? How do you compensate the losers? Or do you?

Planners who design ideal models for metropolitan growth rarely face up to the awesome economic implications of their plans. The most ambitious of these plans are tidily geometric, concentrating development in narrow strips, with huge intervening areas to be zoned as permanent open space. Were the plans to be literally applied, however, the people who own land in the strips would be made millionaires. People on the green side of the line would be told they have a nobler role to play. They are to keep on as they were—farming the soil and tending the landscape for the greater good of the region.

Such plans caricature the problem. But even a well-conceived plan will not resolve the inequities of growth. It will sharpen them. A plan that is any good cannot homogenize the region and provide a little bit of everything to keep each of the parts happy—some open space, some industry, some residential development. Necessarily, the plan will call for imbalances, with development going where development goes best, and other areas remaining relatively undisturbed. It can be added that without a regional plan, market forces would tend to produce much the same imbalances. Shopping complexes, research labs, and light industry—the cream of the ratables—do not spread their tax benefactions, but follow the leader and cluster in a few fortunate townships. The poor may not get poorer, but the rich get richer.

To illustrate, let me note a tale of three villages. One is Cornwall, a sleepy hamlet on the west bank of the Hudson. When Con Edison announced it was going to build a $186 million pumped storage reservoir and plant there the townspeople were overjoyed. In one fell swoop all the town's money problems were to be solved; the tax base would soar, individual taxes would go down, and long-deferred community facilities would be built. For good measure it would get a free riverside park from Con Edison. As to the charge that the plant would ruin Storm King Mountain, Cornwall people did not see it this way at all. The place would look better, they said.

Towns on the east bank of the river were not overjoyed. They would get none of the windfall, but they would get the transmission lines. A number of their citizens inclined strongly to the conservationists' viewpoint and testified that great aesthetic and resource damage would be done.

Later, the Georgia-Pacific Corporation bought a stretch of shore-front property on the east bank, Little Stony Point, and announced that it was going to put up an $8 million wallboard plant. The town, Philipstown, was overjoyed. The plant would provide 300 jobs, solving its unemployment problem. Taxes would go down. Long-deferred community facilities would be built. True, the plant would be far more visible than the Con Ed plant across the river, and it would pre-empt what had long been regarded as one of the best potential sites for a state park and marina. But in this case, the people of Philipstown could see no aesthetic problem.

From a regional point of view, however, this was clearly the wrong place for the plant. Governor Rockefeller asked Georgia-Pacific to look for another site and said the Hudson River Valley Commission and the Commerce Department would help in the search. To the consternation of Philipstown, Georgia-Pacific agreed. It bought an alternate site in a village some miles to the south, and shortly afterwards the state bought the Little Stony Point tract for a park, thereby taking it off the tax rolls. Some of the people of Philipstown were pleased. A number were apoplectic. The fact that the state said it might provide some payment in lieu of taxes mollified them not a bit. Industry is what they wanted.

And who got the Georgia-Pacific plant? It was Buchanan, a small village whose cup was already running over. It had a tax base of such stupendous proportions that it was properly known as the "Kuwait of the Hudson." First, Con Edison bestowed upon it a nuclear plant assessed at $20 million; this tax bonanza had enabled the village to launch an ambitious public improvement program and cut taxes at the same time. Next Con Edison added a second nuclear plant alongside the first one. Then came the news about Georgia-Pacific, and at about the same time, an announcement from Con Edison that it was going to add yet another nuclear plant. Buchanan is now planning another round of public improvements. The people of Philipstown, who are still looking for a plant, think the whole business is grossly unfair.

It is unfair, but these kinds of imbalances are the rule rather than the exception in metropolitan areas, and there is very little that regional planning can do to resolve them. "As long as there is a Chinese wall around each town's ratables," says one regional planner, "I don't see any chance for a rational land-use plan. We can make the plan, but I don't think we are going to get local governments to do anything about the plan that they would not want to do anyway, unless they get the cut."

Why not do away with the local governments entirely? Some people think this is the only logical direction to pursue, and that if the governments cannot be eliminated, there should at least be superimposed over them an areawide authority with the power to enforce its view of proper land-use policy. But a supergovernment does not seem a very likely possibility for large metropolitan areas. If one were set up, furthermore, the basic inequities would still be unresolved. Local jealousies will not disappear if local governments are eliminated. If they were eliminated, furthermore, they would probably have to be set up all over again under a different name.

The problem is not so much the multiplicity of local governments; it is the multiplicity of local tax districts. Local officials want plants and shopping centers for the jobs they create, but what they want chiefly are the additional tax revenues, and if they could get assurances that their communities would get a fair share of these revenues, they might not mind very much if the plants and shopping centers were physically located somewhere else; in some cases, they might be quite happy if they were. (If Philipstown, for example, had been promised a pro-rata cut of the tax ratables of Buchanan, its citizens might have had second thoughts about the looks of the wallboard plant and concluded that Buchanan would be just the place for it.)

We must, in short, find ways of spreading the gravy. One way is to widen the geographic tax base. As an institution, the local property tax will die hard, of course, but it is reasonable to expect more of a shift to taxes levied on a county, special district, and regional basis. One possibility is an area-wide agency for assessing and collecting property taxes, with kickbacks to local governments for purely local services. In time, the states might take a direct hand themselves.

We also are likely to see new mechanisms for providing subsidies to local governments to equalize growth inequities and to provide incentives for going along with regional plans. Federal-grant programs to local governments are already doing this to a degree. Whatever the original purpose of the particular programs, together they are rapidly evolving into an instrument for redistributing revenues and buying local cooperation with metropolitan agencies. Their leverage power in this respect is likely to increase. One proposal along this line, by planner William Wheaton, envisions a "Metropolitan Services Improvement District." This would not be a metropolitan government, the workability of which Wheaton questions, but a vehicle for improving local services by distributing money, the bulk of it federal.

Some people still maintain that metropolitan government is workable and offers the only real solution. The case has been impressively and exhaustively argued for many years—the latest bibliography on metropolitan government runs 536 pages and it is only a supplement. But the idea has not caught on, nor does it appear highly likely that it will in the future. But the search for some kind of metropolitan unification continues; and in a messy, pragmatic way, devices are being worked out. Councils of local governments have been set up in most urban areas and some are beginning to be effective. County governments are playing a much stronger role. There is more "contracting" of services, with larger units of governments, such as counties, providing area-wide services that the local governments previously provided, less efficiently, on their own.

The states have been slow to take a hand, or lend one, and this is why the cities have been bypassing them and going directly to Washington for help. But a change is bound to come. Politics and geography dictate it. As more of the states' land area, and voters, are encompassed in metropolitan areas, the states will of necessity take on the mediating role in urban affairs and reassert many of the powers—such as zoning—they formerly delegated. Rather than have a new layer of government interposed between them and the cities and counties, many of the states will become, in effect, metropolitan governments themselves.

These changes are going to be slow in coming, and in the meantime we face land-use decisions that are going to have to be made now. In the next section, I take up the principal approaches for saving open space and I think it will be clear that there is a great deal that can be done, and will have to be done, with the tools we already have at hand and with the political realities we now face. I also think that by tackling these approaches, we are going to force the larger issues—and that there is no better way to do it.

The Devices

3. The Police Power

>>>

Saving open space is only part of the job, but it is as good a way as any to come to grips with the basic problems of shaping metropolitan growth. For all the host of methods, the essential technical question boils down to this: To what degree can we use the police power to order better land use—and to what degree do we have to use eminent domain, that is, pay for it? We have to use both, of course, and other tools besides, such as tax power and the power to provide services or to withhold them. But to pay or not to pay is the fundamental question.

Broadly speaking, the community applies the police power to see to it that people do not use land in a way that injures the public welfare. Through the official map, for example, the community shows the location of future streets so that people will not put up houses on them. Through subdivision regulations, the community sets minimum standards so that houses will be safe and the streets and pavements wide enough.

For open space, the application of the police power that seems most useful is zoning. Through zoning ordinances, the community can say what land is not to be developed and how much space there should be for each building in areas that can be developed. As with other applications of the police power, zoning does not cost governments anything, or at least it does not appear to. The courts have been increasingly sustaining broader applications of it, and where not so long ago the courts emphasized property rights, they are now swinging to a greater emphasis on the needs of the community. They are even talking openly about aesthetics as a good reason for zoning.

In principle, zoning is invoked to protect the public's health, safety, morals, and general welfare, and under this rubric there would appear to be no limit to the forms of beneficent land control we could with invention contrive. In practice, zoning has so far been used principally for the protection of property interests. The first comprehensive zoning ordinance came about because a group of Fifth Avenue merchants did not want to see garment factories blight the character of their area. They were ahead of their time. Elsewhere the idea of zoning was bitterly fought by conservatives as an encroachment on free enterprise, and only slowly did they begin to see its great usefulness in curbing the kind of free enterprise they did not like and which was contrary to the general welfare. By the 1940s, zoning was established in almost all of the principal metropolitan areas (except Houston, which is still holding out).

The administration of zoning has been terrible. Most zoning maps are a hodgepodge of odd shapes and cabalistic letterings, and in some cities they have been amended so much that it is impossible to get hold of a legible map. If there is a clear map, furthermore, it does not bear much resemblance to the comprehensive master plan for the area. "Stripped of all planning jargon," says Richard Babcock in *The Zoning Game*, "zoning administration is exposed as a process under which isolated social and political units engage in highly emotional altercations over the use of land, most of which are settled by crude tribal adaptations of medieval trial by fire, and a few of which are concluded by confused *ad hoc* injunctions of bewildered courts."

Zoning is a tool that always seems on the brink of better days. Planners, who have a slant on zoning somewhat different from that of property owners, have been constantly pressing for a broader, more public-oriented application of zoning and with some success have been strengthening other variants of the police power, such as the official map and the regulation of new development. New forms of zoning are constantly being invented, and in time, conceivably, they could be orchestrated into a regional design of considerable force. But the prospect is doubtful. For the most part, zoning has yet to emerge from phase one. In most communities, suburbias especially, it is an elaborate mechanism for insuring a satisfactory status quo, or a future reasonably similar.

Let us start with large-lot zoning. This is the exercise of the police power that suburbanites look to as the primary means for saving the open space. Minimum lot sizes vary greatly—what for one community would seem tiny would for another seem excessive—but in general they are as large as local price and incomes can enforce. Some communities go further and set up "green belt" zones, but this is euphemism; most of the green that looks so good on local land-use maps is usually nothing more than large-lot zoning with very large lots of four or five acres or more.

As I noted in the previous chapter, large-lot zoning does not save open space. It squanders it. By forcing developers to use large lots for little houses, the community forces them to chew up much more of the open landscape than they have to. Instead of several tightly knit subdivisions, housing will be spattered all over the place.

The true purpose of large-lot zoning, of course, is to keep people away, or at least people with incomes lower than the majority. It can work very well in this respect, but over the long run the victory is likely to be pyrrhic. The community may shunt developers and middle-income people away, but they will soon fill up the interstices, and the surrounding landscape that the community took for granted will disappear. The community won't be penetrated; it will be enveloped.

At the moment, courts are of several minds about large-lot zoning. Some have struck down one-acre zoning; others have upheld four-acre zoning; and in interpreting the general welfare, the findings differ so much that it is impossible to find any clear agreement as to just what this is. But there is one thread. Whatever the public welfare may be, most courts tend to go along with the idea that it is the public welfare as the particular community sees it.

This parochialism is the great weakness of local zoning, and it seems inevitable that the courts will be calling for a broader view. Events will force them to. If all the separate zoning ordinances in suburbia were put together and carried to their logical conclusion, there would be no place for anybody to go save the inner city or the hinterland. But there are just too many people to be contained. As they press on suburbia, it is going to be increasingly difficult for the courts to swallow the public-welfare argument as justification for excluding the public.

Most of suburbia is already embroiled in a desperate fight against garden apartments, and even worse confrontations are impending. Mobile homes, for example. These are at the absolute bottom of the list of things that any respectable community wants to see around, and most zoning ordinances exclude them. But mobile homes, being the only truly mass produced housing available to date, are accounting for a sharply increasing percentage of the total home market, and for lower-income people they may soon be the dominant form of housing.

Redoubts are going to fall. If the courts won't break down large-lot zoning, the marketplace will. Economic pressures for higher-density development are very strong, and they are going to get more so. If a man can get his property rezoned from two acre lots to one acre, the market price more than doubles immediately, and if the lots go down to a half acre or less, the price can go up a thousand percent or more.

The prospect of such windfalls can convert many people to a more democratic view and it is little wonder that the pressures for rezoning are so relentless, and so often successful. The wonder is that local governments have not been cutting themselves in for some of the profits. They could, for example, slap a tax on the extra value added to a property by rezoning. One such proposal has been made by the Commissioners of Prince Georges County in Maryland. If a man's property was rezoned so that more dwelling units could be put on it, the County would levy a special tax on the difference between the market value before the change and the market value after. To date the Maryland legislature has shown no enthusiasm for the idea.

A more sweeping proposal along this line has been made by Marion Clawson, of Resources for the Future. Sell zoning to the highest bidder, he suggests. "Much is made in zoning cases," he observes, "of possible deprivation of property values to persons whose property is adversely affected. But seldom do we recognize that zoning and rezoning often confer values, and sometimes very large values, on some property owners." The public has created these values, not the owners, and the public ought to recoup the values by putting the zoning of a tract up for open, competitive sale. This would take political pressure off zoning boards, deliver officials from temptation, put the market mechanism to good use, and produce some money for the local treasury. Outrageous? Think it over, says Clawson.

Windfalls or no, rezoning to higher densities can make sense. The trouble is the people who press for the rezoning. In most communities they appear to be the forces of greed versus the forces of good. The responsible, conservative citizens will uphold the large lot zoning. The people fighting it will include the developer, who occasionally will come dressed for the part, polo coat and all; one or two local fat cats who want to mark up their land, and perhaps an official of whom it will later be remarked that he seems to be living extremely well for one his salary. The developer will present the arguments of the liberals and city based planners and will plead that his small homes, or garden apartments, or towers, best serve the needs of middle-income people. He is patently interested in money, of course, and since so much of it is at stake, re-zonings can be squalid affairs. The fact remains, however, that the ultimate force for knocking down large-lot zoning is not the developer; it is the pressure of people looking for a place to live.

In the long run, this will out. It is quite possible that in time we may have ordinances for *maximum* lot sizes. If the community is reconciled to housing more people and wants to save open space, it will have to reverse course and demand that the developer use less land for putting up his houses. In the form of cluster development, steps in this direction are already being taken.

But you cannot save much open space by zoning it for de-velopment. At best, development zoning can help achieve more adequate playground areas, better handling of the open spaces within subdivisions, and a more sensitive treat-ment of the topography. It cannot, however, preserve the countryside. For this, the community has to turn to zon-ing that in one way or another forbids development. And here we get onto very tricky constitutional grounds. Is it really necessary for the general welfare that the land be zoned against development? Or merely desirable?

For one kind of land, the case for zoning is abundantly clear: the flood plains that border our rivers and streams. Fortuitously, they are probably the best-looking parts of most of our local landscapes, and if one were to zone only on the basis of aesthetics, the flood plains would usually be the highest priority areas of all. But there is a public necessity at stake, and it can be documented on quite ob-jective grounds. A flood plain is a great sponge. When the rains and floods come, it soaks up an enormous amount of water, returns a good part of it to the underlying water table, and then over a period of days and weeks slowly releases the rest.

Building on flood plains hurts people. It is not only a question of what happens to the unfortunates who live in the houses that will be inundated but to the people downstream. When a flood plain is covered with streets and rooftops and parking areas, the amount of water that runs off is greatly increased, and the watershed becomes a very "flashy" one. An average rooftop of twelve hundred square feet will shed 750 gallons of water in a one-inch rainfall. Put together a subdivision of rooftops, and you have a veritable flood-producing mechanism; the separate runoffs will be intercepted before they have a chance to soak into the ground and through a network of drains, gutters, and storm sewers will be compounded into a torrent and sent racing downstream.

Flood-plain zoning is clearly a proper exercise of the police power and has been so upheld by the courts, but the application of it has been quite spotty. It is up to the local governments, and few of them worry very much about local governments downstream. Only a fraction of the flood plains in our metropolitan areas are properly zoned, and even those that are zoned are vulnerable to developers seeking variances.

There is much money to be made from flood plains. Partly because of the hazards, the land is cheap. It is usually flat and easy to build on. If the flood plain has been under water recently enough to make the community a bit nervous, the developer can usually calm apprehensions by agreeing to protect the area with a small dike. This further increases the flood potential to the communities down the river, but that is their worry.

It is widely assumed that there is less and less need for any community to worry. Because of the vast amount of dam building that has been going on, the public is under the impression that the danger of floods is receding. But the opposite is true. By allowing developers to waterproof the flood plains, communities have been increasing the flood damage potential faster than the engineers can build dams to compensate. The public pays dearly, both in flood damage and in the cost of dams that otherwise would not have to be built. Just one shopping center and parking area built on the flood plain can create enough extra runoff to require the construction of anywhere from five hundred thousand dollars to a million dollars worth of flood control structures. The public pays the whole bill and retroactively provides a subsidy to developers for building where they shouldn't.

Flood-plain zoning should be made mandatory, and the federal government and the states have enough leverage to see that it is. One thing they can do is to tell local governments that they won't give any more grants for open space and water facilities unless the local government zones its flood plains against development. If a local government won't take this elementary step, which costs it very little, there is no reason it should be given money to make up for its derelictions.

If local governments will not protect the larger public interest, the states should. They have the basic police power, and though they have farmed out the exercise of it to local governments, there are signs they will be taking on more of the job themselves. Connecticut furnishes an important precedent. Its towns have by tradition been very independent, and partly because of this the state has had severe flood problems. Many of its towns were built squarely in the path of the flood waters; and each time they were destroyed, they were promptly rebuilt in exactly the same place, thereby making the damage from the next flood worse. The 1955 floods were so devastating, however, that the state at last decided that the public equity was too vital to be left to the discretion of the separate towns. The legislature enacted a "channel-encroachment line" program for major streams and rivers. On the basis of past flood data, the state's Water Resources Commission outlines the main floodway area that extends beyond the banks of the streams and rivers. Once these lines are established, no one can build within them except by specific authorization from the state. It costs about $6000 a mile in hydrologic surveys to establish the line. This data gives the lines their legal heft, and in upholding the constitutionality of the program, the Connecticut court noted that there was nothing arbitrary or capricious in the designation of the lines.

This program is not the same thing as flood-plain zoning; the state's concern is to keep the floodway clear of obstacles so that there will be a channel open to the sea, and the channel encroachment line does not extend to the full width of the flood plain. But the state has provided the spine for a broader program, and the local governments have been covering the rest of the flood-plain areas with their own zoning. The Connecticut experience would indicate that local governments welcome a strong lead and that it stimulates rather than inhibits local initiative.

Some local governments have pushed flood-plain zoning beyond reasonable limits. It is not true, as many of them believe, that zoning does not cost anything. It may cost landowners a lot, and if it does, the community may have to pay too. The fact that the public may strongly benefit from having the flood plain remain open is important, but the courts must also weigh the harm the zoning might do to the value of the private property. Usually, the public benefits are great, the harm to the property slight, and there is no constitutional problem. Sometimes, however, the zoning may strip the property of any practical use, and unless the owner is content with it as a bird sanctuary or similar "permitted use," he can rightfully argue that he is being taken. Through his loss in property value he is being saddled with a cost that the public should bear. In such cases the courts are likely to agree with him and strike down the zoning as unconstitutional.

News of these decisions can lead people to the impression that the courts are ruling against flood-plain zoning in general. But this is not so. It is the particulars that have concerned them. What the courts have objected to is not flood-plain zoning but the use of it by communities to get something free that they ought to pay for.

Many a community has certainly tried. One indication is the suddenness with which it discovers an area is a flood plain. For years it might not have shown the slightest interest in conserving it. It may have had it zoned as residential, and already have permitted some subdivision on it. But then it sours on the idea of more subdivision. School taxes are out of hand and getting worse. Abruptly, the community discovers ecology and slaps a flood-plain designation on the area. Not fair, the courts are likely to hold. The community's new-found solicitude for conservation is plainly disingenuous. What it wanted was to stop a subdivision.

In one Connecticut case, the community levied an assessment on a subdivider's property to provide new sewers, then pulled the rug out by changing the zoning from residential to flood plain. This cut the value of the property by seventy-five percent. In striking down the zoning, the court observed that open-space preservation was a laudable objective but that the community could not demand such a sacrifice of property rights to achieve it. It was an appropriate situation, the court said, for the exercise of eminent domain. (*Dooley* v. *Town Plan and Zoning Commission of the Town of Fairfield*)

In a similar case, a Philadelphia suburban township changed the zoning on an undeveloped portion of a subdivision from residential to "flood-plain conservation district." The main cause of the occasional flooding of the area, the court found, was a road bank that had too small a drainage culvert under it. Put in a bigger culvert, the court suggested. As for the open-space objectives of the zoning, the court said, they were fine and lawful. It was just that the methods were unlawful. "What is attempted under the guise of police power," the court ruled, "is, in reality, the exercise of the power of eminent domain without compensation for the taking, and, therefore, is unconstitutional." (*Hofkin* v. *Whitemarsh Township Zoning Board of Adjustment*)

In most cases flood-plain zoning is fairly applied, and it does stand up in court. Even so, however, a community is wise not to rely too much on zoning alone. Flood plains need to be used. If they remain vacant land and no more, the vacuum is bound to be filled somehow. Short of purchase, the best way to stave off the pressures for variances is to encourage a compatible use of the land. One community I know of acts as a sort of broker for the properties in its flood-plain zones. Several years ago, when a large holding came up for sale, it went out and found an entrepreneur who would make a commercial golf course of it. Occasional flooding does little damage to the greens and fairways; they help keep down the amount of flooding downstream; people enjoy the golf; and the owner makes a profit. The zoning stands up beautifully.

Marshes and coastal wetlands should also be protected. They are still a no man's land as far as most local zoning ordinances are concerned, and the few citizens who urge their salvation are generally regarded as dotty birdwatchers. To the majority, marshes are so much waste land, and officials are often delighted at the prospect of increased ratables when developers come in with plans to fill them up.

The case for zoning marshes against development is just as strong as that for flood plains. They are even greater sponges, and they are also extremely important for wildlife. Coastal wetlands are among the most productive food producing areas in the world; they are a seedbed for marine life, especially vital for shellfish, and it does not take much dredging, or sewage, to do irreversible harm. In New England the famed Niantic Bay scallop has almost disappeared, and the Ipswich and Essex clams may be next.

Hunters and fishermen had made common cause with conservationists in supporting public acquisition of wetlands. But while the best way to save these lands is to buy them, as a minimum step they should be zoned in the meantime. And here, too, the state and federal governments should take action if the local governments do not. Massachusetts has taken a major step in this respect. Under recent legislation the state's Department of Natural Resources has been given broad police powers over coastal and inland marshes. If a landowner wants to dig or fill a marsh or bank along streams, ponds, bays, or the shore, he has to file his plans with the Department. If it finds harm will be done it can order modifications in the plans. This is to meet crisis situations, of which the state has had plenty. To prevent them from coming up, the Department has been empowered to set standards for the local zoning of coastal wetlands and to impose stiffer regulations itself where necessary. If a landowner thinks the regulations are so stiff as to amount to a taking of his property he can go to court; if the court agrees with him the Department may proceed to buy the land or an easement on it through condemnation. So far the Department has not had to make such purchases.

Wisconsin has taken much the same tack to protect the land along its streams and lakes. Under a 1966 statute, the state took the power to regulate land use along lakeshores and within flood plains away from town boards and gave it to county boards. The state laid down standards for the boards to follow in their ordinances. If they do not apply them, the state will do the zoning itself.

Similar legislation has been proposed for the protection of freeway interchanges. The federal government had a chance to make such protection mandatory when it launched the Interstate System. But it threw it away, and for lack of constraints the local governments have been allowing the roads to be choked with commercial development; and sometimes they encourage it. Since the interchanges are used and paid for by motorists in general, the state ought to protect their interests by demanding proper zoning, and if the local government defaults, the state should apply the zoning itself. Such legislation has yet to pass, but its day is coming.

One state, Hawaii, has gone so far as to institute statewide zoning for all its land. It divides the land into four categories—urban, agricultural, rural, and conservation—and on paper it has strong powers to prevent uses inconsistent with the particular zones. Hawaii is an unusual case, however; there are some very large landholdings there and the owners have welcomed the zoning, and the tax stability it promises. It is still too early to see how well the zoning is going to stand up over the long pull or how applicable it might be to other states.

In most states the major trend will probably be for more back-up zoning, and the threat of it will probably be more valuable than the practice of it. The state's major contribution will be to set zoning standards for local governments and prod them into recognizing the public interest larger than that of the immediate community.

The federal government will be doing more prodding too. So far it has not attached very many strings to its grants; for most grants it does ask that the community have a comprehensive plan, but since it also hands out grants for financing the comprehensive plan, it is no great burden for the community to do the paper work that will get them still more grants. The one thing the federal government hasn't been asking is that communities *do* something about their plans. But now it is starting to. Conservatives who have fought federal grants have always claimed that they were a foot in the door and that before long the government would be laying down stricter rules. They are quite right.

A county board helped bring about the harder line. The board was that of Montgomery County, Maryland, where, not so incidentally, a great number of federal officials live. And it was a very bad board. It had been voted out of office, but in the few days that remained before the new slate would take over, the lame-duck officials went on a rezoning blitz, and approved wholesale a series of applications for rezoning that had been made by developers. In the process, some two thousand acres that had been designated as an open-space reserve were rezoned for high intensity commercial and residential development.

The federal establishment was outraged to action. The

Department of Housing and Urban Development announced it was suspending some ten million dollars worth of grants it was about to give for open space and sewage treatment projects in the county. The Agriculture Department withdrew a grant for a small watershed recreation project. Interior Secretary Udall attacked the board as "a dreary little band of zoning lawyers and political fixers" and threatened to do everything in his power to keep federal installations and money grants out of the county unless the new board set things straight. It may be, as the *Washington Post* charged, that the reprisals were too harsh and that the incoming board would have revoked the action anyway. Federal officials felt if they couldn't act in a case as flagrant as this one, they couldn't act in any. The point is that they did act, they are glad they did, and they will be acting more like this in the future.

Another precedent was set in the establishment of the Cape Cod National Seashore. Some of the towns vigorously resisted the idea of wholesale acquisition, but after prolonged haggling a satisfactory compromise was worked out. The federal government agreed that it would not condemn additional lands if the towns would do a satisfactory job of zoning them against incompatible development. The federal government suggested the standards, and the towns incorporated them in their zoning ordinances. Those who know the Cape and its people will appreciate the magnitude of the achievement; if such accommodations can work on the Cape, the potential elsewhere must surely be tremendous.

Regional agencies are going to play a larger role in zoning. A few, like the Lake George Park Commission in New York, have the power to zone directly. But most regional agencies will do very little direct zoning whether they are authorized to or not. They do not have a sufficient political base of power. They can have leverage power, however, and this can be used quite effectively in drawing up model codes and persuading local governments to adopt them so that their procedures will be more uniform and their standards more representative of the region's interest.

So far we have been discussing land-use situations where the public welfare is clearly at stake. It can hurt the public if stream banks and wetlands are developed. Aesthetics do not have to enter into it; the public's health and safety are involved and it has every reason to apply the police power to the limits of reasonableness to protect such land.

But what about the land beyond—the upland meadows, the hillsides, the woods? Can the police power be used to prevent development here? It would be difficult to prove that the public would be actually harmed if such land were developed. The view might be prettier, but this is not reason enough. To invoke the police power it would have to be proved that the public benefits of leaving the land open would be surpassing, and even then tough legal questions would remain.

But this has not deterred a number of communities from making the attempt. By setting up "conservation" or "open-space" zones, they believe they can successfully retard, if not prevent, development of much of the countryside. They concede that they are pushing the police power very far, but they believe that the courts will eventually come around to their way of thinking, and that, in the meantime, they will save a lot of land. I think they are on the wrong track, but it is good that the experiments have been made. If they do not work, we will know better what will.

The prime example of this approach is agricultural zoning. The case for it is an appealing one. Farmland is the heart of most of our landscapes and for aesthetic reasons alone the public would benefit were it preserved. But there are stronger reasons to advance. On the basis of economics and resource values, it is argued, farmland preservation is not just desirable, it is essential. The farmland around our metropolitan areas is usually the best farmland of all, with the richest soils and the most amenable topography. But it is this irreplaceable prime land and not the marginal land that developers go for first. Everybody loses, yet there is no reason they have to. Exclusive zones have been set up to protect residential areas and industrial and commercial areas. Why not exclusive zones for agriculture?

California's Santa Clara County was the first to try the idea. It had a special reason to. Its flat valley floor is many inches deep with some of the richest soil to be found in the world, and until shortly after the war it was devoted almost entirely to intensive specialty-crop agriculture. Then the subdividers, moving south from San Francisco, began to spill into the valley. By 1954 the place was a mess. The subdividers had taken only a fraction of the land, but they had taken it in bits and pieces, with the result that the farms and subdivisions were all mixed up together, to the benefit of neither.

The farmers were caught in a squeeze. The new subdivisions were vastly increasing the service load on local governments and swamping the school districts with thousands of new children. The farmers did not contribute to the new service load, but they were being taxed for it just the same. Mill rates were going up. Worse yet, assessed valuations were going up too. The assessors, like those in most farm areas, were still appraising farmland mainly on its farm value, but they were coming under strong pressure to raise assessments to something nearer actual market value.

Farmers got together with the county planning commission and worked up a plan for exclusive agriculture zones. In some areas the farms had been so chopped up there was little hope they could survive as farms much longer. But there were still many relatively large expanses left. These were set up as "green belt zones." Within their limits there could only be farming—no subdivisions, no commercial establishments. It was hoped that the designation would make it easy for assessors to continue valuing the land only as farmland and that it would also put a stop to the practice the local municipalities had of annexing farmland and enveloping it in their tax structures. To make doubly sure, the farmers went to the state legislature and got a law which said that municipalities could not annex land in agricultural zones against the farmer's wishes.

The program worked well, for a while. By 1958 some 40,000 acres of farmland had been zoned; by 1960, 70,000 acres. For good measure, the county planners enfolded golf courses and an airport in the agricultural zones, observing that these uses were highly compatible. News of the experiment spread. Other California counties began to apply exclusive agricultural zoning, especially those with highly specialized crop land, like the lettuce farms of the Salinas Valley. Several years later farm groups in the Midwest and East began to see its possibilities, and in a number of areas variants of it were applied.

Back where it started, however, the cracks were beginning to appear. The agricultural zoning had saved large unbroken tracts, and large unbroken tracts were what developers now wanted most. They raised the offers—to $3000 an acre, to $4000, to $5000. Farmers began to ponder. They had gotten themselves zoned; they could get themselves unzoned. They could, among other things, ask the nearest city to annex them. One by one they began to do so. The cities, which had detested the idea of exclusive agricultural zoning from the beginning, went to great lengths to oblige. If the farm was far away, they simply gerrymandered the city boundaries to meet it, sometimes snaking out a strip along several miles of road to do it. By 1965 five thousand acres had been subtracted from the agricultural zones; by 1968 several thousand more.

The county planners have been well aware that the zoning would not hold land open very long and have always argued that other means would be needed. They are glad they tried it; there wouldn't be much open space left to save by other means if they hadn't. And there still is some; if you are in an airplane approaching San Francisco from the south, look down and you will see several large expanses of green where the original zones were established. But they are remnants, and the farmers who have kept on farming within them have put themselves in a most interesting position. (The stakes are now running $8000 an acre and up.) How much longer will they hold out? Whatever the decisions, zoning is not going to control them.

In Santa Clara County it does take some work to get out of a zone. In most other areas agricultural zoning has been mainly a matter of nomenclature, designed to impress the assessor as much as anything else. If a farmer wants to subdivide, he need only ask for a zoning change and he will get it. There are few cases on record where one has ever been turned down. In many cases the farmer does not even have to ask for a change; most agricultural zoning is cumulative, permitting agriculture and subdivision into one- or two-acre lots.

Estate zoning suffers from the same defects. Occasionally a group of large landowners will have their area zoned as an open space or conservancy district with any development restricted to extremely large lots of ten acres or more. For a while, the designation serves the interest of landowners and the community; taxes are kept low for the owners, and the community gets a moratorium on subdivision. When the owners decide to develop, however, they don't want any nonsense about ten-acre lots. They want the zoning changed, and the community is in no position to make it stick. The zoning has not been an exercise of the police power; it has been a ratification of a status quo. Change that and the zoning falls apart.

Why not straight aesthetic zoning? This is what a lot of zoning done in the name of conservation is all about, and some people believe the time has come for a more direct attack. The courts seem more sympathetic. In broadening the concept of the public welfare they have been increasingly disposed to put more emphasis on community appearance. A relatively new form of zoning, historic district zoning, is applied largely for aesthetic reasons, and the courts have sustained it.

What is really new, however, is candor. For years communities put through zoning regulations for aesthetic purposes, but they advanced every reason but the real one to justify them and the courts did their best to go along with the fiction. "The irony," says planner-lawyer Norman Williams, Jr., "is that most of the fuss and legal trouble over aesthetics has arisen from regulating the ugliest things, such as billboards; and yet many more drastic regulations have been upheld on the grounds that they are really concerned with something else, something more conventionally acceptable."

Now the courts are getting franker. The shift in attitude has been particularly important for billboard control. Not so long ago courts that upheld antibillboard ordinances would go through all sorts of tortured explanations to avoid the obvious; ordinances would be upheld on the grounds that the billboards might fall over and hurt somebody or that their back sides would provide trysting places injurious to the public morality. (Somewhat similarly, a California court upheld an ordinance against beach front houses on stilts, noting that the area underneath them might be an invitation to lewd conduct.)

In the aftermath of a key Vermont decision, the courts have been upholding billboard zoning on more forthright grounds. The argument, essentially, is that the public has a right of view. The public, after all, created the view; it built the highway, the landowner didn't, and antibillboard zoning is not taking anything away from him that was rightfully his. If he puts up billboards, he is trespassing on the public's right of view, and ordinances that forbid him to can be held a fair exercise of the police power.

Applying this power, of course, is something else again. The billboard people are an adroit lot, and they have found all sorts of ways to obstruct governments from taking what theoretically should be a very simple course of action. In the 1965 Highway Beautification Act, for example, legislators sympathetic to the billboard people stuck in a clause which said, in effect, that though zoning against billboards was perfectly all right, in certain areas, landowners who already had billboards in these areas ought to be paid for giving up their rights. By indirection, the provision undercut the whole basis of billboard zoning. It also called for compensation far huger than government appropriations committees would ever approve. But all is by no means lost. For all the backward steps, the major thrust of government action is likely to be for stronger control. Most states have not applied the police power to billboards as much as they should, but they are on sound ground when they do apply it, and by all indications the courts will sustain them.

For land control in general, the big breakthrough would appear to be the 1954 Supreme Court decision in the case of *Berman* v. *Parker*. This was prompted by a redevelopment project in the District of Columbia. Berman was a store owner in the area. When his property was condemned, he sued on the grounds that it was in perfectly good shape and should not be torn down to make way for something the planners thought would be better. The court upheld the taking. In Justice Douglas's words, it found that

"The concept of the public welfare is broad and inclusive. The values it represents are spiritual as well as physical, aesthetic as well as monetary. It is within the power of the legislature to determine that the community should be beautiful as well as healthy, spacious as well as clean, well-balanced as well as carefully patrolled."

This is heady language for planners, and some have been too exuberant in projecting its implications. *Berman* v. *Parker* was not a zoning case. It was a case about eminent domain, and Berman did get paid for his property, a point overlooked by those who think the decision is a call for achieving aesthetics through the police power. But the decision did serve to broaden the concept of what the public *purpose* involves. In explicitly taking up aesthetic values, it has opened the door to a more liberal construction of what governments can do about land use.

But there is a limit to what can be done with the police power. To recapitulate: for preserving open space the public can properly prevent people from building on flood plains; it can prevent the filling in of wetlands and of marshes; it can prevent landowners from closing off the view along the rights of way that the public has created. In all these cases the public's welfare is at stake, and, so long as the landowner is not unfairly harmed by the zoning, there is no reason to pay him for not injuring the public welfare.

The land beyond is the problem. We can slap any zoning designation we like on it—scenic reserve, conservation district, agricultural area, or the like—and as long as it suits the owners not to build on it we can maintain the fiction that we are successfully using the police power. But we are not. If it comes to a test, and it usually will, we will have to back down. Were we to try and make it stick, we would be put in the position of telling the owners that we are breaching our tacit understanding; we're not winking anymore—we have now decided that their land is so nice to look at undeveloped that they are jolly well to keep it that way. The owners would be indignant. They would say they had been entrapped and that we were trying to take their land without compensation. And so we would be.

We have gone beyond the limits of the police power. In trying to save open space, we are looking for a positive benefit, not just the absence of something harmful. Here is the vital distinction between the police power and the power of eminent domain. We cannot compel a benefit by the police power, for if we do we are forcing the owner to forego money that he might properly realize and thereby shoulder a cost that should be borne by the public. The law is clear on this point. If we want a benefit, we have to pay for it.

The distinctions are not to be fudged. It is all very well to say that this kind of zoning can buy time. But time for what? New legal devices may eventually be worked out, but by then the land will long since have been lost. The trouble with overextensions of the police power is that by seeming to work for a while they blind us to the very real conflicts of interest that will have to be tackled by other means—and to the urgency of doing it now.

4. The Fee Simple

>>

The best way to save land is to buy it outright—or in legal parlance, buy the fee simple. There are a lot of other ways to save land short of outright purchase, and later I am going to go into them in some detail—in particular the ancient device of the easement. It is obvious, however, that if there is to be any permanent open-space plan, the public, through its agencies, must have the money and the power to buy land. The existence of this power has a very great bearing on all of the other devices. If a local government has the right of condemnation, it is in a much better position to persuade landowners and developers to cooperate on measures that will make condemnation unnecessary. The stronger the stick, the less need to use it. There will even be more gifts of land. Communities with vigorous public purchase programs are usually the ones with the most vigorous private programs.

Public purchase is probably the oldest device there is, but until fairly recently it was generally assumed that a government could not buy land unless the public was going to use it actively—as a park, for example. The courts have been taking a broader view, holding that public purpose does not necessarily require public use. The recent state open-space acts have further clarified the issue by specifically naming the wide range of lands that can be bought and the different kinds of uses to which they can be put, public or private. In most of the big urban states, local governments can buy land that serves a public purpose by remaining open, whether or not the public sets foot on it—such as wetlands, highly productive farmland, land that has great scenic properties. Some of the acts also include land that is valuable for conserving water resources—a category that can be construed to cover almost any piece of ground one might have in mind.

The government can buy the land and then sell it back, subject to restrictions, to the original owner or to a new owner. It can buy lands and then lease them. It can spread out purchase over ten or twenty years, making installment payments to the owner while he still remains on the land. The permutations are almost infinite. So far, these various devices and combinations have not been much explored, but the possibilities, as I will outline in the next chapter, are quite exciting.

And now, at last, there is real money to work with. A good conservationist ought to take the position that there is never anywhere enough, as indeed there is not, but there is certainly a lot more than was ever available before. First, in 1961, the federal open-space program was set up; to date, it has provided some $133 million in grants to local governments in urban areas for open space acquisition. Next came the establishment of the Land and Water Conservation Fund program; since January 1965 it has provided $214 million in matching grants to the states for acquisition and park development.

Meanwhile, the states have been launching large-scale open-space programs of their own; in the last six years, voters in twenty-four states have approved bond issues for a total of some $455 million, and by an average plurality of 63 percent. Some states, such as Wisconsin, have earmarked special taxes for financing acquisition.

Most of the state programs include grants-in-aid, and as a consequence, local governments can multiply every dollar they put up for open space by three or four matching state and federal dollars. Terms vary from state to state, but generally it works out that the federal government pays 50 percent of the cost, the state 25 percent, and the local government 25 percent. The grants have only a few strings. The community cannot bar people from the open space on the basis of race, creed, color, or residence, and if the open space is not kept open, the community has to provide comparable land or pay back the money.

There are many other kinds of grants to be had for the asking. The Department of Agriculture, which is now quite eager to get its share of the urban problem, offers "Greenspan" grants for bearing half the cost of converting excess cropland into local parks and conservation areas. It also provides money for recreational areas around dams put up under the Small Watersheds Act. There are federal grants for landscaping open spaces; federal and state grants for park development. This by no means exhausts the list; the basic manual listing federal grants available for communities runs to some 413 pages. There are so many different kinds of grants, indeed, that some local officials are confused to the point of not applying for any. A number of enterprising communities have people working almost full time on searching out grants, and some retain consultants for the task. It has become almost an occupation in itself with an arcane lingo of its own. ("First, we'll try HUD for a 701 for $50,000 and follow up with a Title 7 for $300,000 . . .")

For the federal government's own park and forest programs Congress has been authorizing expenditures at a great rate; in the three years since January 1965, some $2.7 billion worth of recreation projects. Appropriations of actual money, however, have been something else again, totaling only $131 million. Congress has been gearing its appropriations to the revenues earmarked for the Land and Water Conservation Fund—entrance fees and park permits, taxes on motorboat fuels, and sale of surplus federal property. Entrance fees and permits have fallen far below expectations and the total receipts for the Fund have been averaging only about $100 million a year.

To beef up the Fund Congress is thinking of other revenues to tap. One munificent, and relatively painless, solution would be to earmark the money the government gets from offshore oil and gas leases. These revenues, which now go into the miscellaneous receipts of the Treasury, are running at about $300 million a year and before long should be up to $500 million a year. The administration is asking that $200 million of the annual revenues be given to the Fund. Some in Congress, notably Senators Jackson and Kuchel, would like to see all of the oil money go into the Fund, and more besides. It would be none too much, they say, and the more of it provided now, the less the land would cost in the long run.

While appropriations for land acquisition have been rising, the price of land has been soaring. On the average, land prices have been going up between 5 percent and 10 percent a year and the price of the open-space land that is best for parks has been going up much faster. For one thing, it has more speculative potential left in it. Most suburban land suitable for development has already been rather fully priced, some of it exorbitantly so. The kind of marginal or wooded land suited for recreation, however, starts from a much lower price base, and once it is in the wind that the government is thinking about it, asking prices start to soar. A guaranteed buyer is on the horizon. To be sure, the government may eventually condemn the land if it does not like the price, but it will have to pay fair market value, and there are all sorts of ways for owners to elevate this figure.*

* "Quick take" procedures used by many state highway departments could be of help. Where these are authorized, the public agency can condemn the land and take possession without having to wait until the size of the award is settled. But the agency has to have the funds in hand; it cannot quick take land in anticipation of getting money later.

They will have plenty of time to do it, too. There is usually a very long interval between the time a park acquisition is first proposed and the time the negotiators can go to work. For federal acquisitions, the period is measured in years, and in some cases, decades—the Indiana Dunes proposal, for one, was first considered by Congress thirty years ago. Even in what could be called the final stages, there will be lengthy hearings, sometimes stretching over two or three years—for the Cape Cod National Seashore, the hearings spanned some four years. When the park is finally authorized, there will be much cheering over the action, but this step is only the beginning.

Most citizens fail to realize the tremendous difference between authorization and appropriations. The basic act may authorize many millions for the project, but it is nothing more than a permit for the proponents to go before the Appropriations Committee and see how much of this they can get in actual money. The committee takes its own good time. Nine months or more will go by before it votes some money. It will not be the full amount either, but a modest down payment. Planning and negotiation will consume yet more time. Usually two to three years will elapse between the time of authorization and the first purchases.

Prices will long since have started to take off. The people of the area, some of whom probably fought against having a park there, are on to a good thing and they know it. Local officials could zone some of the area against commercial development, but in most cases they are not inclined to any kind of zoning, and especially zoning that would curb the property rights of the local landowners, some of whom may be officials themselves.

Owners who only a few years ago would have been very happy to unload their land at $100 an acre, develop a sudden interest in the commercial potentials of their land. A favorite device is to have a civil engineer draw up a development plan for the property. Some of these are quite imaginative, with sketches of ski tows, marinas, resort villages, and shopping centers to demonstrate the great development potential at stake. The landowner may have no intention of going ahead with the plan or the capital to do so. But this is immaterial. The purpose of the plan is to get the price up. Obviously, says the owner, fair market value is now at least $1000 an acre. This may not impress the government negotiator, but it can be very useful in arguing for a sizable condemnation award.

In some cases, the owner will go ahead and start putting up buildings. Either way, he can't lose. If the negotiators decide the property is too expensive to buy, he ends up with a prime chunk of land beautifully protected by surrounding parkland. If the land is condemned and the buildings have to be torn down, he will still get more money than if he had not built at all.

This is what happened at the Point Reyes National Seashore in California, one of the more flagrant examples of escalation. When Congress authorized purchase in 1962, the total cost was estimated at $14 million. By the time this money was available, however, speculators had driven the cost up by double the amount. In 1966, Congress came across with another $5 million, but the gap was wider than ever. Total estimated cost is now $58 million—leaving some $38 million to go, *if* prices don't go up anymore, which they assuredly will.

What is to be done? Bigger appropriations, of course,' would help. What agencies want most, however, is to have money faster, whatever the amount. To beat rising prices, they need money in hand for down payments. Rather than wait until the full sums are appropriated, two to five years later, they would like to be able to go ahead and purchase the key tracts or options on them just as soon as the project is authorized.

Congress is making a partial move in this direction. It proposes to give the Interior Department permission to contract for parkland in advance of appropriations. The check will be by no means blank, however. The project will have to have been authorized by Congress and no more than $30 million a year is to be obligated by such contracts. But legislators are chary of widening the door further to this kind of anticipatory spending. They call it "back door" financing. They might favor it for their own particular measures, for it means bypassing the hurdle of the Appropriations Committee, but in general principle they are against it.

The Appropriations Committee is most especially against it, and it has ways of visiting its wrath on any government agency that gets away with it. (In the original open-space grant provision of the Housing Act of 1961, authorization was given for a "contract financing," that is, spend the money and Congress will have to pay the bills. The Appropriations Committee brought everyone to heel by threatening not to appropriate money to pay the light, heat, and salaries for the people administering the program.)

One solution is a revolving fund. The legislature provides the agency with an initial stake for making tactical purchases of land in advance of need. Later, when the legislature makes regular appropriations for the projects involved, money covering the cost of the purchases already made will be credited to the fund, thus replenishing it for additional advance work. The advantages are many. It helps the agency beat out speculators for land it knows it is going to have to buy eventually. It also gives its negotiators much greater latitude in dealing with the land market. Often it is best to wait until a property comes onto the market. Then the owner wants to sell, perhaps urgently. If the negotiator can take advantage of such situations as they come up, he will do far better than if he has to force the market later, and on a lot of properties all at once. By the advance buying, he will also have spared the public from having to pay extra for any additional building that may have been done on the properties.

A good example is the fund the California legislature set up in 1952 for the advance acquisition of highway rights-of-way. The Highway Commission dips into this to buy properties that look as if they are about to be developed. It then rents them until it is time to build the highway, which may be as long as ten years in the future.

During this time there will be some landlord and tenant problems, and the Highway Commission will have to devote a good bit of its rental revenues to keeping the properties in shape. Overall, however, it saves a tremendous amount of money. With the fund the Commission has so far acquired approximately $72 million worth of properties. If acquisition had been put off and the properties developed, it estimates, the cost would total about $400 million. There are other savings, too. The Commission will have to spend less demolishing new buildings for highways; it will have fewer people to be displaced; fewer stop-the-highwaymen controversies.

But Congress and most state legislatures have not been very keen on revolving funds. They detest giving "blank checks" to the executive branch, especially when it is run by the other party. Legislators do not want the executive branch to spend money on any project they have not specifically reviewed and authorized. As a consequence, the capital budgets for forest and park acquisition programs are usually drawn up in minute detail ($220,000 for purchase of inholdings in Forest A, $85,000 for purchase of a six acre addition to Beach Park B, and so on). Up to a point, there is good reason for demanding such detail. The trouble is that even the heftiest budget is rarely accompanied by so much as a token amount in free funds.

For lack of such flexibility, normal budgeting procedures discourage new approaches. The pity is that not much money would be required. Check the plans of most state agencies and you will find that the imaginative programs involving new tools or a joint effort by two or more agencies add up to a fraction of the total program—one percent would be a generous figure. But it is precisely these kinds of projects which get cut out in the usual budget process. When the time comes to submit the first draft of a capital budget, agencies may stick some of these projects in, but their real concern is the shelf of projects for which they did not get enough money in the past—adequate parking facilities for a state park, for example. When the governor's office says everyone is asking for too much money and to cut thirty percent, everything but the conventional projects go—even before the legislature has had a crack at the list.

Because they do not have any discretionary money to speak of, acquisition agencies are inhibited from experimenting; they are also inhibited from grabbing the most obvious kinds of opportunities. A relatively small amount of money at the right time could save many times that amount later—and land that might not be available later at all. There is hardly any acquisition agency, state or federal, that cannot document this in dismal detail. Back in 1952, to cite one example, the Forest Service was offered a piece of property for $12,000. It wanted the property, and the price was fair. It did not, however, have any appropriation for the purchase. Helplessly, it watched the property change hands over a period of ten years, gathering improvements with each successive owner. In 1962, the Forest Service finally obtained funds. It bought the property for $198,000.

Unless they have free funds to tap, agencies are also unable to exploit unforeseen opportunities. Hurricanes, for example. These ill winds occasionally do blow some good, for in ravaging coast lines, they often clear many stretches of beachfront that had been sealed to public access by low-grade shanty-type development. If officials could move in quickly, they could compensate the owners right away and secure the land at moderate cost. But they do not have any money for this. The legislature might well be disposed to give it to them, but the legislature probably will not be in session. By the time it does meet again, which could be two years off, real-estate people will already have snapped up the shorefront lots and put up a new strip of buildings.

A ready fund would be invaluable if there were a bust in land prices. Such a possibility is not even countenanced by planning staffs, almost all of which take it for granted that land prices will continue to rise. This is one more good reason for anticipating an interruption. It could be spectacular. The price of unimproved land is now so inflated that in many cases it has gone beyond the level that is economically sustainable. Developers cannot raise housing prices enough to make up for the increase. This is especially true of second-grade land that is not well located, for the price of it has risen proportionately more than that of the prime tracts.

A shake-out is overdue. If one comes, and I think it will, the times will probably be tough for public finances as well and thus it will be all the more important to have had a ready fund already established. It is just at such times that bargain opportunities for acquisition present themselves. It was not in the prosperous twenties, but in the depression years of the thirties that some of our greatest acquisition programs were accomplished.

For enlightened opportunism, private groups have been best. Some have revolving funds of their own and often use these to pre-empt land for later public acquisition. The best example is the Nature Conservancy, a national organization with local chapters. It will buy land public agencies would like to have; and when the legislatures get around to providing the money, sell the land to the agencies and put the proceeds back into the revolving fund.

Because they operate without any fanfare, the private groups can often strike much better bargains than public agencies. Recently the Western Pennsylvania Conservancy set about acquiring some nine thousand acres of land for a regional park. It didn't say a word about its plans. Parcel by parcel it proceeded, so quietly that over the two years the acquisition took, speculators never caught on to what was happening and prices remained stable. The Conservancy is now turning the property over to the state.

With good lawyers and little money, private groups can also do a lot to obstruct speculators' acquisition plans. A good example is the foiling operation staged by the Philadelphia Conservationist on the New Jersey coast. With its ready fund, it snapped up seven areas with the idea of eventually turning them over to the state or federal government. A certain two-and-a-half-mile stretch of barrier

rangements. The National Park Service has made extensive use of this device. Often it will buy the property with the proviso that the present owners can continue to use the land, subject to normal restrictions, for a stated period of years or as long as they live. (In return for the tenancy, the Park Service reduces the purchase price somewhat. Regular formulas, known as the Inwood Tables, are used to figure the amount of the deduction.)

Still another variant is purchase and sale-back. Under the excess condemnation laws of some states, the state can buy more land than is needed for a particular purpose—such as a highway—and then lease back or sell back the land for uses that will make it serve as a buffer zone. So far, very little use has been made of this approach.

Many planners think it might furnish the major tool. They would like to see wholesale public acquisition—not merely as a means of keeping open space but of determining what spaces should be developed and how. As time went on, the public agency would sell or lease land to people who would build in accordance with the comprehensive plan for the area.

From the planners' point of view, this would be the ideal, and they can point to many European examples as evidence that the results would be excellent for the public. Stockholm is one of the best. In 1906 it started buying up the farmland that surrounded it and then leasing it back to farmers. As the city grew, the planners were able to determine which areas would stay open, which would be developed with new towns, and how. The city, in effect, owns its suburbs and a great deal of the still-undeveloped land beyond.

Municipal land acquisition of this order of magnitude is beyond reach here. It is not that the public would recoil from this as socialism. Aided by appropriate euphemism, we have been expanding the concept of public ownership rather markedly—urban redevelopment, to cite one example, is as drastic a use of eminent domain as may be found in any country, socialist or otherwise. The trouble is that the time is too late.

Our cities have, if anything, practiced a reverse procedure. Where they did happen to have land, they did
not bank it but sold it, and often for a pittance.* Land is
now in such short supply they are having quite enough
trouble getting sufficient money to acquire the high-priority
recreation spaces that are needed. Even were we to assume there would not be further price escalation, it is
extremely difficult to see where the money would come
from for the vastly greater amount of public acquisition
that would be required for industrial and housing development.

This qualification aside, however, it is entirely practical
to urge cities to do much more with the purchase and
lease-back approach. One possibility is a revolving land-
bank operation. One agency would buy land for future
needs, rent it out or manage it in the interim, and then
transfer it at cost to specific agencies. Such an operation
would require a hefty initial grant to get it started, and
there would undoubtedly be some intragovernmental bick-
ering as to what agency is to get what land, comprehensive
plan or no.

But federal support, very very slowly, is moving in this
direction. The housing people have been pushing the idea
of public development corporations for new communities.
Aided by federal grants, communities would acquire land
for new town development. The parts to be developed
would be sold or leased to the developers who would hew
to the general plan. When this idea was first presented to

---

* A flagrant example is the rape of Staten Island. New York
City had acquired large amounts of land there through tax
foreclosures on ill-fated subdivisions of the 20s and 30s. This
gave the city a superb chance to gain open space and to ensure
amenable development when the next building surge began after the war. It threw it away. The city sold off the parcels in
dribs and drabs and as a consequence the obsolete street patterns planned for the defunct subdivisions laid the pattern.
There is still hope for some of the unbuilt land. The city recently adopted a cluster ordinance and is encouraging a "new
town" type development for one area. But it is very late in
the game.

Congress in 1961, it so outraged some members as to endanger the more modest open-space grant proposal. It keeps coming up, however, and though the basic idea is regularly beaten down in Congress, a few steps have been taken. The FHA is now authorized to underwrite loans to developers for land assembly. The Department of Housing and Urban Development can give grants to communities to pay the interest charges on money they borrow for advance land acquisition. Because of restrictions in the law, however, few communities have applied.

For the present, the principal difficulty with purchase and leaseback is that the capital has to be put up all at once. Though the long range rewards of such projects are great, they are long range and in the meantime officials have lots of projects of more immediate use to think about. Since there is rarely enough money to go around, it is the immediate projects that usually win out.

One way to get around this problem is to buy the land on the installment plan. The best example is furnished by the Maryland-National Capital Park and Planning Commission. When its budget for long range park acquisition was cut back it dreamed up something called the "option-agreement plan." Instead of waiting until it has enough money to buy a farm it would like to have for later park use, it goes to the owner and proposes that he sell it to the Commission in takes—so many acres a year for a given number of years. If the period is for ten years, he will sell a tenth of the property each year. During this time he remains on the land and continues to farm it. He gets his capital gains spread over ten years instead of one, and since the Commission takes title to the land at the beginning, he does not have to pay local property taxes any more.

The Commission nails down the land for only a fraction of the money it ordinarily would have to put up and it freezes the cost of subsequent payments—the price of the last acre ten years hence will be the price of the first acre. The Commission does not have to spend any money to maintain the land; the farmer maintains it. As part of the bargain he agrees not to cut down trees or otherwise change the character of the property. Until the land is needed as a park, it is kept in productive use, and the landscape is the better for it.

The Commission has secured 2000 acres with this technique and expects to secure 5000 more over the next twelve years. Escalation or no, the program should be satisfyingly retroactive. Currently, the Commission is negotiating new option-agreements for rural properties at about $1000–$1200 an acre and that is what it will be paying for these particular properties in the mid-seventies. In the meantime, thanks to earlier agreements, it is still buying land at the $300–$400 an acre prices of the early sixties.

Another technique is pre-emptive buying. There is, let us say, a large tract of land bordering a river. It is semiderelict land consisting of many patches of marshland and an abandoned gravel pit or so. It would make an ideal shoreside park, and the cost of the land is still fairly reasonable—$500 an acre. The public agency does not have enough money to buy the land now, but it would very much like to nail it down somehow.

Unfortunately, this kind of tract can be immensely attractive to speculators. They will have to spend a lot on land and improvement, for they will have to dike and fill the marshland to make it suitable for commercial development. But it still will be an excellent deal. The speculator will pay $500 an acre for the land, another $1000 an acre in land improvement, and then mark it up to $10,-000 an acre.

Because he has to do so much diking and filling, however, the speculator is highly vulnerable to one simple ploy. The public agency does not have to buy up the land to forestall him. All it has to do is buy a few strategically placed parcels. Once it gets title to these, the public agency—or for that matter, a private agency—can start raising all sorts of legal mischief to enjoin surrounding development; at the very least, the speculator would have to go to great added expense in his diking-and-filling operation to protect the parcels that are not his.

The fish-and-game department of one New England state is especially adept at this kind of tic-tac-toe. In the absence of sufficient money to buy prime coastal wetland areas, it has bought time with a spoiling operation. Its negotiators, who vastly enjoy what they call their dirty-tricks project, have very skillfully picked up enough isolated tracts to effectively seal many thousands of acres against development that otherwise would be inevitable.

Wetlands are particularly suitable for this kind of operation. Land holdings of this kind usually have very cloudy titles, particularly so along the Eastern Seaboard where titles date back to the early colonial times. The original parcels were often laid out in long strips most of which were subsequently chopped up into smaller and smaller bits. The original surveys, which were in metes and bounds, read something like a clue to a treasure hunt. "From the large oak tree, thence nearly along Watkins Creek Road and bounded severally by the tract owned by Wilkins and the Point Road, so called." It is difficult enough to figure out what the present boundaries of the tract are; it can be even more difficult to try to find who owns it. Heirs are dispersed all over the country, and just to clear title in one tract can involve literally hundreds of people. This makes it very tough for the speculator to assemble his land in a reasonable period of time. It's tough for a public agency, too, but it has one ace card that the speculator does not. It can condemn land and automatically clear title. For this reason there are many "friendly" condemnations, for even though the seller and the public agency are agreed on price, the condemnation will clear up questions of title.

There are a surprising number of landowners who would give land if someone asked them to. It is not quite as simple as that, of course; the man who is doing the asking has to know a great deal about legal and tax matters and

he must be a good salesman. There are few such people. Training them takes time and money, and there have
been few efforts to put real backing behind this kind of
operation. Yet there is probably no greater leverage opportunity to be seized.

It has been mistakenly assumed that the day of large-
scale land giving is pretty well passed. Over half of our
existing park holdings were donations, but a large proportion of these date back to the days when income taxes
were low and there were many wealthy people with huge
landholdings. There are still a few left, but not very many,
and as the big estates have been broken up and sold off
by heirs, land that once might have ended up as parkland
is being taken over for schools and convents.

But the gift potential is as great as ever, and in considerable part because of taxes. While large-scale landholdings
have diminished, there are a great many moderately sized
landholdings the owners of which have a very strong feeling for the landscape, city people especially. That is why
they bought the land. To be sure, some of them also
bought it as something of an investment, and the increase
in market value provides a strong temptation to sell for
development. But this same increase also makes giving
more attractive; because of recent changes in tax and investment procedures, people who give land gain important
tax savings—in some situations, more in savings than the
value of what they are giving up. It is rare that people
give land just for tax reasons, but for those who would *like*
to give, the benefits can provide a fine additional stimulus.

But there is no regular mechanism for getting to these
people. Here and there, individual negotiators do an excellent job. A state-park man that I know makes it his avoca-
tion to find out who owns various parcels, and he spends
much of his off hours dropping around to visit with these
people. He is particularly well-known among his colleagues
for his ability to charm elderly ladies. "I play a waiting
game," he says. "I plant thoughts. I suggest to them what
a wonderful nature preserve their land would be and how
it ought to be named after them or in memory of their

husband. Then I get them to thinking about what their heirs might do with the land. I don't push them. After a while, they'll call me."

People who would like to see their land in safe hands can also call on private groups for assistance. Some will take title to the land and maintain it. Others prefer to hold the land on an interim basis and then turn it over to a public agency. A good example of the latter is the Massachusetts Trustees of Reservations, which since 1908 has been operating a sort of revolving land trust. They have secured key tracts—including some of the best parts of Cape Cod—and then, after rousing public interest, have turned many of them over to public agencies as parkland. In recent years there has been a sharp increase in the number of local land trusts, most notably in New England. These are tax-exempt organizations that will receive land from donors who are fearful of what local officials might do with the land once they got their hands on it.

Generally speaking, however, it is the landowner who must take the initiative. A few private groups have people working for them full time, but in most cases the work is done by volunteers. And while some of these are pretty good at twisting landowners' arms, most groups have neither the staff nor the resources to follow through on any systematic basis.

Recently, a group of people in the New York metropolitan region decided to organize such an effort. Most of the privately owned open space left in the region was held by about ten thousand people, or only 6 percent of the population. This was still a lot of people, and with some foundation money the group set up the Open Space Action Committee and started after them. The story of what ensued is worth telling in some detail. To save open space, the Committee had to write the book on the art of solicitation.

The first step was an "every owner canvass" in several test areas. Committee staff members, assisted by a corps of volunteers, went to the tax records and traced the ownership of all holdings of twenty acres or more. They then sent each owner a letter explaining what they were up to and a folder about "Stewardship," an excellent book the Committee had prepared on ways owners can preserve their land and the psychic rewards of doing it. Owners could have it free if they would merely check the Yes box on the enclosed post card.

The people who mail back the cards are the live prospects. The Committee sends the book, waits three weeks, and then follows up with a phone call. A lady of great charm and persistence handles this. After a warm-up conversation she tells the prospect that she might be able to have one of the executives of the organization personally pay a visit. Would an evening be suitable or would daytime be preferable? One out of four times, on the average, she secures an appointment. (Lawyers, she finds, are among the easiest to deal with; doctors, the most difficult.)

The field man calls. He suggests to the owner that they go off and walk the property together. This is important, for owners are usually very proud of their land and of their knowledge of its trees, plants, geological history, and they are apt to become quite expansive on such a tour. By the time it is over the field man will have a good idea of what heirs the owner has and what he thinks of them —a most critical point for the Committee—and what his inclinations for giving might be. The field man will offer the Committee's services as a middleman; it is not after land for itself, but it will assist in drawing up a conservation plan and finding suitable recipients to help carry it out.

The first round of solicitations was encouraging. It turned out that many owners had already been thinking about giving their land but had never gotten around to doing anything about it. Some landowners who had made the attempt discovered that it is not always easy to find somebody to give the land to. Counties are usually not interested in small or medium tracts, and towns are often not interested in any size tract unless they see immediate use for it. In several instances, owners had offered land to towns and had been flatly rejected, the town preferring taxes on the land to the land itself.

To bring the parties together, the field men spend almost as much time working on potential recipients as they do on givers. They make it their business to know local officials, members of school boards, private conservation groups, and find out from them what kind of land they might be interested in receiving and under what conditions. If they are not interested, the field men keep after them.

With this market in mind, the field man will make a detailed analysis of an owner's property and submit an "advisory memorandum" and sketch maps illustrating what might be done with it. He approaches this task in much the same spirit as eighteenth-century English landscape architects. Like Lancelot Brown, he will see capabilities—*great* capabilities. Here, adapted from several reports, is the way he might suggest them.

This unusually magnificent and well-cared-for property is beloved by many people. This is because the farm buildings and the meadows dotted by cattle make the view for motorists as they crest Edgmont Hill on the Parkway just west of the property. There is a special charm to such a landscape in an area in which practically all other farming has disappeared.

Considering the size of the tract there is an extraordinary variety of land forms and buildings and for this reason we suggest that you consider a multiple-purpose program that would involve several recipients:

Historical Museum: The 1787 main house would be an ideal headquarters for a museum for the Bellfield Historical Society. The wing added in 1828 could serve as offices and library.

Arboretum: This would be the area immediately south of the main house and would include the pond, the beautiful grove of mature hemlocks, and all of the present landscaped portion of the property, eight acres in all. Planning and maintenance could be done by the Bellfield Garden Club.

Town Park: Directly south of the Arboretum area are approximately twelve acres that would be most suitable as a recreation area for the town, with tennis courts and picnic areas in the stand of woods. There would be direct access from the east road.

Model Farm: The barn, the silo, and the stables would make the nucleus of a splendid educational center for the children of the area. There is a possibility that the school district might be interested in the acquisition and operation of the farm area under a grant through the new federal Title III program of the Education Act of 1965.

Nature Area: The low, moist ground and swamp area in the southwest portion should be left as a nature-study area with self-interpretative trails and one or two exhibit and lecture areas. This would provide an adjunct to the science curriculum of the school.

In summary, the property lends itself ideally to a multiple-use situation; the separate uses fit together, and would represent a much more effective use of the property than were it turned over to one recipient as a park.

At the very end of the report, the field man will tuck in a section on the mechanics of transferring property. Then he will take up the income tax advantages. He will treat these details in a low-key fashion, and well he can afford to. Most owners will already know the pertinent part of the Internal Revenue Code [Sec. 501 (c) (3)] backward and forward. Thanks to the 1964 revision of the code, the owner may now deduct up to thirty percent of his adjusted gross income for donations. If the value of the gift is over thirty percent, the excess can be carried forward as a credit and averaged out over a five-year period. Previously, any excess would have been lost as a deductible item.

In computing the value of the land he is giving, the owner does not appraise it merely on its open-space value, but on its full market value, including its "highest and best use" for development. He gets the maximum advantage of the rise in value that has taken place since he bought the property. However, since it is a donation, he is exempted from payment of a capital-gains tax. In effect, he gets a capital-gains tax in reverse.

The field man outlines the different ways the owner may maximize his gifts:

1. You can give all the property now and retain a life tenancy for the house and immediately adjacent area.

2. You can give the property less the main house area and designate the latter as a donation in your will.

3. Instead of giving the property all at once, you may give it on the installment plan. You may, for example, give an undivided interest of ten percent of the property each year for ten years, or five percent for twenty, or whatever arrangement would best suit your income-tax needs. Your will can deed to the recipient the undivided interest that remains.

4. You can give a positive interest to the grantee, affording use of the property with full title to be awarded to him as a testamentary gift.

5. If you would like to have your children have use of the main house area, this could be provided for in your will by stipulating a life-tenancy arrangement or a lease-back to them at a nominal charge.

Whatever the specific arrangements, your general intent for the conservation of the property can be protected to a considerable extent by the use of a rewritten will or a clearly written codicil. It should make clear to the heirs that you wish to protect the natural beauty of the land. The Committee, via its experienced legal counsel, is ready to help you and your attorney construct such a codicil.

To ensure that the open space you are giving will be used as you intend, you may wish to include a reverter clause. This would specify that if the land is converted to another use, ownership of it will pass to a third party. We suggest either the Nature Conservancy or the Bellfield Land Trust.

When you give land to tax-exempt organizations, you will no longer have to pay property taxes on it to the town. We recommend, however, that you consider a gradual rather than abrupt cessation by providing some payment to the town for several years in lieu of taxes. Such payments, it might be noted, can be entered as a deductible item on your income tax.

These recommendations can only sketch the various possibilities. As the next step, we suggest that you hold preliminary discussions with your attorney, the school board, the Bellfield Land Trust, the Nature Conservancy, the Garden Club, and the Audubon Society.

As to the role of the town, Supervisor Polanski has expressed strong interest in the joint conservation project for the property and is going to take the matter up with his Board. However, this is a local election year and the political situation is unusually turbulent. It may well be that further discussion will not be fruitful until November has passed.

The Committee wishes to express its gratitude to you for permitting these recommendations to be made and assures you that it would be happy to assist further in the follow-up work.

During the first year and a half of this program, the Committee worked up recommendations for the disposition of some 7000 acres worth approximately $30 million, and a good part of this land has already been pledged or given. In one sense this first phase was the easy one. The Committee went first to landowners wealthy enough to be able to give their land and occasionally an endowment fund for its maintenance as well.

Now the Committee is concentrating on the critical middle range of landowners, and they do not have this kind of money. Many say they would very much like to see as much of their property saved as possible; still, they do have their old age and their children to think of, and they cannot help but think of the money their property is now worth. Is there, they ask, some middle way they could give without it hurting too much?

To save land, the Committee is finding, one must know how to develop it. Field men now try to visualize uses of the parts of the property that would be profitable to the owner yet be compatible with preservation of the rest of it. In some cases, golf courses provide a happy solution. In most, however, some form of residential development would be involved.

The cluster principle, as I will take up in more detail in a later chapter, is providing a most useful lever. For one owner the Committee has recommended a plan that would preserve the bulk of the property and its key natural features and concentrate groups of houses on the remaining part. The owner could make more if he sold all of it for development, but not so very much more; by applying the cluster principle, development of a third of the tract can return him almost as much money as conventional development of the whole tract would.

There are difficulties to surmount. This is unfamiliar ground for conservationists; in addition to the usual parties at interest, they have to find imaginative site planners and enlightened developers, neither of whom are in strong supply, nor are they the most seemly of allies. When a plan is agreed upon, furthermore, it is likely to provide resistance from the local zoning board. But the members of the Committee think the new approaches worth the risks and that there is probably more to be lost by not trying them. If the "stewardship" idea is to be expanded, they believe, it will be largely through approaches that meet a landowner halfway, and sometimes a little more.

Private groups in other metropolitan areas are coming to the same conclusion. It is the intermediate ways to preservation that most interest landowners for now they see alternatives that they did not know existed. Multiple-use plans tailored to their land, and their circumstances, are opening up opportunities that the all-or-nothing approach could not, and many local governments as well as landowners are becoming increasingly receptive.

5. Easements

>>>

In discussing gifts and purchases of land, we have been talking largely of the fee-simple acquisition. This is the clearest and surest way to save land, but it can take us just so far. The number of landowners who can afford to give away their land is limited, and though more should be walked up the mountain, only so many will go along. Nor can we buy up the land. There is not enough money. Even were public acquisition funds tripled, they would fetch only a fraction of the landscape. If we did have the money, furthermore, what would we do with all this land? How would we maintain it?

But we do not need to buy up the land to save it. There is a middle way. Through the ancient device of the easement, we can acquire from an owner a right in his property —the right that it remain open and undeveloped.

To understand the device, let us go back to the origin of the term "fee simple." In medieval times, a great lord would grant a man a tract of land to use in return for which the man would be obligated to perform certain services, or fees. The land with the fewest strings attached—the simplest fee, you might say—was the closest to outright ownership. But there were always strings.

There still are. The fee simple has never been absolute or indivisible, nor, *laissez-faire* economics to the contrary, have landowners inherited license to do anything they please with the land. What the landowner has is a bundle of rights—the right to build on the land, for example, or the right to grow timber on it, or to farm the land. Some rights he does not have: his riparian rights to a stream running through his property may not include throwing a dam across it. All of his rights, furthermore, are subject to the eminent domain of the state.

When we wish to acquire a man's property, we usually buy the whole bundle of rights from him—the fee simple. But we can buy less. To achieve a particular purpose, we may only need one or a few rights in the property. We buy these, in the form of an easement, and leave the rest of the bundle with the owner.

One class of easements is positive; that is, we acquire the right to do something with part of the man's property. A public agency may buy a right of way for a public footpath or a hiking or bicycle trail; it may buy the fishing rights so the public may use the banks of a stream. Utilities may buy a right to lay a pipeline or high-tension wires across the property, and they have not the slightest qualms about using condemnation powers to do it. Businessmen may buy rights to cut timber on the land, to graze livestock on it, or to dig minerals under it. They may buy air rights to build a structure above it, or to make sure that nobody else does. When a property is being subdivided, municipalities require the developer to give easements for sewer lines and roads. There are few properties that do not have some sort of easement on them.

The other main category of easement is negative. In this case we do not ask for physical access to the property; what we do is to buy away from the owner his right to louse it up. Through a conservation or scenic easement we acquire from the owner a guarantee that he will not put up billboards, dig away hillsides, or chop down trees; with a wetland easement, we acquire a guarantee that he will not dike or fill his marshland. Except for the restrictions, he continues to farm or use the land just as he has before; one of the main points of the easements, indeed, is to encourage him to do just that.

To understand the benefits of the easement approach, it is important to understand its limitations. One of the reasons some observers have been critical of the device is that they have asked too much of it. They have considered it as a means for sweeping control of whole regions. In this scheme of things, a public agency would acquire easements for all the open land, not merely to keep it open but to stage development; phase by phase, certain easements would be relinquished so that development would be encouraged to go where the master plan indicated it would be best to go. This would be a terribly complicated procedure, as the British found when they tried something like it after the war. But the problem is not the limitations of the easement device; it is the expansiveness of the goal.

The approach to be discussed here is a more modest one. It is to tailor easements very closely to the pattern that has been set by nature and by such man-made features as highways. They would not be applied wholesale to blanket vast areas; in many cases they would be applied only to portions of individual properties.

Let us take a stream valley as an example. It is a beautiful valley on the edge of suburbia, still unspoiled, with most of the land in farms and small estates. The meadows on either side of the stream are a flood plain; and quite properly they have been zoned against development. The rest of the valley is zoned as low-density residential, with minimum lots specified at two acres. There are no subdivisions yet and landowners are still assuring each other that they would not dream of selling out. Most of them believe it.

Obviously, the place is ripe for development. Technically

speaking, the upland meadows and hills are quite suitable
for housing, with excellent soil percolation characteristics
for septic tanks and good drainage. We know development
is going to come, whether we like it or not. But there is
still some time to work with. We would like to use it to
secure the key spaces in the heart of the valley, the network of streams that run down to it and, perhaps, several
wooded ridges on the rim of the valley.

We have, then, three kinds of land: the flood plain that
can be kept open by zoning, the highly developable land
that probably cannot be kept open, and the in-between
land where there is a fighting chance. Here is where the
easements can be most useful. No one landowner has to
give up very much. He is not asked to give an easement
on all his property, but only on that part of it which falls
within the conservation zone along the streams.

The community benefits in a number of ways. It preserves the heart of the open spaces of the valley without
having to buy the land outright. The land remains on the

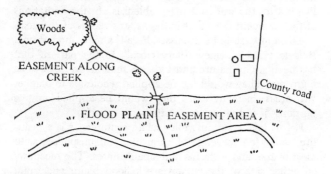

local tax rolls. There is, furthermore, no maintenance
burden: The owner, by continuing to farm the land, maintains the landscape, and the net result is far more pleasing
than were the whole thing formally manicured and maintained in conventional parkway style.

There are considerable benefits for the owners. The most
obvious is that they keep their land, and by agreeing to

the easement they forestall the necessity of outright acquisition. The possibility of such action can have a persuasive influence on the landowner. This is a tricky matter for public officials to deal with, for it is easy to get landowners' backs up. But in several instances where possibility of a condemnation has been softly raised by officials, landowners have become so enthusiastic about an alternative that they have offered easements as gifts.

Landowners may get more out of easements than they give up. By agreeing not to develop the most scenic portions of their property, they may enhance the value of the portions they might develop. It would be just as well, perhaps, if they didn't want to develop at all, but it can be pointed out that if later they did wish to build, they would have a more marketable proposition than otherwise. And subdivision, let us remember, is not necessarily the highest and best use. The market for estate land and relatively modest tracts for gentlemen or parttime farmers is a very flourishing one, and the supply of such land is getting smaller. Those who take the long view in this respect may do very well for themselves in the years to come.

Another important benefit for owners is the flank protection that they get. This is an important selling point in estate country, for owners there are often nervous about the intentions of some of their neighbors, and there are few things that worry them so much as the thought that they will wake up one morning to see bulldozers hacking into one of their favorite views. Where the easement program is tailored to the natural features and thereby involves a group of landowners, all benefit. This is another reason why it is good to have the power of condemnation in reserve. It can chasten holdouts who would exploit their neighbors.

Then there are the tax benefits. If a man gives an easement on part of his property, he can enter the value of it as a charitable deduction on his income tax. More important is the local property tax. If a man gives an easement, he will not necessarily get a reduction in his present

taxes; in all likelihood, the assessor has been valuing the
land only at its open-space value. What the easement does
is ensure that he will keep on valuing it that way and not
raise the assessment on the basis of the development
potential. Some states have passed laws to that effect, but
in principle they should be unnecessary. In most state
constitutions, there are guarantees against assessment at
more than fair market value. If a man gives an easement
on certain portions of his land, the assessor should recognize this in computing market value. He cannot rightly
value it as developable land if there is a binding agreement
that it is not developable.

Easements are very binding indeed, and there should be
no sugar-coating the fact. This is why they work. The
deed forms must be explicit as to what is granted and what
is not, and there can be no open-end clause by which the
purchaser can make up new conditions for the landowner
as time goes by. Such flexibility would appeal to administrators; it would not to the landowner or to the courts.
They frown on loosely drawn easements, particularly those
so loose that it is difficult to determine how much the
landowner is letting himself in for and, thus, how much he
is entitled to be paid.

Easements "run with the land," and their conditions
apply to subsequent owners of the property. Unlike cove-
nants, they are held by someone with a truly proprietary
interest in seeing that they are enforced. (One legal
complexity that some lawyers like to fondle is the matter
of "gross" versus "appurtenant" easements. What this boils
down to is whether or not you can acquire an easement
on a man's property if you don't have property yourself
nearby. Gist of opinions: Yes, you can, although it is often
helpful if you have a piece of property as anchor.)

Most easements are for perpetuity. Some people blanch
at the thought of such a commitment and would like to see
short-term easements. But the sale of the fee simple, or of
most anything else, for that matter, is for perpetuity, and
there are practical reasons why easements should be too.

If they are not, the landowner is likely to have trouble persuading the assessor to overlook the development potential. Nor will the landowner be able to get capital gains treatment. If the payments are for a lesser period they will be taxed as income, just as lease payments are.

Short term easements can also create problems for the purchaser. Public agencies have found that it is as much trouble to renegotiate an easement that is about to expire as to negotiate one in perpetuity and be done with it, and agencies that used to secure short-term easements are now switching to the long term. They find that it costs them no more to do so.

And perpetuity does not last forever. In almost every easement deed there will be a reverter clause to the effect that if the purpose for which the easement was acquired is abandoned, the easement will then automatically be voided and all rights will return to the owner of the fee simple. Many of the old interurban trolley lines were laid down on easements; now that the trolleys have gone, the easements have long since reverted. The people who own the land are often unaware of this, and in many areas these ghostly traces can still be found, weedy and unused.

The device, to repeat, is an ancient one, and its application to conservation goes back many years. In 1900 Charles Eliot had easement provisions incorporated into the Massachusetts Bay Circuit Act. At the urgings of Frederick Law Olmsted, a number of scenic easements were acquired in California. In 1930, through the Capper-Cramton Act, Congress authorized easement acquisition along the streams and parkways of the national capitol area. In the thirties, the National Park Service used scenic easements along many stretches of the Blue Ridge and Natchez Trace Parkways.*

* This was a pioneering program without enough pioneers. The National Park Service laid down excellent specifications for the rights-of-way, but the actual job of acquiring them was up to state highway departments, with the result that many of the easements were negotiated by people who did not much

But attempts were sporadic. By the late forties the device was almost forgotten. Conservation and park officials were not particularly interested in exploring its potentials, nor did there seem at the time a great reason to do so. The great postwar building boom was gathering force, but state and federal park acquisition was still largely in rural areas where fee-simple costs were low; anything over $150 an acre was considered very expensive land.

What prompted the new interest in easements was the outward push of suburbia, and the initiative for action came as much from land-owning groups as from public officials. The history of the open space acts is illustrative. In Monterey County, California, a number of landowners, alarmed at the threat to their magnificent coastline, warmed to the idea of giving easements on key scenic tracts to the County. There was some doubt, however, as to whether the County could accept such easements, and there was a feeling some sort of legislation would probably be necessary.

At the time, a lawyer and I had just finished drafting a model easement bill for Pennsylvania. It was not getting anywhere in Pennsylvania, a large-scale study project being then in process, and now that we look back on it, there were quite a few holes in the bill. But it was something on paper, and the Monterey people saw it as a lead. Their state senator, Fred Farr, was an ardent conservationist,

_____

believe in easements. The variance in attitudes showed up in the costs: in Mississippi, for example, easements averaged only three to ten percent of fee simple costs; in Virginia, forty percent. Negotiators did not follow a standard practice for appraisal and when farmers later compared prices with each other a number got mad because they felt they had been out-dickered. Exposition of the device was spotty. When the National Park Service took over the parkways, it found that many landowners had been given no clear idea as to what they could and could not do on the easement land. This caused enforcement problems, particularly with woodland. Over the years, the parkways have proved out very well indeed, but for quite some time these early easement problems were widely cited as reason for experimenting no further.

and with state planner William Lipman, he worked up a bill for the California legislature.

It was a great improvement on the Pennsylvania proposal. For one thing, it specifically authorized not only easements but the purchase of land for the purpose of selling it or leasing it subject to restrictions. Second, and perhaps more important, it greatly broadened the public purposes for which open space could be acquired, whatever the techniques, and clearly established that the purposes were by no means restricted to the traditional concept of immediate public use. It did all this, furthermore, in ringingly affirmative language. Here are the first two sections:

"It is the intent of the Legislature in enacting this chapter to provide a means whereby any county or city may acquire, by purchase, gift, grant, bequest, device, lease or otherwise, and through the expenditure of public funds, the fee or any lesser interest or right in real property in order to preserve, through limitation of their future use, open spaces and areas for public use and enjoyment.

"The Legislature finds that the rapid growth and spread of urban development is encroaching upon, or eliminating, many open areas and spaces of varied size and character, including many having significant scenic or esthetic values, which areas and spaces if preserved and maintained in their present open state would constitute important physical, social, esthetic or economic assets to existing or impending urban and metropolitan development."

There were only a few days left before the legislature was to adjourn, and ordinarily such a bill would not have had a chance. Because his fellow legislators had just voted down a billboard control program Farr had sponsored, however, they were feeling somewhat contrite, and the word was passed around that the next time it would be Fred's turn.

This was the next time. The bill passed unanimously. If it had been written in Chinese, Farr says, it would have passed unanimously.

As these things often happen, the particular local cause that prompted the bill ran into snags, and it was not until several years later that the Monterey program got going. The moment the bill became an act, however, hundreds of copies were made and sent to conservationists and planners in other states. It was fine news to them, and emboldened by the unanimity of the vote, they went to work on their own legislatures. In less than a year, New York had passed a similar bill, and in short order Maryland, Connecticut, and Massachusetts did likewise. Others were to follow—and eventually, I am happy to note, Pennsylvania.

While most planners welcomed the acts, some felt they were an invitation to rash action, and a few seemed gripped with the fear that communities would start saving too much land in advance of a comprehensive plan to determine what land should be saved. They need not have worried. Lead time on these things is very slow. There was no rush to precipitate action, nor was too much open space saved.

But here and there local and state governments stuck their necks out. They were not interested in being pioneers; they were trying to solve a particular situation and found easements would be useful. The news spread. Others tried the device. More enabling legislation was passed.

Now, at last, the breakthrough has arrived. Even highway departments have come around. Just in the last few years, the highway departments of most of the big states have embarked on large-scale scenic easement programs. The momentum should pick up. There is still self-reinforcing skepticism in many park and conservation agencies but no longer do they have a dearth of precedents to complain about. The key propositions about easements have been put to the test, and most of the important questions that stilled resolve have been answered.

How much do easements cost? The greatest single obstacle

to greater use of the device has been the assertion that it probably would cost as much to buy an easement as to buy the land outright. This is simply not true, but it has been repeated so often in the literature, accumulating footnotes along the way, that it has become a fact in itself. It gives officials just the discouragement they need.

Actual experience bears out what common sense would indicate. Easements are worth what the landowner is giving up. Sometimes this is a good bit; sometimes it is very little.

The rule of thumb for estimating the value of an easement is to figure the "before and after" value of the property; the difference between what the property is worth without the restrictions and what it is worth with them is the value of the easement. This depends on time and place. If you want an easement forbidding development on a piece of prime land in an area that is ripe for development, the owner is giving up a major part of the value of his property, or thinks he is, and you could pay through the nose. At the Antietam Battlefield the National Park Service has been offering landowners up to thirty percent of the fee value of their land for scenic easements, but the landowners have not been interested; they think the development of value is going to increase much more. In cases like this, it often makes more sense to buy the land outright.

In the rural areas where there is yet little development pressure, however, the cost of easements has been quite modest. A good example is the success Wisconsin has had with easements on the Great River Road along the Mississippi. Originally, the highway department was going to buy a wide right-of-way so the landscape could be kept to parkway standards. For a number of reasons, including the protests of sportsmen (who were afraid they would be sealed off from the river), the department decided to have a smaller right-of-way and protect it with scenic easements extending 350 feet from the center line on both sides of the road. Between 1951 and 1961, easements were secured along fifty-three miles of the road. Prices paid to landowners averaged $16 an acre, versus $41.29 for comparable land in fee simple. Since 1961, an additional 100 miles have been secured and though land costs in general have been soaring, prices paid for easements have risen only moderately, to an average of $21 an acre.

The Wisconsin highway people have learned a lot about keeping easement costs down. The most important factor, they emphasize, is clarity. Original costs and later enforcement costs depend very much on how well owners understand the device; violations are almost always the result of misunderstanding and ambiguity, not willful transgression. The highway people have kept such instances to a minimum by careful, and continuous, explanation of the terms of the easement. Recently, they revised the deed form to clear away the legal jargon and put into simpler English exactly what rights the landowner is yielding and what rights he is not.

As the highway people have been seeking more precision in the instrument, they have been applying it more flexibly. Instead of acquiring a uniform strip 350 feet on either side, they now tailor the easements to the contour of the view. If a nearby ridge foreshortens it, they buy no further; in other cases they may extend the easement to 700 or 900 feet. They will also zig and zag when they run up against unusual situations or very high-cost land. In areas just beyond town limits, for example, they do not try to buy all the development rights but secure an "urban scenic easement" permitting houses spaced three hundred feet apart. Where there is merchantable timber, they will buy the full fee simple, and will do the same with land that is of so little use that even the fee cost is nominal. (This is one reason why comparisons between fee and easement costs can sometimes be misleading.)

There are still problems to be licked. Appraisal costs, of fee purchases as well as easements, seem to have gotten out of hand. The highway department has recently professionalized its appraisal staff and one result is such a display of zeal in survey and documentation that it frequently costs as much or more to figure out what an

offer to a landowner should be as the offer amounts to
itself. Condemnation has posed no great difficulties—it has
been used in only about ten percent of the acquisitions—
but juries can be extremely generous at times; one recently
upped a $250 award to $6000. The highway department
would like the option of disengaging from the purchase
when juries ask that kind of money, but under present law
it has to go through with the deal.

On the whole, however, the economics have worked out
as well as the aesthetics, and for the landowners as well as
the public. Had there not been an easement program,
many stretches of this road would long since have become
rural slums. Nobody would have made much money out of
it—a few dollars for leasing billboard sites, some income
from a trailer camp—and everyone would have paid in
future values. But the desecration has not taken place, save
in stretches within town limits. Along most of this splendid
road each man's property enhances his neighbors' and the
whole is the greater for these parts. Landowners have not
had their values diminished. A check of sale prices indicates
that land covered with easements has been fetching as
much as comparable land not covered by easements. Some
people believe that in time the properties protected by
easements might actually fetch more.*

The constitutionality of the program, furthermore, has
been successfully tested. One group of landowners brought
suit against the state, charging that the easements were
only for aesthetic goals and that this was no proper public
purpose since the public didn't get to use the land. In a
decision of great importance to other states, Wisconsin's

---

* Experience along the earlier Blue Ridge Parkway has not
been as satisfactory. In the *Appraisal Journal* of January 1968,
Howard L. Williams and W. D. Davis report that a study of
land sales along the parkway in one county in North Carolina
indicate that portions of property covered by scenic easements
fetched appreciably less on the market than comparable land
without easements. They also found, however, that owners did
not suffer any loss of value, or "severance damages" on the
remainder of their properties.

Supreme Court upheld the easements. They did serve a
public purpose, the court held, providing "visual occu-
pancy"; they were not imposed by the police power, but
were paid for under eminent domain, and the legislature
had laid down proper standards for their application
(*Kamrowski* v. *State*, 31 Wis. 2d. 2456; 1966).

People who want to know the costs of scenic easements
should study the costs of actual scenic easements—those
along the Great River Road, for example. This would seem
obvious enough, but there has been a persistent tendency
among officials to look away from the obvious. They
hypothesize what easements *might* cost, and without
making clear what kind of easements they are talking
about. Officials who want to stick with straight fee acquisition sometimes arrive at alarming generalizations
about the cost of scenic or conservation easements by using
the costs of quite another kind of easement and they sometimes forget to mention the unusual circumstances involved. They are particularly fond of cost data about flood
easements. With these the public buys from landowners
the right to flood private lands around reservoirs if it
becomes necessary. Most of the time it is not necessary,
but the landowners are obviously yielding rather considerable rights, and the easement costs are likely to run
to about eighty percent of the cost of the fee. If the land
is suitable for recreation the public agency would have
good reason to pay the additional twenty percent to secure
it outright.

It hardly follows, however, that easements in general
cost eighty percent of the fee simple. There are no easements in general. Each is specific. It is one thing to ask a
man to keep his land looking nice and quite another to tell
him you want to put it under water, and to talk of the
costs of one by using the data of another is to talk of apples
and oranges.

People who want to use easements can be similarly
imprecise. The most frequent error is a failure to distinguish
between a scenic easement and an easement that grants
public access. The two rights can be combined in an ease-

ment deed for a particular tract, but the two can't be had for the price of one. Several years ago a town conservation commission found that the owners of parcels that made up an especially attractive meadowland were quite receptive to scenic easements; most, indeed, said they would give the easements. The commission members were so encouraged by this proffer of good will that they got a little greedy and decided that for good measure they would add to the deeds a provision for public access. The landowners stiffened. Who would pick up the trash? How would the hordes be kept away? The gift offers were withdrawn; some landowners said they would be damned if they would give the easements at any price. The program was stalled for three years, and only now, on a more modest scenic-easement basis, is it at last getting underway.

Another key variable in costs, and one that is rarely noted in studies, is the man who is doing the negotiating and, sometimes more important, the man who runs the department. In tracking down scenic-easement costs I have been struck by the relationship between such presumably objective data as payments to landowners, engineering and survey costs, incidence of court appeals and the like to the attitude the officials have toward easements. In those states where officials welcomed the easement approach, cost figures have been moderate, there has been little litigation, and enforcement problems have been minor. In those states where officials didn't welcome the approach, cost figures have been notably higher, and there have been recurring maintenance and enforcement problems.

The Wisconsin experience sheds further light on this phenomenon. In 1962 Governor Gaylord Nelson proposed a $50 million conservation program, and noting the Highway Department's success with the Great River Road easements, he called for a broadened use of the device by other agencies.

"In addition to scenic easements," he said, "I propose that we purchase public access rights, public hunting and fishing rights, use and alteration rights of headwaters and spring heads, wetland drainage rights, scenic overlook rights, fencerow rights for the protection of game cover, platting rights along trout streams, subdivision and timber-cutting rights along lake shorelines, and development rights to protect lands adjacent to state parks and camp grounds from the clutter of billboards, taverns, and concessions."

The state conservation department was not enthusiastic. At the hearings before the legislature, a top official said he and his colleagues yielded to no one in applauding the over-all goals of the program; however, they did wonder whether this was the time for untried devices, or for a program of such magnitude. They recommended more study.

The program passed. The draftsman of the act, Harold Jordahl, was a student of administrative behavior and he had so worded it that the conservation department very well had to turn to. There were no escape clauses. The act gave each division some mandatory pioneering to do; specific sums were allocated to specific easement programs in specific areas and if the money was not spent, it would revert. For many officials it was a wrenching assignment to ponder.

I remember well a two-day clinic on easements staged for state agency people. Some were still in a state of administrative shock. Here was this damn easement business they had fought and now they were stuck with it. In an atmosphere of truculent curiosity, the reluctant pioneers learned for the first time that an easement program had been operating in Wisconsin for some years, and quite successfully. They were shown the cost figures on the Great River Road program, and learned that no, costs were not almost as high as the fee simple; they were low. Legal obstacles? The late Jacob Beuscher, an authority with a gift for direct English, assured them the statutes gave them leeway to do far more than they had yet attempted. Easements would work, went the charge, just about as well as they wanted them to work.

That is the way it has turned out. Both the over-all effort and the easement programs have been successful, and it is a pleasure to read the conservation department's bulletins on its part in the pioneering work. But some of the easement programs have worked significantly better than others. Many factors are involved, but it is evident that the skill and enthusiasm of the personnel involved are probably the most important of all.

Park people, who were the least enthusiastic about easements, have only recently begun to make progress. Fish-and-game people, however, have done extremely well. They have secured easements on 200 miles of lake and river frontage and at a fraction of the fee simple cost. For each dollar they get about three and a half feet of frontage with easements; only a half foot with fee simple. They have also covered some 9000 acres with wetland and hunting easements at an average cost of $8.30 an acre. (Comparable fee simple costs; $26.00 an acre.)

Easements can be made to appear much more expensive. It depends on how much in the way of engineering and overhead costs the particular agency decides to cram into the figures. On one series of projects it looked as though everything but the main office light bill was included; the extra costs attributed came to more than the money paid for the easements themselves; on other projects, by contrast, officials were able to achieve the same end with much more economy of effort. One particularly good negotiator has sewed up as many easements as a number of others combined, and at very reasonable costs.

Occupational bias is important. The attitude that agencies take toward easements depends a great deal on whether or not they have been used to working on a continuing basis with landowners. In most states the highway engineers want to buy land in fee and be done with it. Recreation and park officials tend to feel the same way. Forest service and fish-and-game people, by contrast, have been more used to working with landowners and tend to be receptive to any tool which helps them in this mutual relationship. They have been responsible for some of the most successful easement programs, though the news not always seems to reach other conservation agencies down the hall in various capitals.

An excellent example is what the Fish and Wildlife Service of the Department of the Interior has been doing in the "pothole country" of Minnesota and the Dakotas. This is the great nursery for the ducks of this country, for the thousands of little holes left by glaciers make a unique habitat for the breeding of wild fowl. For farmers, however, these wet patches have seemed a nuisance and a waste of cropland, and after World War II they began filling them in at a rapid rate.

To counteract this, Congress passed legislation by which the revenues from the sale of duck stamps could be used to conserve these wetlands. The Fish and Wildlife Service started out by negotiating twenty-year leases. It quickly found that it would be easier to obtain easements in perpetuity. Farms change hands frequently (in that area, the Service discovered, about every six to eight years on the average); owners preferred a lump sum in hand to income payments stretched into the future.

The Fish and Wildlife Service settled on a conservation program involving both acquisition of the fee simple and of easements. Where there were large wetlands it would try to buy these in fee as "nucleus areas." For the smaller wetlands it would use easements.

The easements stipulate that the farmers won't burn, fill, or drain the wetlands on their property. So far 102,000 acres of wetland have been bought outright and 500,000 acres covered by easements. Field men have done an outstanding job working with the farmers and have been getting the easements at an average price of $11.50 an acre. Enforcing them over so vast an area promised to be a problem, but the Service has solved this by aerial surveillance. Periodically, field men fly over the area; by checking previous aerial photos they can quickly spot where a farmer has filled in a hole or touched a match to the brush.

In a quietly effective way, New York State's Conservation Department has been buying fishing easements along trout streams. The easements give fishermen the use of the strip stretching thirty feet from either side of the stream. They do not have access to the rest of the property. Where parking areas are needed the state buys parcels in fee simple. Since 1950, it has secured easements along 1000 miles of stream; acquisition costs are currently running about $1000 a mile.

The negotiators, who conceive of their job as essentially a direct selling operation, spend a good bit of time casing an area. Before making the first call they will know all the local gossip about the farmers, their financial situation, the history of the properties, and the state of their titles. They go to work first on the "Elmers," the most influential of the farmers, and then work down the list. The man they have been told will give them the most trouble they leave to the last, by which time he will be feeling so left out he will be almost pathetically eager to be included. Negotiators do not haggle. They make each offer on the same price-per-foot basis as the other offers in the area, regardless of how good the land is as farmland. This saves time and money in appraisal costs, and since farmers are quick to compare notes with each other, no one feels that he has been had—a matter of particular importance in farm country.

In states that have followed New York's lead, negotiators have had similar success. In Minnesota they have been securing fishing rights from almost all of the landowners they have approached, and for the minimum consideration of one dollar per easement. In Wisconsin, fish-and-game negotiators used to lease strips along streams for twenty-year periods; they now find it more economical to secure easements in perpetuity. Since 1961, they have obtained easements along 170 miles of stream, at a cost of 30 cents per foot of frontage, as opposed to $2.38 for fee-simple acquisition.

So far I have been emphasizing the opportunities in rural

areas. For a long time many people assumed that in urban areas easements might be prohibitively expensive. (So did I, and I have been chagrined to see an earlier study of mine quoted by officials on this point as justification for not inquiring further.)

On the face of it the case would seem open and shut. It rests primarily on the very high average cost of open land in urban areas. Wherever land is selling at $2000 and up an acre it is obvious that the development potential accounts for most of the cost, and, ergo, it would appear that an easement stripping this development potential would run almost as much as the fee simple.

The conclusion tends to be self-fulfilling. Several years ago, for example, one state that had just put through a program providing for easement purchase commissioned a university study to determine where, if anywhere, the state might buy easements. The man who did the study took what he called the macro-view and charted average land costs for large areas. Where the average price was over a thousand dollars—which is to say, most of the urban area of the state—the charts said No go. (For good measure the study also ruled out the areas where land value was very low, the theory being that there was so little development value there would be no point to purchasing easements.) The state's easement program died aborning.

This is the kind of result you get when you do not look at the land itself. If you do, you will find that average land costs can be highly misleading, for they mask all sorts of variations and unexpected opportunities—and it is the developers, of all people, who are now teaching us this lesson. Just in the last few years it has become apparent that in the urban areas we may find some of the best opportunities of all for less-than-fee acquisition. Here is where the pressure for more intensive land use is strongest, but it is because of this fact, not despite it, that all the ingredients for some excellent bargains are at hand.

Let us take a suburban area, where the going price for land ranges anywhere between $2000 and $10,000 an acre. As farmland, it is not worth more than $150 or $300 an acre. Thus the development value, on the average, also runs somewhere between $2000 and $10,000 an acre.

Let us take a closer look at the land. Assume a tract of 100 acres for which a developer paid $500,000. The average value was $5000 an acre. But is each acre worth $5000? This figure is only an arithmetic average, and it covers a wide variation in the value of different parts of the tract—variation assessors usually take into account as a matter of routine. It is the frontage land, the highly buildable part that the developer was after, and in some cases only a third of the tract may account for the bulk of the value.

The chances are that some of the property is not worth building on at all—a patch of swamp, perhaps, a stream, or an extremely steep hill. What is the development value of these acres? They may have no development value; and if there is any value, the bulk of it will have to be realized by the developer through extensive grading, diking, filling, and such; and this costs him a great deal of money.

This marginal land may have great value as open space, and aesthetics aside, the developer is better off if he does not have to build on it. If he can concentrate his building on the buildable parts, it is to his self-interest to keep the land as an open space and recreation area, or deed it as such to a home-owners association or a special district. And this, with unexpected fervor, is just what developers are trying to do.

The open-space acts have been a help. When the original act was put through in California, the sponsors were not preoccupied with helping the developers. They were supposed to be the dirty guys. One of the first consequences of the act, however, was to make it easier for developers to give away open space. A number of them had been offering to deed large parts of their tracts as permanent open space if they could cluster their houses on the remainder. Communities, however, were suspicious. Just how permanent, they wondered, would the open space be?

The easement device, several California communities found, could resolve the impasse. Whether the developer held the open space himself or deeded it to a home-owners association, he could prove his good intentions by deeding a conservation easement on the open space to the municipality, guaranteeing that it would forever remain open. Developers liked the idea and have been helping to spread it to other states.

The new interest of developers in cluster planning has important implications for landowners, and the fact that there is a pocketbook motivation makes it all the more compelling. Until not so very long ago one had to argue hypothetically with a landowner that if he were to agree to the conservation of certain parts of his land he might not necessarily be damaging the over-all development value of the property for enlightened developers. Landowners would be skeptical. Where were these enlightened developers? As far as landowners could see, most developers wanted to develop every bit of ground they could get their hands on, and they'd pay less for a property if they couldn't. As for cluster, fine idea in principle, but it might never come about.

Now it has come about and the case for easements is no longer hypothetical. The landowner can be shown, with concrete examples, that conservation of the natural features goes hand in hand with a development layout which is not only pleasing but commercially profitable. He will not, in short, be giving up very much. Even though he may not intend to sell for development, the assurance that easements would not prevent him from doing so will make it much easier for him to take the altruistic view.

The gift potential for easements has been stronger than was generally expected, and it has turned out to be strongest in the urban areas. Again, the initiative has come as much from landowners as from public officials. In some cases the latter have been so sure that easements would be outrageously expensive that when landowners actually offered them as gifts they found it too hard to believe, and it was the landowners who had to do the arm twisting.

One of the best examples of the trickle-up effect is the evolution of the government program for the protection of the view of Mount Vernon. Back in 1959 an oil-tank farm was planned for the Maryland shore just opposite Mount Vernon. Representative Frances Bolton of Ohio was so exercised that she bought the property with some of her own funds, and with some neighboring landowners set up in the Akokeek Foundation to expand the holdings. Everything went well until 1960, when the Washington Suburban Sanitary Commission announced it was going to condemn land along the shore and build a sewage plant there. This precipitated a tremendous outcry. Representative Bolton and others pressed the federal government to make a park of the area, and many of the landowners in the area pledged that they would give easements free if the federal government would act. In 1961 Congress passed a resolution authorizing the Secretary of the Interior to acquire land and interests in lands to establish a conservation area, Piscataway Park, and to receive gifts of easements from landowners in the area. He would acquire 586 acres in fee, secure easements on surrounding land.

To the considerable surprise of many government officials, the landowners made good on their pledge of easements. The owners of 167 properties pledged easements on 1215 acres. The easements specified that the land was not to be subdivided into lots of less than five acres, and strictly regulated future land uses and buildings. They also provided that no trees thirty feet or higher could be cut without permission of the Secretary of the Interior.

Officials of the county, Prince Georges, liked the easement plan and thought that it should be encouraged in other areas. To provide a carrot, the county passed an ordinance in early 1966 providing a fifty percent tax reduction on properties covered by such easements. Landowners along another scenic stretch, the Patuxent River, indicated they would like to give easements too.

But there was one important condition to all this. The Piscataway landowners who had started the whole business insisted on a *quid pro quo*. They made their easement deeds contingent on the federal government's going through with its part of the bargain. If the government purchased outright the 586 park acres within five years of the original resolution—that is, by August 1967—the easements would become perpetual; if not, the easements would expire.

It was a good thing that the landowners insisted on the proviso. The government, or to be more accurate, the House Appropriations Committee, reneged. Though Congress had authorized $937,600 for the purchases, the Committee appropriated only $213,000. This was nowhere near enough to buy the land, and over the next few years rising land prices widened the gap further. Additional appropriations were denied in 1963 and 1964. By 1967 the market values of the unbought land had gone up so much that to finish the job Congress was moved to authorize $2.7 million. In May, a subcommittee of the House Appropriations Committee struck out every penny. By thus kicking a gift horse, the Committee not only jeopardized the easements that had been given but the possibility of additional gifts. The Patuxent landowners, for example, announced they would have to rethink their easement plans.

This is the same committee that has been scolding federal agencies for not making their acquisition dollars go further. Since the Piscataway project happened to be an outstanding effort to do just that, the cut stirred vigorous protests and just before the deadline a House-Senate conference committee restored $1.5 million. This was enough to reassure the landowners and the easements were left in force.

Another important confrontation took place several miles farther upstream. The Merrywood estate, a wooded tract with a dominant position on the heights above the Potomac, was bought by developers. They applied for a zoning change so they could put up high-rise towers. There was fierce protest, for towers would change the whole character of the area, but the local authorities made the zoning change, and that seemed to be that.

Then, in one of those acts of affirmation that change everything, Secretary of Interior Udall moved in. He had his lawyers find the right statutes, invoked the right of eminent domain, and slapped a scenic easement on the property forbidding high-rise development. The situation was by no means ideal for an easement; because of the recent zoning change, development values had increased considerably, and the government had to pay $745,000.

What was gained, however, was far more than the stopping of several towers. The action was an important precedent, and it started a chain of responses. Landowners in the area offered similar easements as gifts to the government, and this in turn led to a long-awaited ruling by the Internal Revenue Service. One of the donors asked for a ruling on whether the value of the easement could be entered as a charitable deduction on the income tax return. The Internal Revenue Service said that it could and made the ruling applicable to similar gifts of easements throughout the country.

One thing does lead to another.

I do not want to overstress one device. There are other ways to achieve the same results and sometimes it might be better if they were used. For shoreline land, for example, we could use a procedure that would be the mirror image of the easement approach. We could acquire the land in fee and then sell or lease the rights to use it.

Another possibility would be "compensable regulations." Under this proposed device the police power would be used first. An area would be zoned for open-space or low-density uses. Later, when a landowner in the area sold his property he could put in a claim for compensation. If his property had suffered a loss in market value because of the restrictions imposed on it, he would be paid the amount of the loss. In effect, an easement would be retroactively purchased from him.

But technique is secondary. I have been emphasizing

easements not because I think they should be the major tool but because they are probably the clearest illustration of a basic approach. What we are essentially concerned with is finding ways of working with the people who own most of the landscape so that private interest will be coupled with public interest. If officials are really interested in seeking the middle ways, they will find that there are plenty of them and that they will work if they want them to.

The point is combination. Alone, any single device is limited; together they strengthen each other. If we zone flood plains, for example, it will be much easier to buy open space in them later and the price will be more reasonable when we do; if we buy land in fee simple, it will be easier to buy easements on land that buffers them. Each step makes another easier.

To illustrate, let me conclude with a brief account of what happened along the Sudbury River. The river winds through a lovely valley on the outskirts of Boston. Along its banks lie beautiful expanses of marshlands, which from earliest times have tempered the floods, nourished wild life, and delighted the eye. In the 1950s, developers began eying it, and the Massachusetts legislature passed an act envisioning their protection by a combination of state and federal action. The key wetlands were being bought in fee simple by federal Fish and Wildlife Service. The rest of the job would be up to the state.

The then Conservation Commissioner of Massachusetts, Charles Foster, did not have much money to spend for acquisition and being very much a Yankee, he wanted to see what could be done without spending any money at all. At a public meeting in the Sudbury area, he made a proposal to the local people. He said he was prepared to buy or condemn the additional wetlands in fee. But was this necessary? He noted the job that already had been done by conservation commissions and private groups in the area. (One group, the Sudbury Valley Trustees, had been buying swamps.) Foster suggested that maybe the local people could work up a scheme that would preserve all of the wetlands. He wasn't too concerned what devices they used just as long as there was a real guarantee of permanence. He would give them a year to see what could be done.

The response was almost instantaneous. Within a matter of weeks all the owners who had land along a key stretch had voluntarily given easements on the wetland portions to the local land trust.

Much has taken place since; strengthened wetland zoning, more gifts of easements and gifts of land in fee. There is such a dense mix of public and private efforts, indeed, that it is impossible to chart them clearly on a map, or to assess which have been most responsible for the saving of the area. And that is the reason it has been saved.

That is how hundreds of other areas can be saved. Officials who are really interested in exploring the possibilities with landowners will find that between zoning and outright purchase there are all sorts of middle ways, in all sorts of combinations, and that if they want them to work they will work. But they have to try them. Where they are not we should be building fires to see that they do.

6. The Tax Approach

>>>

Many people believe that the real key to open-space preservation is not to be found in zoning or in buying land or
rights in land. The best way to save open space, they
believe, is to take some of the tax pressures off the people
who own it. The approach they recommend is "preferential assessment" and it is simplicity itself; while the wording
of the statutes gets extraordinarily verbose and complicated, the guts are contained in one sentence: *Assessors
shall assess open space only at its open-space value.*

Through this small change in the law, it is believed,
great expanses of farmland and open space that would
otherwise be developed may be saved for years to come—
and without the expenditure of any public money. Politically, the vision has proved most persuasive. Seven states
have already adopted preferential assessment in one form
or another and by all indications more will shortly be doing
so. Farmers have been the prime movers, but conservationists have been lending enthusiastic support, and even

city people and suburbanites, when the question has been put to them on the ballot, have voted in favor.

I think they are being had. As part author of one of the state statutes, I believe there is a good case for open-space assessment—if it requires a land-use plan using a whole range of devices, and if it sets up tight safeguards against speculative abuse. But most of the statutes that have been passed do not do this. They offer tax benefactions but do not demand any real *quid pro quo* for the public in return. The public is not getting what it is paying for. What it is getting is the appearance of open-space preservation. These laws were passed in good faith, but in effect if not in intention, they are creating new speculative pressures on the countryside and the groundwork for some major land scandals to come.

In the constitution of almost every state there is a provision holding that one man's land should be assessed on the same basis as another's. That basis is *ad valorem*—at its value, or, as sometimes defined, "cash value," or "highest and best use." To compute this, the assessor takes many factors into consideration, recent sales of comparable land being one of the most important, and estimates the amount a willing buyer would pay a willing seller for the property. In a purely rural area the willing buyer would probably be another farmer and the most he would pay would be several hundred dollars an acre. In such cases farm value and market value are apt to be synonymous. On the edge of suburbia, however, developers would be not only willing but eager to pay one thousand dollars an acre for the same kind of land. The higher value is what the assessors should consider.

That is what the law says. But most assessors have not been hewing to the law. If they had, some will tell you, they would have been run out of their communities long ago. On the suburban fringe assessors have been valuing farmland only on the basis of its current use. Sometimes they do this on a flat-rate basis: $175 an acre for pasture, $75 an acre for woodlands, $50 an acre for marshland, and so on. Assessors have been similarly sympathetic in their treatment of golf clubs and large estates. They may slap a high valuation on buildings, but they value the land as though there were no market for it, save as farmland or golf clubs or large estates. Some assessors make it a point not to recognize the subdivision potential until bulldozers start to work.

But the pressures on the assessors have been rising. With communities desperate for more tax revenue many an assessor has been forced to raise the valuations of farms to something more closely approaching actual market value. This is particularly the case when communities decide to have a revaluation of the whole grand list and bring in outside consultants to help with the job. The consultants have no empathy. *Ad valorem* is their watchword. They are hard-nosed about any kind of undervaluation and the result of their labors invariably comes as a shock to land-owners, the farmers most of all.

Farmers argue that full assessment is iniquitously unfair to them. They have a hard enough time, they say, if the assessor values their land only on its farm value. If the assessor is prodded into considering full market worth, their position can become untenable. A vicious spiral gets under way. A nearby farm is sold to a developer for $800 an acre, so the assessor decides to up the valuation of the other farms a bit, from $200 an acre, say, to $300. Next the tax rate goes up. The developer's subdivision is producing many more children who have to be educated, and the community has to spend more for a variety of additional services—much more, probably, than it gets back in taxes from the subdivision. School-district bonds are floated; mill rates are raised. Another farmer sells out, this time for $1500 an acre. Another subdivision goes up. The tax rate rises again. So do assessments. Another farmer sells.

Farmers are of two minds about this spiral. On one hand, it means that they may eventually get a fat price for their land. Farmers like this part. What they do not like is what happens to them in the meantime. If they want to continue farming, they can afford to pay very little more in taxes if they are to make any profit from their operations. The speculative demand raises land values and taxes; it does nothing at all to raise farm income. If the farmer had the capital he could afford to lose a little while he waited out the market. But he does not have the capital. He is forced to sell too early in the game, and he gets only a small part of the increase in land values. It is the people who buy the land from him who get the real money.

The farmer says that he is being punished when he should be rewarded. The reason the taxes have to go up is those new people in the subdivisions. They are the ones who need the extra sewer lines and the schoolrooms and the fire engines. He does not. His property, indeed, is a boon to the community. By keeping it open, he provides scenery and breathing space—and he spares the community the burden of yet another subdivision. Why, then, sock him? It would pay the community to keep his taxes low just to have him stay around and keep the land open. Come to think of it, some farm bureaus have suggested, it would pay the community not to tax him at all.

In the fifties the farmers were worried enough about the specter of full assessment to press for corrective legislation. There were basically two approaches open to them. One was a form of tax deferral similar to the "severance" tax procedures some states had adopted for forest land. These were passed to encourage landowners not to cut their timber prematurely. As long as the owners do not log their land, they have to pay only a minimal tax; when they cut the timber, they pay a tax based on the worth of the timber. Conservationists were keen on this approach and thought it could be applied to farmland. While it was farmed, the owner would be taxed only on farm value; if and when the land was developed, the owner would retroactively pay the additional taxes that otherwise would have applied.

Farmers liked another approach much better. They

thought it would be simpler to press for straight "preferential assessment" legislation. This would make it mandatory, rather than illegal, for assessors to keep on valuing farmland only on the basis of its farm use. Lately farmers have become uncomfortable with the term "preferential assessment"; they fear that it conjures up the thought that they have been asking to be singled out for favored treatment. That, of course was precisely the idea—the low use value was to apply only to farmer's land; nobody else's. Since it was so bald in this respect there was a strong likelihood that eventually the courts might object on constitutional grounds. But the farmers, who had not dominated state legislatures without learning a thing or two, decided to get the statutes on the books and worry about the courts later.

The first test was in Maryland. In 1956 the General Assembly, by a large majority, passed a straight preferential assessment statute. Four years later the Maryland Court of Appeals struck it down as unconstitutional. The court held that the statute violated the uniform taxation clause, unduly favored farmers in suburban areas, and in general was wanting in reasonableness and public purpose.

But there was a way to get around the courts. The General Assembly drafted, with alacrity, two amendments that would put preferential assessment into the constitution itself. The amendments were to be submitted to the voters on the ballot for the November 1960 elections.

In describing the public purposes to be served, the legislators threw in the works:

"The General Assembly hereby declares it to be in the general public interest that farming be fostered and encouraged in order to maintain a readily available source of food and dairy products close to the metropolitan areas of the State, to encourage the preservation of open space as an amenity necessary to human welfare and happiness, and to prevent the forced conversion of such open space to more intensive uses as a result of economic pressures caused by the assessment of land at a rate or level incompatible with the practical use of such land for farming."

Citizens were responsive to this line of reasoning; those who lived around cities surprisingly so. Most of them did not give a hang about the agronomic argument, but they cared very much about the lovely Maryland countryside and they saw preferential assessment as a way of saving it. There was some opposition: one group took out newspaper ads warning that the amendments amounted to a steal; that they would raise other people's taxes and inflate the price of non-farmland.

But leading conservation and citizen groups supported the measures. So did the newspapers. Maybe the farmers might be getting a bit of a break, went the editorials, but this was a small enough price to pay to keep Maryland green. When the votes were cast in November there were 334,888 for the amendments, only 123,636 against—and the pluralities were as high in the urban areas as in the rural.

Farm groups in other states were encouraged to new efforts. One of the states was Connecticut, where, it so happened, I was working up a program of conservation legislation for Governor Dempsey. High on everybody's agenda was some form of tax legislation to save open space; and as part of the 1963 legislative package I was asked to prepare an open-space assessment bill. I thought other measures far more important—a bond issue for buying open space, for one—but there was going to be a tax bill in the hopper in any event, and there was an opportunity to have a good one.

I did not think straight preferential assessment was right; aside from the legal problems it posed, there was a strong possibility that it would not do what it was supposed to do. A study by the U. S. Department of Agriculture of the first effects of Maryland's statutes had already raised warning signals. A broader approach, involving tax deferral, seemed more in order for Connecticut and I so argued.

But the farmers were on the scent. They had had poor luck before in getting a preferential assessment statute. Now there was a strong tide of public interest in the saving of open space, and they felt they deserved to be the beneficiaries. As in Maryland, city and suburban people were keen on saving the farm countryside and were inclined to support any measure that promised to help. Preferential assessment did have the virtue of simplicity, and on this basis had the support of several assessors. As to the Maryland experience, farmers believed everything they heard about how well it was working there and were convincing others as well as themselves.

But was it really working? To do my homework on the Connecticut bill I went to Maryland and spent several weeks reconnoitering the countryside and checking with assessors in the courthouses of the principal counties. Here is what I found:

Out in the rural farm countryside, preferential assessment was having little effect one way or the other. Assessors were continuing to value farmland only as farmland. Like everything else, however, the price of it was going up, and for this reason, not because of any development potential, assessors were raising valuations. In one county the assessor found that the price farmers were paying for farms had advanced so much since the last revaluation that to make up for lost time he had to double most farmland assessments. The farmers were very upset about this but they had no legal redress. Preferential assessment was what they were getting, only at a higher level.

For farmers in the suburban area, however, preferential assessment was making a big difference. It was not so much that farmers' assessments were being reduced, though some were, and substantially; the important effect was to prevent raises in assessments that otherwise would have had to have been made. And they would have been steep raises. The value of farmland for farm use had risen to somewhere around $250 an acre for prime land, not

much more than it was in rural areas. Its real value in
the open market, however, had risen to many times that.
Thanks to law, the assessors had to ignore the obvious.

One effect was a considerable reduction in potential
taxes for the counties. In Montgomery County, for example, the assessors' official value of farmland in 1961 was
$17 million; had there not been preferential assessment,
the assessor said, the sum would have been $32 million.
Since then the disparity has increased greatly.

In some part the tax loss has been hypothetical. Law or
no law, many assessors probably would have continued
to under assess farmland. Farmers can further argue that
even if the loss in tax revenues was large in dollars, relatively speaking it was a trifle for the rich suburban counties.
Precisely because these counties were developed, office
buildings, subdivisions, and plants accounted for the great
bulk of the tax base; farmland only about two or three
percent.

The key question was whether open space was being
saved. The question could not be answered with any exactitude; there was no way of knowing for sure what would
have happened in these particular areas had there not
been preferential assessment. As far as these eyes could
see, however, preferential assessment was not saving open
space. Maryland counties were being developed at about
the same rate and the same fashion as suburban counties
elsewhere; subdivisions were going up in the usual scattered pattern and to judge from the "for sale" signs that
were to be seen on the farms, the scattered pattern was
certainly going to continue. I did notice one difference.
In most transition areas you usually see many patches of
farmland that have reverted to second growth while awaiting development. In the Maryland counties there seemed
to be fewer such patches. Whoever was buying the farms
was farming them.

But who were these buyers? Not farmers. As a cursory
check of the real estate pages indicated, ads for suburban
farmland were talking about the amount of road frontage,
favorable zoning, and similarly non-agricultural factors.

Most revealing was the price, $2000 an acre and up, mostly up. As the lawyers say, the thing speaks for itself. Patently the land was being bought for development; at those prices there was no other way to make money out of it. Farmers were not buying; none of the assessors I talked to could remember a single farmer-to-farmer sale in recent years.

Some assessors had tried valiantly to separate farmers from speculators, and on the basis of criteria developed by the State Division of Taxation, denied preferential assessments to a number of landowners. When assessors got tough, however, landowners went to court, and the courts generally upheld the landowners. The courts said it was not up to the assessors to interpose administrative criteria; the ruling phrase in the statutes was whether the land was being actively farmed or not. If it was, the land was to get preferential assessment and that was that.

The landowners took care that it was actively farmed. Some had a neighboring farmer do the job; in some places the owners contracted with a canning company to come in and conduct a farming operation. Such activity not only kept the owner's taxes low, it returned enough money to pay the taxes. This was not wholly a bad bargain for the public; the speculators and developers would have bought the land anyway and preferential assessment did at least give them an incentive to keep it productive a while longer. Farmers got some extra work and the countryside looked the better for the husbandry.

But it was a Potemkin Village kind of countryside. Looks belied the reality. I remember especially one large tract of farm country astride an interchange on a new freeway. It was not very good farmland and ordinarily would have long since reverted to a mixture of second growth and scattered developments. But the area, which was designated as an open-space reserve on the Washington-area master plan, was still being farmed. When I asked the assessor about this, he laughed hollowly and showed me his books. A New York real estate syndicate had bought the land from the farmers. It had told them, however, that they could keep on farming there until it was time to develop it; as a matter of fact, the syndicate insisted on this part of the deal. The syndicate had paid over $2000 an acre for the land; the assessor had to value it at only about $200 an acre.

Thus the illusion of open space. Assessors knew well how temporary it would be. "I've been all for keeping farms going," one assessor said to me, "but what sticks in my craw is the way these builders are getting away with murder. Why, when the land is zoned commercial, they'll come in here and with a straight face say they want to farm it." Said another: "I've a fellow here who says he's a Christmas-tree farmer. The money he would get out of those little trees is peanuts. He's just sitting on that land until he can make a killing."

Even when an owner had platted his property for a subdivision and put up signs advertising it, he would demand farm assessment until actual construction began. If he were only developing part of the property, furthermore, he would ask for farm assessment on the parts he was not developing just yet.

Most of the "new towns" in the area benefited from this procedure. The building of them was planned in stages, a neighborhood at a time, and the developers took care that the undeveloped portions were actively farmed. (At James Rouse's Columbia, for example, a staff of agricultural and forest experts was put together to supervise a model farming operation.) By keeping down carrying charges on the land, the developers could argue, preferential assessment helped them take the long-range view and discouraged premature subdivision.

Whatever the incidental benefits, it was clear that preferential assessment was primarily benefiting speculators and developers and it was not doing what it was supposed to do. I felt at the time that the abuses were so palpable they would soon provoke corrective legislation. I was wrong on this point. Since 1963 several efforts have been made to tighten up the Maryland statutes so that only true farmers would qualify, but the efforts have not gotten very far. The public is being had, but the galvanic revelation is yet to come.*

I reported to the Connecticut people what I had found out and suggested an approach that would eliminate the shortcomings of the Maryland procedure. It had three principal features. First, the open space assessment would apply not simply to farmland, but to any land the openness of which would benefit the public; principally, farmland, recreation land, water-supply land, and forest land.

Second, open-space assessment was to be geared to the land-use plan of the local government. The open-space assessment would not be automatic. It would be up to the community, through its zoning and planning machinery, to determine what open spaces should qualify. Just because a piece of land was open would not necessarily commend it for open-space assessment. It might be the only tract left that was suitable for industrial development, or it might be a piece of land obviously being held for subdivision.

* It may not be long in coming. From the *Washington Post* January 22, 1968: "FARMLAND TAX REFORM SOUGHT IN MONTGOMERY. Montgomery County legislators are trying to tighten the Maryland farmland assessment law after the county's program coordinator reported that the law resulted in a loss of $5.6 million in county tax revenue last year. The report, by William H. Hussman, showed that the amount of property assessed as farmland increased by 5902 acres in 1967 despite the spread of the suburbs. Hussman lists the owners of about 1700 acres that are under the farm assessment even though zoned for commercial, industrial, or apartment use. The list includes major building and land development firms and leading county political figures. . . ."

Early in 1968 the Maryland legislature responded to the pleas of Montgomery County and passed a modest reform measure. Preferential assessment will be denied a property that is subdivided, rezoned, or sold for more than seven times its farmassessed value. The legislature also authorized Montgomery County to levy a transfer tax of up to six percent on the sale price of property previously assessed as farmland.

The community should be given the chance to withhold open-space assessments in such cases.

The third provision was for a partial recapture of taxes when open space was converted to another use. The argument against this had been that in time the back taxes would become confiscatory. But this objection was easily met by limiting the time period. When and if an owner developed his land or sold it to developers, he would have to pay only the taxes that he had been forgiven the previous four years.

Actually, a roll back would be no great deterrent to development, with or without a time limitation. The amount of extra taxes a man would have to pay would depend largely on how whopping a profit he made on the sale and the taxes would be only a tiny fraction of this. But the roll back would be important nonetheless; it would not demand the suspension of the *ad valorem* principle, and it would assure the public some recompense for the tax breaks it was giving.

I worked up a bill incorporating these features. At first the farmers were fairly receptive. They very much liked the idea of including other kinds of landowners. They recognized that if they were encompassed in this broader approach they would no longer seem to be asking for special-interest legislation for one group. The legislature would be more likely to pass such legislation and the courts would be more likely to sustain it.

But farmers said they did not like all that rigamarole about zoning and planning. Why give planners the right to determine if a man could keep on in farming? Most especially, the farmers did not like the roll back. It was not the money, they said. Most of them maintained that they neither wanted nor expected to sell out, and I think most of them were sincere in this belief. Their argument was technical. They showed a great solicitude for the assessors and the burden that a roll back might put upon them. The assessors would have to keep two sets of figures on each property, one for farm value and the other for market value, and this, presumably, would be much too onerous. I have talked to many assessors about this problem and the only conclusion that I have been able to come to is that assessors who believe there should be straight preferential assessment see great technical problems in a roll-back procedure; and those who do not like preferential assessment do not see great technical problems.

What really irked the farmers about the roll-back provision was its acknowledgement that there was a difference between farm value and market value. They took the curious position that there was no difference. At several stormy meetings with the farm bureau people, I heard men expostulate, one with a pounding of fists, that farmers' land was in fact only worth the low farm value. They wanted a ringing affirmation of this proposition written into the law. I thought they would paint themselves into a corner if they got this into the books, but they did not agree.*

The final act was a hybrid. As I had recommended, open-space assessment would apply to several categories of land, and it would be geared to the community's land-use plan; to qualify, the land would have to be designated as open space by the local planning commission. (Forest

---

* Such clauses pose an interesting legal inconsistency. It is fine for farmers to have a statute saying farmland is not worth much when they are figuring how low the value of their land is for tax purposes. It is not so appropriate when they are figuring how much a buyer ought to pay them for the land. The state itself, for example. The state is supposed to pay full market value. But now there are statutes that say that market value is no more than farm value. To be consistent, the farmer should tell the state's appraiser to disregard the $4000 an acre prices developers are paying for land across the way. The property is worth only its farm value of $400 an acre. Pay no more.

Farmers are not likely to press this point. Taxpayers may. If there is a new state law saying farms are worth only farm value, suit can be brought against the state for paying more than this. The courts would probably hold that the constitutional proviso for fair compensation would be paramount. Such a test, however, would make the new law look inconsistent, and a bit silly.

land would qualify under an earlier law or under the new one, with the state forester validating the owner's application.)

But on two critical points the farmers had it their way. The roll-back clause was eliminated. Further, they were exempted from bothering with land-use plans or planning-commission approval. Unlike other landowners, farmers would eventually qualify. They would get preferential assessment.

But there was sweet along with the bitter. The farmers were not ingrates about the wave of public interest they were riding; they supported the other measures for open space rather than fought them, as farmers in other states have been prone to do. Tucked away in their tax bill, furthermore, was a short but potent clause giving communities the power of eminent domain to acquire easements and fee title to open space. Farmers had strongly opposed just such a provision in previous years, and of all places to put it, a tax bill seemed the oddest. But justice was served. The farmers were too happy about the other parts of the bill to complain, and despite the last-minute efforts of some legislators, the clause was kept in.

Preferential assessment has been going on the books in other states. In New Jersey, where preferential assessment was earlier ruled unconstitutional by the courts, the voters in 1963 approved an amendment to make it constitutional. Because of the insistence of Governor Hughes, however, there is a roll-back provision: On conversion to other use, owners have to pay the taxes they got out of for the preceding two years. So far, the state's tax division reports, assessors do not seem to have had any great difficulty administering the roll back. In 1965 Oregon and Pennsylvania passed similar statutes but with a five-year roll back.

In 1966 voters in Texas and California approved preferential assessment amendments. The Texas amendment calls for a three-year roll back. California's, which was dubbed the "Breathing Space Amendment," has no roll-back provision but it does lay down one stiff requirement:

To qualify, the lands must be "subject to enforceable restrictions as specified by the legislature." At this writing, the legislature has not yet drafted the enabling act.

Hawaii has instituted the most elaborate procedures. First, it set up statewide zoning, with land classified into "agricultural," "conservation," and "urban" zones—later weakened by the addition of a catchall "rural" zone. Assessors were supposed to assess land only on the basis of the existing and permitted uses. This did not, however, protect farmers who were in an urban zone. In 1963, an act was passed giving owners the option of dedicating their lands to a given use. Under this act, a farmer could bind himself to keep the land in farming for a minimum of ten years and even if he was in an urban zone he would be guaranteed farm-use assessment. But there are no real teeth in the provision. The farmer can sell out whenever he pleases; all he has to do is pay back the taxes forgiven plus a five percent surcharge. The tax division thinks the penalty would have to be as high as fifty percent to be effective.

Criticism is mounting. Tax experts and land economists never did think preferential assessment was a good idea and they are surer than ever that they are right: significantly, the economists who have been most critical are those of the Department of Agriculture. Conservationists are still hopeful—the Sierra Club, for example, went down the line for the California amendment—but a number are beginning to entertain second thoughts. Planners are becoming more critical. They dislike the way preferential assessment bypasses planning, and they dislike its lack of teeth.

Of all people, it is the builders who have become the most censorious. Some of them, as in Maryland, have benefited from preferential assessment but the great majority are not in a position to benefit. Builders work on short-term credit and they do not have the money to stockpile land. They buy from the people who do have. Preferential assessment, the builders charge, enables the

speculators to hold choice land off the market; this not only
jacks up the eventual price to outrageous levels, it makes
the builders leap-frog over the close-in land that should
be developed to the open land that properly should not be
developed for years to come. The result: more urban
sprawl. If we really want to curb it, maintains *House and
Home,* the leading trade journal, far better to turn assessment policy the other way around. Assess open space to
the hilt, it says. Borrowing the old single-taxers argument,
it maintains that full-value taxation would force the most
developable land into development earlier, and thereby
relieve the pressure on the further-out land. The result:
more orderly development, less urban sprawl.

Whether or not preferential assessment accentuates sprawl
is still a question. The returns are not all in yet. The
Maryland experience has yielded some important clues,
but one cannot argue by analogy that the results will
necessarily be similar elsewhere. The newer statutes have
only been in operation for several years and the results are
highly inconclusive. In Connecticut, for example, the farmers have had their taxes reduced; this has cut into the
grand list of many towns but at no appreciable cost to the
state's grand list. Most assessors have complied with the
law readily; some have fought it. Courts have upheld
the landowners in four out of seven cases, though so far
there has been no challenge to its constitutionality. Has it
saved open space that otherwise would have been lost?
Opinions are mixed.* They are similarly mixed in other
states.

* My good friend Joseph Gill, Connecticut's Commissioner
of Agriculture and Natural Resources, thinks I may be unduly
pessimistic in my judgment. He believes the law needs more
time to work out and that it will work out. "Our main problem,"
he says, "is a handful of assessors who just don't like the law
because they believe it is a 'giveaway.' They are the ones who
have been trying to get the legislature to change it. We would
like to see the law remain as it is until we get a clear perspective
on its good points and bad points. If there are defects, time
will bring these out."

My own guess is that preferential assessment is going to do very little to halt the conversion of open space. Even if the speculator is weeded out and only the true farmer benefits, the true farmer is going to do what anybody else would do. When the price is right he is going to sell out, low taxes or no. And why should he not? He is not going to forswear a large capital gain so suburbanites will have pretty scenery. Unless there is some compelling incentive, he is going to relocate.

With the money, he can often create a more efficient farming operation farther out. This is what most farmers have been doing and will continue to do. "The real commercial enterprises," says Edward Higbee, "the twenty-two percent of the census farms which account for seventy-two percent of all production . . . will tend to move back into the country as the city moves forward. They will use their capital gains to develop even better farms on cheaper but equally productive soils. They will not expose their farms as buffers against urban sprawl."

One can concede this point and still argue for preferential assessment as a delaying action. Even if the farmers are being given more of a tax break than they warrant, it would not be the first subsidy they have received and if it stayed the execution of the countryside for any appreciable period, it would be well worth it. This point was forcibly argued in Connecticut and with some justification: I know of several large farmers there who have resisted tempting offers because they really do care about the land and low assessment has helped them stay on.

Praise be to such men. But there are not many of them. The statistical record on farmland conversion indicates that so far as most farmers are concerned any holding action induced by preferential assessment is apt to be of short duration. Worse yet, by maintaining appearances, it can lull a community into a mistaken sense that all is still well.

If it wants to save open space, the community could do it less expensively by buying it. In Maryland, economist Peter House found that in 1965 one county lost $2,343,000 in tax revenues because of preferential assessments. With this amount of money, it could have bought about 1500 acres of farmland, or one percent of the total farmland in the county. As percentages go, such figures do not sound large, just as the reductions in the grand lists do not sound large. Accumulatively, however, they amount to a lot of money over the years, and a lot of land not saved that could have been.

Preferential assessment buys time, it is said. But time for what? One appealing proposition is that the holding action will save land for communities to buy later, when they have more money. But such deferment carries a steep price. The low assessments will not keep the market values from rising. Were the community to buy the land later, it would have to pay for all the increase in speculative value that took place while it waited. It might not have the money.

If communities do not realize how fleeting is the opportunity for effective action, the opportunity will slip through their fingers. There may be reprieves—a bad slump in the housing market, for example, might slow things down a bit—but the only safe assumption is that time is running out, very, very fast.

The only possible way we can save much open space is to use every tool we can get our hands on and use them together. There has to be a unifying plan, and we must be as hard-boiled as the speculator in framing it. We must identify what cannot be saved, what can and should be saved, and tackle the job as though there will be no reprieve.

7. Defending Open Space

>>>

Once land is secured, how can it be kept secured? Thanks to new federal and state programs, we are saving open space at a greater rate than ever before. Unfortunately, thanks to other state and federal programs, at an equally growing rate we are losing open space we already saved— to highways, cloverleafs, dams, sewage plants, post offices, commercial parking lots, and public projects of one kind or another. On balance, we are still adding more open space than we are losing, but not by so very much and there is a qualitative loss that can be immeasurable. Most of the additions to open-space acreage have been in the outlying areas; most of the losses have been in the urban areas where open space is most precious and where there is little more to be had at any price. There is every indication that the situation is going to get worse rather than better.

So far, the highway men have been doing most of the taking. To a degree, they have had to, and they have often been maligned when, in fact, they had no alternative.

Under the Interstate Highway program, it is practically impossible for state highway planners to draw a line from City A to City B without crossing parkland somewhere along the way. In the open country where land costs are relatively low, the planners can sometimes detour around parkland, but they won't detour very much, for if they did, the Bureau of Public Roads would say that the alignment was too costly and would withhold the ninety percent federal-aid funds until the engineers straightened things out.

The real problem is in the urban areas. Here the engineers are positively attracted to parkland and if there is any detouring to be done it is toward the parkland, not away. The attractions are compelling: parklands are not built up and thus require far less demolition; there are no homeowners in the path to form protest associations and put pressure on the politicians. Best of all, the land is cheap. If it is public land, the highway men sometimes do not have to pay anything for it, and where they do, it is usually scant recompense for the loss of the irreplaceable.

There has been little redress. The highway people have money and they have procedure. The key decision that route A-B is the best one may have been made very far down in the echelons of the department, but once made, the decision has juggernaut force. Protest groups will be formed; newspapers will rage. But the highway people are inured to such abuse: They are professionals, usually of high technical competence, and they are fortified by the conviction that their decisions are based on objective data. They know they will clash with bleeding hearts, bird lovers, sentimentalists, and people who want the road to go anywhere except where they live. To the professional, this is an occupational cross, to be borne with patience and fortitude.

There will be public hearings, but these come very late in the game and are predictably futile. Members of Citizens for Parks will get up and make impassioned statements about the impending desecration of the last valley in the county. Municipal officials will plead for an alternate route. Experts will testify to the ecological importance of the riverland and marshes. A homeowners group, which is very happy the route will bypass their area, will warmly support the highway department. So it will go long into the night. The highway people, who are in the position of being judge as well as defendant, will dutifully note everything in the record and then go ahead and do exactly as they had planned all the time. There are very few cases of a highway department's voluntarily reversing itself because it was persuaded by the logic of those who wanted another alignment.

Sometimes they do change their plans, but it takes an extraordinary amount of hell-raising to make them do it. San Francisco is a case in point. Over widespread local protest, the state highway department built an elevated freeway that ruined the view of the old Ferry Building and, in the opinion of many people, a good bit else of the city besides. San Francisco lost that one, but the people were so mad that when the state proposed to run a freeway through Golden Gate Park, there was a truly massive civic revolt. The entire freeway project was canceled.

These controversies often have a valuable side effect. Even though the highway people eventually have their way, they provide the villain that is often just what is needed to unify various local groups into common cause, and the civic passions that have been thus stirred sometimes lead to planning and conservation programs that might not have been launched otherwise. In Monterey, California, for example, the state highway engineers proposed a gigantic interchange—locally termed the "can of worms"—that would destroy part of the town to improve access to it. Just about this time, the highway people further invigorated the townspeople by digging up a hillside and chopping down a beautiful stand of trees to complete a nearby highway stretch. Conservation became a great popular cause. The highway people withdrew the can of worms proposal but such a head of steam had been built up as to propel the Monterey area groups to some outstanding conserva-

tion efforts—including, eventually, scenic-roads legislation
they hoped would prevent the highway people from
ruining scenic roads.

Another example is Glen Helen, a nature reserve at
Antioch College in Ohio. The best thing that ever happened to it was the announcement by the state it was
going to run a highway through it. The campaign launched
to knock this down gained the reserve far more support
than it had had before and sparked a new effort for a
"Country Common"—a program to buy land and easements
to protect the surrounding area. To make matters better,
as soon as the highway proposal was beaten, municipal
engineers proposed to run a big sewer through the area.
The defeat of this gained even more support and the
whole Glen Helen program has been thriving ever since.

But the fact is that engineers usually win. Their decisions
are usually beyond review by the courts, and review by
elected officials counts for little. There have been several
cases where it appeared that virtually everyone from
citizens and officials of the area to the governor of the state
himself have been unable to overrule the engineers. For
the new route I-87 in Westchester County in New York,
for example, the state highway department wanted an
alignment that would bypass two nature preserves. So did
most of the towns in the area and a well-heeled and powerful group of landowners. A district official of the Bureau of
Public Roads, however, did not. He said it would be unnecessarily costly and insisted on the shorter alignment. A
vigorous campaign was launched to get the decision over-
ruled. The road is going exactly where the district engineer
wanted it to go.

What is to be done? Some conservationists argue for a flat
restriction against diversion of parkland anytime, anywhere,
and in most sessions of state legislatures, the hopper is
filled with bills which would put parkland beyond the
reach of eminent domain for other purposes. They do not
get anywhere.

People of the touch-not-one-blade-of-grass school perform a valuable service as a counter force. But as a general policy, their position is not really tenable. In the abstract, it is impossible to declare that any piece of land is beyond reconsideration for any purpose in the future. The public acquired the land; it should have the right, however tempered, to meet new conditions. In the case of the state and federal governments, furthermore, a fiat against taking parklands would not stand up in the courts. The state and federal governments have the sovereign right of eminent domain. The exercise of this power can be made less draconian, but the power cannot very well be taken away from them.

The practical approach to encroachment is not to make it illegal but to make it much more difficult. Basically, there are two ways to do this. One is to fight each encroachment as it comes up, case by case. This is fighting at the last ditch, but it will always be necessary and the prospect of it does chasten the engineers somewhat. But the best way is to stop encroachment before it comes up. To do this we must use the machine itself, and by good legislative draftsmanship make bureaucratic inertia and conservatism work against encroachment instead of for it. Here are some proposals to this end.

A first step is to raise the cost of taking parkland. Under the doctrine that municipalities are creatures of the state, states can take municipal land without paying anything for it, and that is what most of them do. Some states do pay compensation, but even so, the municipality usually comes out on the short end. In principle, the state is supposed to appraise the land at market value, but since the land is not available for commercial development, it is usually appraised at a level far beneath that of comparable land nearby.

Another reason municipalities accept niggardly awards is the original cost of the land. Most parkland was bought years ago at a fraction of today's prices, and a great deal of it was given by citizens. This should not affect the taking price; indeed, it should make local officials even more adamant. But a low book value can make a relatively low award look like something of a bargain—$100,000, for example, for twenty acres that cost $8000. For this reason, municipal officials in many communities have allowed themselves to be conned into outrageously low settlements.

Replacement value is the key. The agency that is taking the parkland should be required to provide comparable land, or the money to buy it. If it takes, say, ten acres of downtown parkland, the payment should be based on what it would actually cost the municipality to acquire ten acres of similarly located land. Alternatively, the agency should make payment in kind. If it has land to provide in trade, it should not be allowed to palm off ten acres of unused institutional land on the outskirts as a fair recompense. If the downtown ten acres would cost $300,000 to replace, and outlying land was valued at $1000 an acre, a fair swap would call for some 300 acres. Even this wouldn't really make up for the loss of the downtown parkland, but it would be a stiff requirement for the taking agency, and were officials faced with it, they would likely be much less hasty to covet parkland. Their own cost-benefit formulas would now inhibit them.

Another step is to open up the taking of parkland to judicial review. In an excellent report on possible legal approaches,* Lawyer Lois Forer points out that everything is stacked in favor of the officials who are doing the taking. If the state or federal government takes private land, citizens whose property interests are affected can go to court and try and enjoin the taking. If it is public land that is being taken, however, the citizen has no such redress—in legal parlance, he has no "justiciable interest" —and thus, for want of a plaintiff, many an unreasonable taking has gone uncontested.

Taxpayers can bring suit to prevent an improper use of public funds. But this is rarely the issue in takings of

* "Preservation of America's Park Lands: The Inadequacy of Present Law," New York University Law Review; December, 1966.

parkland—one of the main troubles, indeed, is that often no funds at all are exchanged. "The real interest of the citizen who seeks to sue," says Forer, "is not the expenditure of funds, which may be minimal, but the loss of the park. Under present law, this is precisely the interest that the courts refuse to remedy." She recommends legislation that would permit citizens to go to court to question the necessity of a proposed encroachment. To cut down on crank suits, a minimum of ten citizens would be required to initiate suit.

There is another legal vacuum to be filled. When a qualified plaintiff, such as the municipality itself, does get to court to protest a condemnation, the court will consider many matters, but the one thing it will not consider is whether the condemnation is a good idea. The court will want to be satisfied that due process is being followed and that the condemnation is for a public purpose. It almost always is, of course, and that will be that. The court will not go into the question of whether the new public use is a better or more necessary one than the one it is displacing, or whether the officials who decided on the condemnation could not have achieved the purpose by taking land somewhere else. This, the courts say, is not their line of work; it is the legislature's.

Even when officials display palpably bad judgment in their choices, the courts feel they have to go along. A case in point is the new post office in Cape Girardeau, Missouri. Whoever in the post office department was charged with picking the site thought that a dandy place to take would be the town square, all of it. There were plenty of other sites that could have been used and the square was the one place most prized by the town. It sued to stop the condemnation. The matter finally ended up in the Supreme Court. Whatever their opinion on the wisdom of the taking, the members of the court held that the choice of the site was not a matter for the court to pass upon; a post office was a public purpose, and due process was being followed. Under such circumstances, the court reiterated, a decision of a public official made in good faith is not reviewable. (*U.S.* v. *Carmack,* 329, U.S. 230, 1946)

The courts are stuck with this position because the legislatures have given them no directives on the matter of priorities. Are parks a higher purpose than public parking lots? Sewage plants? Government office buildings? Should officials be required to investigate alternatives? Unless the legislatures make policy declarations, the courts have nothing to go by, and the determinations will remain with officials—the officials who build public parking lots, sewage plants, and government office buildings.

What is needed is a basic policy statute by the federal and the state governments declaring that parkland serves one of the highest public purposes and should not be taken unless there is no alternative—and that the burden of proving there is no alternative should be on the taker. This would not prevent condemnation of parkland. It would deter it strongly, however, and it would subject such condemnations to the rigors of judicial review.

Such a requirement has been adopted by Connecticut. In 1963, as part of an omnibus open-space program, the legislature passed a statute saying that if the state takes municipal park or conservation land for highways or for other purposes, then the state must to the extent feasible provide the municipality with comparable land or money to buy it. Two years later the legislature added a stiffener: If the municipality does not agree to the taking, the state has to go to court if it wants to get approval of the condemnation and establish that there is no other land that would serve its purposes.

The Highway Department put to this test happens to be one of the best in the country, and it feels quite put upon. Unlike many highway departments, it has always paid for municipal land, and as far as state land is concerned, it has given more than it has taken—between 1949 and 1964 it subtracted 249 acres from the state's parkland and forests, but added 755. In dealing with local governments, the department feels that it has always bent over backward to cooperate (in one case, it wryly notes, it routed a projected freeway so it would go through an industrial area instead of the local park; the town wanted it the other way around, however, and so the park was taken.)

Why, then, the department asked, pick on it? In urging defeat of the statute, it argued that the restrictions would severely curtail its freedom of action, perhaps even to the extent that it would have to abandon some projects and leave intermittent highway strips going from nowhere to nowhere. The Bureau of Public Roads, fearful such precedents might spread to other states, viewed with predictable alarm: It said that the state restrictions might conflict with the bureau's regulations and as is custom for the bureau in responding to such situations, it hazarded the possibility that federal highway aid for Connecticut might be put in jeopardy.

As things have worked out, the restrictions have not proved an insupportable burden to the Highway Department. They have made more work for the department's lawyers and have slowed takings in two instances.* But there is no evidence that the highway planning is being adversely affected: More likely, it will be the better for it. The net effect of the statutes is not to prevent necessary takings, but to ensure that they are in fact necessary, and in calling for a rigorous examination of the alternatives, the statutes advocate nothing more than what highway planners claim they would do anyway. The difference is that now it is law.

The difference is important. In all likelihood, most community open spaces would be secure against highway encroachment, law or no law; the point is that now people believe they will be secure, and because of this assurance, they are more inclined to support action for getting

---

* In one case, the officials of the city of Meriden were amenable to the taking of part of a park for a highway rerouting. A number of citizens were not, however, and taking advantage of the new statute, they have sued to enjoin the taking. In another case, the city of Norwalk voted against a proposed taking, and the Highway Department will have to go to court to proceed with the condemnation.

additional open space. In rousing enthusiasm for acquisition programs—particularly those requiring bond issues—one of the toughest objections to counter has been the fear that the highway people would come in and take the best part away. The fear has been exaggerated, but it has inhibited many a community, and it has inhibited many would be donors from giving land to the community.

In providing assurance on this score, the statutes have strengthened local planning. Instead of being presented with a highway plan they cannot do much about except protest, communities are consulted early enough to be able to think realistically about possible alternatives. "It gives us," one official says, "time to catch our breath."

California provides another good example. It has had highway rows on a really grand scale, but partly because of this, it now has some of the best legislation for preventing them. As part of a reform package sponsored by Assemblyman Z'berg, the California legislature passed an act declaring parkland as a "highest and best use"; if condemned for any other use, the courts can be required to rule on the taking. Another act removed from the statutes the rigid directive that highways be routed "in the most direct and practicable location."

This small change had big effects. At the time that the act was passed the Highway Commission was stubbornly pursuing a scheme to run freeways through several of the state's best redwood groves; citizen protest mounted, but the commission seemed to pay no mind. Then, in 1967, to the vast surprise of everyone, the commission announced it was withdrawing the plans: "Conserving the beauty of the state's natural resources," it said, "has to be thought of as well as modern safe transportation." The change in the law, one of the commissioners later explained, helped them to change their position.

Federal legislation has been long overdue, but thanks to Senators Jackson and Yarborough, an important step has been taken as far as highways are concerned. An amendment to the Federal Aid Highway Act of 1966 declares that it shall be the national policy for the federal government to make maximum effort in the highway program to preserve federal, state and local government parklands and historic sites. A similar, but even stronger measure was included in the act setting up the new Department of Transportation. It specifically directs that no highway program be approved that takes conservation or parkland when there is a feasible alternative. The Bureau of Public Roads was not very happy with these restrictions, and some of its friends in Congress tried to soften the effect of the measures in floor debate, but to no effect. The measures are law and their language is so clearly mandatory that there should be little room for administrative reinterpretation by the engineers.

But who is to blow the whistle on them? What is missing is a provision for enforcing the directives; citizens have no legal standing to go to court to protest violation of these directives by the engineers. There is not much other government agencies can do either. There is not even a review board to which disputed cases could be taken. The Citizens Advisory Committee on Recreation and Natural Beauty has recommended a review board that would serve as an administrative court of last resort; it has also proposed machinery for ensuring that the engineers will involve conservation agencies in the early planning stage, before positions have hardened.

Similar measures should be drafted to cover other public works. There have been some partial moves in this direction. In 1962, an administrative order instructed all federal agencies dealing with water-resource projects to give as much weight to aesthetic, recreation, and wildlife values as to development values. In the Water Resources Planning Act of 1965 Congress required that river-basin commissions consider "all reasonable alternative means" in planning their projects. These directives appear to have had some beneficial effects on the engineers. For real muscle, however, the declarations in the Highway and Transportation Acts provide the best model, and if they are coupled with enforcement provisions they could be broadened into excellent statutes for the state governments.

So far, we have been talking about encroachment of parkland by the federal and state governments. One of the biggest problems, however, is self-encroachment by local governments. Additional legislation could help; Lois Forer argues for a state statute that would, in effect, put all municipal parkland off limits to any other use, except in extraordinary cases. There is also much more that can be done under existing law—better legal draftsmanship in municipal codes and explicit dedication of parklands. People who give parkland can tie strings to it more effectively, with reverter clauses and such devices as giving the fee simple to the municipality and simultaneously giving an open-space easement as insurance to an interested third party, such as a land trust or the Nature Conservancy. Occasionally citizens do have access to the courts to prevent local encroachment, and if they have a property interest they can claim is injured, their lawyers can raise hob.

In a legal monograph on open-space preservation,* Allison Dunham gives a wonderful account of the way Chicago's lake front was saved by the contentiousness of Montgomery Ward. In 1890, Ward brought suit against the city to prevent it from filling up the lake front with public buildings. As the owner of two and a half lots on the edge of the area, he claimed he had an easement in the open space. Back in 1836, the commissioners of Illinois had drawn up a subdivision map of the area for the purpose of selling off lots, and for reasons now obscure, they left much of the lake-front area blank. In 1839, another subdivision map showed additional vacant land, with the notation, "Public ground, forever to remain vacant of buildings." Neither map said anything about a park. But Ward's case did not hinge on the land's being a park. His

---

* *Preservation of Open Space Areas*, published by the Welfare Council of Chicago, 123 West Madison Street.

point was that he had a property right in the open land—the right to enjoy unobstructed light, air, and view. The court sustained him.

Civic leaders were outraged at Ward. He eased up to the extent of not fighting the building of an art institute in the open area, to his later regret, but when the city went ahead on plans for armories and libraries and such, he resumed the fight. "Ward expressed the belief," reported an exasperated civic leader, "that it was better to have this great tract of land as a place for people to go and lie around on the grass than to make it the point of Chicago's scheme of beautifying the city. Yes, he did actually!" Three more times Ward went before the court. Three more times he won, and that is why Chicago still has an open lake front.

There is more need than ever for this kind of obstructionism, and now, as then, it is the good cause that is the worst threat. It is not too difficult to rouse citizens over plans to divert parkland to parking lots, garages, or commercial uses: The problem is to get them to resist respectable incursions, like museums, cultural centers, memorials, and statuary, especially when they are offered as gifts by high minded citizens. New York's Central Park, for example, would have been long since filled up with buildings if it were not for the vigilante groups, for the official guardians have not always resisted the benefactions thrust upon them. The latest example is the gift proffered by Huntington Hartford of a restaurant to be built in a corner of Central Park. This would be a clear case of encroachment, but the then park commissioner thought it was a good idea too. When the matter was taken to court, the judge thought so too. Fortunately, the new mayor and his park commissioner did not like the pavilion idea, and it never got built. But there will be more gifts to come.

There are some things to be encouraged about. The recent statutes telling government departments to lay off parkland and pay more attention to aesthetic and recreation values are beginning to have some effect down the line. For one thing, engineers are at last beginning to overhaul their cost-benefit formulas and give some weight to social and aesthetic values. The figures they have been using for judging the pros and cons of alternate routes have dealt almost entirely with what each will do for cars: how many vehicles each will attract, savings in vehicle miles of travel at 9¢ a mile, and so on. But they have not had figures for such things as the impact on neighborhoods, loss of park space, number of trees each route would destroy. (The National Shade Tree Conference wants the engineers to figure these at about $6 per square inch of cross section.)

It is difficult to quantify some of the environmental values, but it can be done. And it is not a bad thing for the engineers if it is done. It gets them off the hook. Under conventional practice, they can be accused of wasting taxpayers' money if they go to extra expense to avoid parkland, or spend additional sums on aesthetic considerations. New formulas would protect them; the compensating benefits would be demonstrated, with dollar signs and decimal points. In broadening their formulas, the engineers would not only gain more elbow room in their planning, they would broaden their constituency and get more groups to support their projects, or at least not fight them so much. Agencies that build dams, for example, find that if they add recreational and aesthetic benefits, they can work up a more compelling economic case for what they want to do. They also get the conservationists off their backs.

Some of the heralded change, of course, is more in the labeling than the approach. Conservationists are particularly skeptical about the highway engineers. The speeches are fine, but when it comes to cases, the engineers seem as insistent as ever on the "least costly" route. But one must be hopeful. It will undoubtedly take a long time before there is an effective change of emphasis—it usually takes about a decade, or the time for a junior echelon to advance to seniority, before a government agency fully embraces a new task. Glacial as it may be, however, a change is under way.

One sign is the "Urban Concept Team" advanced by the Department of Transportation. This came about as a response to the fierce resistance put up by people of Baltimore to additional freeway construction. To help unsnarl the situation the department awarded a $4.8 million contract for a joint planning operation that will bring highway engineers together with planners, architects, landscape architects, and social scientists. The team will be headed by architect and conservationist Nathaniel Owings. A similar team is in the works for New York City. Such groups will not have the power to tell the engineers where the freeways will go—the engineers have already decided that—but they can have a considerable effect on how they will be designed and how they will fit into the surrounding areas.

Many fights, of course, lie ahead. Engineers are by no means delighted at having other people help them plan, and the planning that lies ahead of them includes the most controversial routes of all. So far, about 3500 miles of interstate freeways have been built in urban areas; but another 2200 miles is still to be built. The toughest miles have been saved for last.

As with so many problems, however, highway encroachment may be gaining maximum attention just about the time the peak of the cycle has been passed. Whether or not the engineers change their ways of planning, by the early 1970s they will not have many more freeways to plan. Unless a whole new highway program is superimposed on the interstate system, which seems unlikely, the bulk of the damage to parks and neighborhoods will already have been done.

But what government gives with one hand, it is going to take with the other. As highway construction phases out, the slack is going to be more than taken up by increased demands for land of all sorts of worthy public purposes—airports, new campuses, government research and defense installations. This kind of pressure is almost totally overlooked in most of the current year 2000 regional

plans, with their vast wedges and green belts. These are
to hold the speculators and jerry-builders at bay. But it's
the good guys who will do them in. With due process.

The encroachment problem, in sum, is going to get
worse. The new safeguards and restrictions can be offsetting; *if* they are enacted, and *if* they are enforced,
public agencies will take relatively less parkland than
otherwise they would. But there will be more agencies
seeking more land, and in absolute terms—in actual acres
—the pressure for taking parkland is going to get worse.
We had better attend to the defenses now.

The Plans

8. The Year 2000 Plans

>>>

I have been talking about ways and means of saving open space. Now let me turn to the question of what open spaces should be saved and how the choosing of them should be done. One would think this would be the easy part. It is not. Planners now see open space as a key to the design of regions and the process of selection has become a technically formidable task. Therein lie some of our difficulties.

Open-space planning used to be simple. In the archives of every city are series of plans, many dating back to the City Beautiful movement at the turn of the century and some a half century before. The plans vary according to the fashions of the period but the open-space proposals are all very much alike. If you put the successive plans on acetate at the same scale and lay them on top of each other, the areas marked green usually coincide.

The idea was to get the land that would be most useful for recreation and looked the best—"pleasure grounds," to use an old term. In most cases this meant highest priority was to be attached to the stream-valley network, and decade after decade there have been repeated recommendations for sewing up stream valleys with parks. Some communities did so, to their everlasting good fortune.

But planners now look on this approach to open space as much too simplistic. They are all for recreation and scenery, but they regard these as secondary functions of open space. They believe the primary function is to shape and structure to metropolitan development; which is to say, the great benefit of open space is not what it will provide, but what it will prevent. Where there is secure open space, unplanned growth cannot take place.

The challenge that excites planners today is the design of whole regions. Development is one part of the design; open space the obverse. Crudely stated, the technique is to figure out what kind of growth the region should have, where it should go, and to designate the areas in between as permanent open space.

This is an extraordinarily ambitious kind of designing, for it calls for vast amounts of open space and, in some cases, a rather radical rearrangement of existing growth patterns. But the very boldness of this vision has fired planners' enthusiasm and it has also prompted some interesting technical innovations in the planning process. Planners no longer attempt to come up with just one good over-all design. This is "normative" planning and is old hat. They design alternatives. These are tested against each other and the best of the lot is chosen.

The most celebrated prototype of this kind of planning is the Year 2000 Plan drawn up for the Washington metropolitan area by the National Capital Planning Commission. I want to go into this in some detail, for though I think it is a bad plan, a great many people have thought it a good plan; more to the point, they have been borrowing the basic approach and applying it to the design of other areas.

But here is a case where it is in order to examine the particulars of a situation. If it is good principle, it ought to apply, and to the place being planned for most of all. There are some problems in the Washington area that are unique to it—the mixture of governments for one—but the mess the planners confronted was the same kind of mess that has afflicted every metropolitan area: a scattered pattern of development oozing over the entire countryside.

Could this development be structured? The planners' base proposition was that it very definitely could be and in a number of different ways. The question was not if, but which; the challenge was to make the choice.

It has become possible, the report said, to shape the metropolis: "A metropolis can now choose to grow in any one of a variety of ways. . . . New tools of design are being created continually. . . . Used in concert, the means within our reach can shape the region and each of its parts into the form we desire."

To arrive at the best form, the planners hypothesized seven possible forms and began weighing the pros and cons of each. They considered a "restricted growth" pattern. This was rejected out of hand. People would not accept it, they said, and the natural increase in the present population would be just too much to contain.

Next, they considered siphoning off the growth by setting up entirely new metropolitan areas seventy or so miles from Washington. This pattern was rejected, with commendation. The creation of such new cities might be a good national policy, the planners suggested, but would be too big a job for the region to undertake.

The planners turned to alternatives they deemed more realistic. One was "Planned Sprawl." This is what would occur if present trends were continued, but with somewhat more guidance. The planners obviously did not think much of this, but the projection was not made entirely horrible. The growth would spread over most of the region but ribbons of open space would run through it.

The planners then considered what might be done with new towns. One possibility was a "Dispersed Cities" pattern. In this, new towns would be set up ten miles or

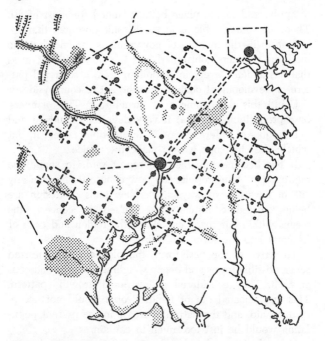

more beyond the present built-up areas. Each new town would be laid out in concentric form. In the center would be a business district; around it would be rings of progressively less dense development, and on the outer edge, a belt of preserved open space. In microcosm, each would offer most of the advantages of large cities so there would be less need for people to travel, less dependence on automobiles.

Another way to arrange the new towns would be a "Ring of Cities" pattern. This would push the new towns even farther from the center city. The remoteness, the planners surmised, might make it easier to keep the intervening land from filling up. This pattern would give regional development something of a doughnut shape. The new towns would be set in a circle, some thirty miles out or more.

As in the plan for London, they would be separated from the core by a large green belt. Thus:

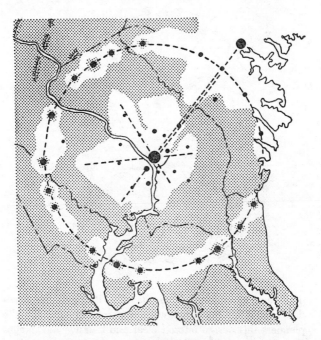

Another variant would be "Peripheral Communities." In this pattern the new towns would be put much closer to the city, and they would be linked with a network of diagonal and circumferential freeways. The planners were not too keen on this, however. There would not be the clear division between town and country that other alternatives offered. It would be a compact form of regional development, the planners noted, probably too compact. To see how they sketched it see page 158.

After weighing all the foregoing (and finding them wanting in some respect or other), the planners came to the final alternative. This was the "Radial Corridor Plan." New development would be concentrated in six corri-

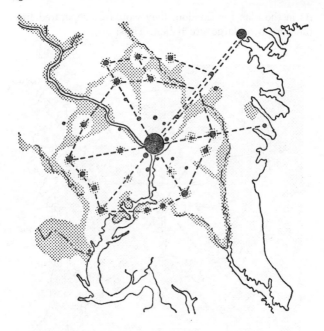

dors running outward from the city. Between the corridors would be the large wedges of countryside. To the planners this design offered clear and decisive advantages over the others. It would maximize access to the core, best exploit mass transportation, and would make feasible the preservation of significant stretches of countryside.

To make developers stay in the corridors, all other land would have to be posted against trespassing and the wedges, accordingly, were designated as "controlled open space." There certainly would be a lot of it. Within the immediate planning area the wedges cover over 1000 square miles of map space, and if they were extended outward later, the increase would become geometrical.

Some who saw the preliminary plan were awe-struck by the size of the wedges and suggested that the plan was too hazy about the positive uses to which they would

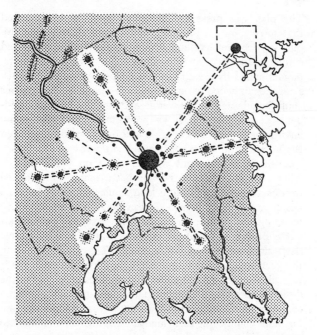

be put. The planners noted that recreation and other compatible uses would in time be found for parts of this land but that to overemphasize these would blur the main point. The primary function of the wedges, the planners said, was to give order and form to the region.

The land would be frozen so development would have to go into the corridors. Farmers could continue to use the land for farming, and existing small towns and crossroads settlements would remain. Some might even be a bit enlarged. But not much. Basically, the wedges were to be made inviolate.

But how in the world was this to be done? A very good question, the planners said. There certainly were some interesting problems involved. But the ways and means would come later, in the implementation stage. The important thing was to get a consensus on the over-all idea.

The plan was presented in 1961. It might be expected that so sweeping a proposal would have stirred up a tremendous controversy and opposition. Instead, it provoked a remarkable amount of acclaim. Civic groups and newspapers hailed its breadth of vision; local planning commissions began working up studies to see how their plans could be adapted to the wedge and corridor pattern; President Kennedy hailed it as promising "the finest living environment America can plan and build," and he pledged the administration's wholehearted support.

Even more important was its effect on planners elsewhere. Some criticized the approach; many more looked to it as a model, and before long similar efforts at regional design were being launched elsewhere. Not all have fastened on the same forms—some have favored circular patterns; others, more linear patterns. But the efforts have been similar in three key respects. They look ahead to the year 2000 as the target date; they look on open space as a means for regional form, and they use the alternative design approach. The principal difference is the degree of elaboration; the second-generation Year 2000 Plans are far more complex in their analysis and the alternatives are programmed for computers.

But the Year 2000 Plan has long since been doomed. Much obeisance is still paid to it, and since the plan was in favor of a number of things that would probably happen anyway—more large-scale planned communities, for example, more intensive development along the traffic arteries—it can be accounted as a partial success.

The biggest element in the design, however, has had the props knocked from under it. The wedges have already been spoken for. The farmers who were to keep the land rural until the planners figured out what to do with it have been acting like farmers in every fringe area; they have been selling out to builders and speculators. You would not always know it from looking at the land; much of it is still being farmed and you can easily get the impression that there is plenty of time left. There is not. The farming is a holding operation, and in some cases, downright fraud.

When I was looking into tax-assessment policies in the area several years ago, I was struck by the number of farms that were still operating in part of one of the Maryland counties. It was marginal farmland, the kind that usually would have been marked by second growth and scattered development. The land happened to be smack in the middle of one of the proposed wedges, but this was not the reason for its sylvan character. When I checked with the county assessor, I found that most of this land had been bought up by a real estate syndicate for well over $2000 an acre. The syndicate was allowing the farmers to stay on the land—in fact, it insisted they did as part of the deal. As long as someone is making a show of farming, the assessor has to evaluate such land at no more than its farm value, about $150 an acre. The syndicate can afford to bide its time. The charade may continue for a while longer, but when the syndicate is ready to start cashing in, the transformation will be swift.

The same kind of transformation will take place in other of the wedges. Developers have not been paying the slightest attention to the wedge boundaries. Most of the farmland has long since been bought for development and as many new subdivisions seem to be going up in the wedge areas as in the corridors.

Government agencies could put a stop to this by using eminent domain and putting the wedges into public ownership. There would be a money problem, however. The land involved totals about 1000 square miles or 640,000 acres. At current prices, the bill would be astronomical. It would be astronomical even if prices were somehow rolled back to those prevailing at the time the plan was first proposed; at $1000 an acre, the bill for the wedges would be roughly $640,000,000. (James Rouse paid about $2000 an acre during 1961–62 for the land he bought for the new town of Columbia.)

Nor could the land be zoned against development. For one thing, many local governments would have to be persuaded that it would be a good idea for them to tell developers and industry to take their money and go spend it in some other jurisdiction. A superbody with area-wide zoning powers could in theory get past this hurdle, but there would still be the courts to contend with. Where land is clearly unsuitable for development—flood plains and marshlands, for example—the open-space zoning could stick. But it could not be applied all over the wedges. Landowners would argue that this was condemnation without compensation, and the courts would agree.

Even if such wedges could be frozen, there is another question to be answered. *Should* they be? And *why*? To the planners, of course, one reason was paramount: "The single most important aspect of open space," they affirmed, "is its use as a means to structure metropolitan form." This doctrine, however, does not appeal greatly to the uninformed and the planners make much of the secondary benefits to be enjoyed. Among other things, the wedges are to conserve natural resources, encourage continuation of the farm landscape, and provide visual amenity.

But they would not do it very efficiently. Great expanses of land are not uniformly scenic, and this is very much the case with the wedges. Some parts of it are very good looking indeed. Some are not. Most of the land the syndicate bought up, for example, is rather scrubby tobacco land which does not look like much, nor is it especially productive.

If the beauty of open space is to be invoked, one must get down to specifics. What are the key features which define it, such as ridges and valleys? How does it read to the eye? Would it hurt scenic values if some parts of the space were developed? Which parts? In the Year 2000 Plan there is no indication of what the whole looks like. There is no indication of what the parts look like. There is no sense of place.

One clue to the workability of an open-space plan is irregularity. If it is geometric and balanced it is probably not very good for nature is not geometric and balanced. In the Year 2000 Plan you would have a hard time deducing what the topography is like from the outlines of the open spaces. The area is rich with stream valleys but there is no map of them. The various alternative plans do have lines indicating the existence of the principal river and one large creek but otherwise give little clue of the drainage pattern and run counter to it as often as not. Soils and gradients are similarly ignored; no effort seems to have been made to figure where land conditions are amenable to development and where they are not. Nor does very much attention seem to have been paid to the previous open-space plans of the local governments of the area.

Thus the vulnerability of the wedges. It may seem very wicked of developers to buy up the land in them, but they are pursuing a logic too, and it is not necessarily the wrong one for being commercial. Much of the land in these wedges is very developable; the gradients do not require too much earth moving; the soil is good for building; interchanges are near and downtown Washington is only twenty or thirty minutes away by car. And this is why the speculative pressure on this land is so intense.

It does not follow that because land prices are steep the highest and best use is development. Some of this land should be kept open however great the cost. But there is a limit. High land prices are a discipline, and people with good causes have to heed it as well as anyone else. When the competition for the use of land is so intense, there must be some very compelling reasons for keeping it open.

Is it possible to extinguish these development pressures? A number of people wish it could be done by fiat.* Lately

---

* The Year 2000 Plan for Paris seems vulnerable on this score. It calls for two parallel belts of development along the Seine, and these can be lengthened if the growth turns out to be greater than anticipated. To help constrain the growth in this pattern, however, large areas around Paris are designated as "zones of deferred development," and through use of the police power the government is to prevent any additional building in them. Since French landowners are as zealous of property rights as any, it will be quite a feat for the government to freeze these rights without paying anything for them.

there has been agitation in Washington for legislation that
would curb speculation, deflate the price of hoarded land,
and make it easier for the good people to deal with the
bad people.

But this is dealing with symptoms. There is a strong
case to be made for improving acquisition procedures and
for changing the laws so they won't be rigged in favor
of the speculator, the tax laws especially. But the basic
pressures would still remain. For it is not the speculators
who cause the increase in prices. The increase is due to
a rising demand for a finite supply of land.

Some people believe complete public ownership of land
would change all this. There should indeed be more public ownership, especially of land that is to be kept per-
manently open. But public ownership does not itself reduce the competition for land. It puts it under different
auspices.

Developers are not the only ones who have their eye on
open space. Even now there is no threat to open space
more formidable than the projects of dedicated public
servants. They act as they do for the highest motives, and
there is the rub. If the official plan is counter to what
they think is right, they will fight it, and no super-body will
eliminate these conflicts of high purpose. A regional housing authority, for example, would be just as covetous of
the land in the green wedges as the developers, and would
be a lot more difficult to deflect.

The plan was bound to fail. There is too much open space
in it. A good argument could be made that the plan
would be far better if it were reversed, that is, have the
relatively thin corridors of open space and leave the large
wedges open to development. To call for less open space
may seem a curious position for an open-space advocate
to make, and let it be conceded that in stimulating public
action it is often useful to ask for more than you think you
can get. But it is very important to have a pretty good
idea of what you can get, for otherwise there will be no

point to the campaign. This is the trouble with the Year 2000 Plan. It is all or nothing.

Utopian goals are supposed to be useful in provoking people to action, but they can also divert them from action. Before the Year 2000 Plan was drafted, a number of excellent plans had been made for open-space acquisition. The most notable was launched by the passage of the Capper-Cramton Act in 1930; this provided grant aid to local governments to secure the lands along the stream valleys of the capital area. Over the years there has been some action here and there, but Congress has not followed through with decent appropriations, and the bulk of the key valley land is yet to be acquired. If the kind of energy and imagination that went into the Year 2000 Plan had been applied to getting action on the more modest and realizable acquisition plan, the truly vital open spaces of the region would have been saved.

The planners are now back at the drawing board. While the Year 2000 Plan is still official, the gap between what it says should be taking place and what has actually been taking place has become embarrassingly wide, and efforts have been launched to recast, or "further evolve" the plan. In the process, the original geometrics are apt to be quietly evolved away altogether. They will have to be. Recently completed highways have already made a hash of the plan. The beltway around Washington has stimulated development in such a fashion that it is running athwart the corridors more than it is going out along them. A major new transit line is to slice into one of the wedges.

Regional bodies in the area are reconsidering their fealty to the plan. The Maryland-National Capital Park and Planning Commission, originally one of the most enthusiastic supporters, has concluded that the wedges and corridor pattern is clearly unworkable. Its planners now believe that the inherent growth pattern takes a quite different shape. They see it as a "star and circle" pattern and believe it would make more sense to work with its trends than against them. The suburban centers, they suggest, could be joined laterally with strips of new development. These strips would make up the star; the circles would be the present beltway, a projected outer beltway, and, beyond, encircling open space.

The rapid obsolescence of the first Year 2000 Plan has not daunted believers in the approach. So there have been some bugs. It is not the particulars of the Washington situation that should concern one, they say, but the basic planning process. But that is just the trouble. The plan has not failed simply because the wedges were too big or in the wrong place, or a highway went this way when it should have gone that way. The plan has failed because of the assumptions of the basic process, and similar efforts being made elsewhere are likely to fail for the same reason.

The fundamental assumption in comparing alternative designs for a region is that it is in the power of the planning process to bring them about. This is a very satisfying premise for those doing the planning, but it does tend to give people a sense of control they do not in fact possess or ever would. The marginal effect that planning can have on growth can be very important. But it is limited. Most of the factors involved are what the planners call exogenous—that is, there's damn little the planners can do about it.

This has certainly proved true in the city, but the experience does not seem to have been chastening. Now that planners have turned to the design of whole regions, there seems to have been a resurgence of optimism about the capabilities of the planning process, and this is shared by citizens as well as professionals. Whatever form these orderly diagrams may take, the fact they are being shaped, and with such confidence, can be comforting to the citizen. Looking at them on the map, one gets a satisfying feeling of man in control of his destiny.

But how realistic are these designs? The only one that could be achieved with the tools at hand is "planned sprawl." But while many plans pose this as an alternative, they usually do this only to scare hell out of the laity, and the accompanying pictures often conjure up the worst of today's suburbia. Thus do the planners box themselves in. It is a shame, for planned sprawl is probably the most challenging alternative they could tackle. If they decided that it would be best to roll with the punch, the planning tools available would have great leverage effect for they would be applied to dominant trends rather than against them. I am not advocating planned sprawl as a goal, but since it might be the most likely of all alternatives to take place, it does seem worthy of more serious attention.

The alternatives the planners really want to choose from are *new* forms, and these all demand sweeping governmental reorganization and legal tools yet undevised. If systems of satellite towns are going to be put up across political boundaries, there is a tremendous amount of preliminary legislative work that will have to be done. Regional design plans are very hazy on this score. They are end-state plans. There is no indication of what the intermediate plans would be or how they would be accomplished. Only the final grand design is shown.

There is nothing to be lost by considering final goals, it can be said, and certainly there is merit in hypothesizing various possibilities. It dramatizes the fact that choices must be made, and it can sharpen our thinking. It can also lead to a certain autointoxication. Once you start moving blobs around on a map as if you could order their counterparts in reality, you tend to become rather Olympian about ways and means, and the choices you pose can be highly unrealistic.

There is no point in discussing choices if the choices are not there to be made. Those open spaces, for example. In Year 2000 Plans, they are not only big, they are sometimes bigger, and more virgin, than what we have today. But where is all this space? How can it be frozen to development? If there is no satisfactory answer to this question or even a glimmer of one, we are embarked on a journey to nowhere.

The matter can't be fobbed off by saying that if we agree on goals we can then worry about techniques. This is the fallacy of considering ends without means. The two are inextricable; they must be considered together and at the same time. Conceivably, twenty years from now the means might be at hand. But that would be twenty years from now. The new techniques might be at hand; the open space wouldn't.

All these plans presuppose that a consensus will be worked out on the political measures necessary and there has been developed a quite elaborate concept of how this consensus is to be achieved. Planners, who have a strong penchant for graphics, love to set down elaborate flow charts and diagrams, the central premise of which is that the communication of facts to the various governmental and private parties at interest will in time lead to the necessary agreement. It all seems very sequential: the definition of the problem areas, the hypothesizing of tentative goals by the planners, the presentation of the goals to the opinion leaders in clinics and workshops and seminars. And feedback—oh, the feedback! On the charts, arrows and reciprocals go back and forth, showing the flow of new information, or inputs, for the reformulation of the goals and construction of alternatives to carry out the goals. Eventually, there is supposed to be an implementation stage— which, when reduced to a figure, generally is set no earlier than 1975.

What all this amounts to is a lot of public-relations activity, and the consensus it produces is illusion. A revealing aspect of these projects is that though the plans call for the most sweeping exercise of governmental power over commercial and business interests, they are roundly applauded at their unveiling by commercial and business interests. As a matter of fact, these interests often form the core of the various advisory groups and steering committees and the other forms of preventive participation with which these enterprises are customarily laden. I have attended many of the civic ceremonies staged for the presentation of these plans, and I am always amazed at the euphoria which characterizes them.

I think the main reason is that the plans are so sweeping. They get everybody off the hook. If they had to make a decision on just one element of the plan, the whole edifice of consensus would come tumbling down. But the plans do not confront people with immediate and difficult choices. They vault over the messy present and near future. They take the big view. They make everybody feel bold.

Which brings us to another disadvantage of the year 2000. It is too far off. You can project current trends with some assurance for a few years and do some educated guessing about things that could and should be done. Once past five or ten years, however, projections become increasingly risky. There almost always seems to be a cross-up, and sometimes the very certainty of the forecast influences people to do things which make a hash of it.

But Year 2000 Plans betray few misgivings on this score. For all the to-do about taking all possibilities into account, almost every Year 2000 Plan proceeds on certain common premises. These seem reasonable enough at first glance— sharp increase in population, greatly increased car ownership, more leisure time, and so on—but it is a little unsettling to see the confidence with which these trends are extended decade by decade ahead. How can people be so sure? Even if they are right about the basic direction of a trend, there could be some unexpected changes in degree, and as with the tiny error in a compass reading, even a small shift can make for a huge margin of error twenty or thirty years hence.

There is also the possibility that they could be wrong about the trends themselves. Population, for example. The past track record of the experts has been miserable. Back in the thirties, the best informed opinion was that the then low birth rate would continue and that this country probably would never have more than 150 million people. Population decline was a problem many thoughtful people worried about, and one of the arguments then advanced for new planned communities was that they would furnish environment that would stimulate more child breeding.

But the birth rate increased. Experts thought this might be temporary. In 1945 they predicted that the birth rate might rise for a few years as the soldiers came home but that it would then drop back. The birth rate rose, and kept on rising for fifteen years.

It is this momentum that has been built into most current projections. But the momentum may already be spent. Since 1957 the birth rate has been going down, not up. The decline may be reversed, of course. But it may not. It may even accelerate. In bracing ourselves to meet a huge population surge, we may have set in motion some subtle but powerful counterforces.

The same kind of turnabout may affect many other trends. Can we be so certain that leisure time is going to continue at the rate it has been? Will land prices continue their seemingly inexorable rise? Maybe they will, but we should remember that these trends we take so easily for granted as constants have been influenced by one of the most extraordinary postwar booms in history. The main body of economists assures us that this condition is more or less permanent and that a major depression is unthinkable. This does not necessarily mean we will get a depression, but it is enough to make one think.

Is it inconceivable some reversals may take place? I have not seen a single plan that considers even the possibility of an interruption. Subsequent events may prove the omission of no consequence, but the planners would be prudent if they considered other possibilities. But they just will not do it. Recently, in a clinic to get layman feedback on an ambitious regional plan, the chief economist was asked if he did not feel uneasy over the quite optimistic projections on which the plan was based. Just for the hell of it, it was suggested, the staff ought to put a man on detached duty and have him speculate on plans that would be called for if the trends did not go the way they were expected to. The economist thought the idea frivolous.

But it is anything but frivolous. Some highly practical

suggestions for contingency planning might come out of such an inquiry. Suppose, for example, that a real bust in the price of raw land were to take place between now and 1975. What kind of action would be in order? A reserve acquisition fund? What lands would most likely become tax delinquent? Questions like this are worth hypothesizing too.

Year 2000 planners do not follow their own precepts. The idea of hypothesizing all the realistic possibilities and then comparing them is an excellent one. In most cases, however, the hypothesizing is done in only one direction. This would not be so bad if the planners recognized that they were engaged in advocacy, or old-hat "normative" planning. The elaborateness of the apparatus, however, fools even the practitioners into believing that the end product is the result of hard facts and objective analyses.

The increasing use of the computer, helpful as it may be in many respects, will not eliminate this defect. The final design that is arrived at through today's comparatively crude procedures does tend to be quite similar to the kind of design the planners had leaned to before the exercise. So in the future. If in the 1970s the fashion is for, say, a "parallel cities" design, you can be sure that the computers will be feeding out tape objectively favoring this design as the optimum.

When we are dealing with the growth of a region, we have almost an infinity of variables to consider. Some of these are measurable and computers could be helpful to us. (Which kinds of dams can best regulate water flow.) But some of the most important variables are not really measurable. (Future attitudes toward family size; the use of leisure.) If we try to crank all these factors together into the machine, the statistical precision of the product does not mean much and the farther we project this in time, the sillier it becomes.

It is not the future that is being measured. It is the present. The Year 2000 Plans are a mirror image; the statistical underpinnings are a projection of what has been happening, only more so, and the solutions are a set of orthodoxies that have passed their prime. For the future that we can do something about, they are beside the point.

9. The Green Belts

>>

The most ambitious effort that has been made to apply
the containment principle is the London Green Belt. How
it has worked out is a matter of considerable relevance
for us. Most of the regional designs now being worked
up for our metropolitan areas borrow heavily from English
theory. The New Town and green belt concepts were not
only pioneered in England but also have been applied
there on a large scale, and it has been widely assumed
in this country that the application has been quite successful.

It has not been, but the assumption is important nonetheless. It buttresses planners' belief that the reason similar
plans have been stalled here is due mainly to the fact
our planners have not had the kind of powers and money
that their English counterparts have had. It should be a
matter of catching up.

First, a definition of terms. In this country the term
green belt is loosely applied to any kind of open space.

In England it has a fairly precise meaning. A green belt is a large swath of permanent open space surrounding a town or city. It contains publicly owned land but the bulk is private land on which the government has placed restrictions against further development. It provides parkland and landscape, but these are secondary purposes. The main purpose of the green belt is to contain the city and channel future growth.

The English green belt is a great achievement. Any American who sees some of the lovely countryside that has been saved should be envious. By having ventured so much, the English have secured for themselves choices the likes of which most of our cities have long since squandered. Many options are still open for the English and they are now in the happy position of being able to entertain second thoughts about the green belts.

The point is that they are having second thoughts. The green belts have provided much amenity but they have not done what they were primarily meant to do. Since we are now just beginning to attempt similar programs, we should attend well to the English experience, for we have much to learn.

The history of the English green belts is a series of swings between emphasis on use and emphasis on containment. The earliest proposals put use first. The English have always had a strong affection for the landscape as an end in itself. Even Ebenezer Howard, who passionately wanted to contain cities, argued for green belts on the basis of their positive values. He urged that the government purchase green belt land so that city people would be able to use it and enjoy it, as a sort of townsman's countryside.

But the English have also inclined strongly to the idea of containment. Since the time of Elizabeth, who banned all new building within three miles of London's gates, the English have habitually viewed with alarm the growth of their cities and sought ways to keep them to size. It was on this basis that in the late twenties the government called for study of an "agricultural belt" around London.

The incidental benefits of husbandry were invoked but the main idea was to say to London, This far and no further. Any future development would have to take place in satellites beyond the farmland.

But when action finally came, the emphasis was back on use. The man who was asked to draw up the government plan, Sir Raymond Unwin, did not think much of the agricultural containment idea. He argued successfully that the really vital need was for open spaces that Londoners could use for recreation and amenity. In his plan of 1932 he proposed a "green girdle" of spaces within easy reach of the built-up areas. These are the spaces he sought:

This plan differs from the present green belt in several important respects. The spaces to be secured, while not vast in acreage, were meant to be purchased for public use. The spaces did not form a continuous belt; the pattern was roughly circular but it was essentially a series of spaces based on the drainage network, and they were woven into the built-up areas. Because of this, the linear amount of space—or "edge"—would have been greater than is the case with the present green belt.

This plan led to the 1938 Green Belt Act and in the

years before the war some 38,000 acres were purchased or effectively controlled. The second major push for green belt action was to come after the war, and by the time it came the planners had a different purpose in mind. They had become acutely concerned about the growth of London. Too many people were coming to it from the rest of England; there was too much industry in the area and there threatened to be more. Starting with the Barlow Commission report in 1939, there was a succession of proposals that the government take drastic action to stop the growth and disperse it away from the London area.

The planners now saw a much greater role for the green belt. Instead of a modest series of recreational spaces, London would be encircled with a huge restraining ring. In the 1944 plan for greater London, Sir Patrick Abercrombie drew a series of concentric rings with the green belt ring roughly five miles deep separating the inner city and suburbs from the outer countryside. He assumed that there would be no more industrial growth in London and that the population would, if anything, decline somewhat. It was recognized, however, that there would be some "overspill" from London. This would be accommodated by the creation of new towns beyond the green belt.

The question of function was no semantic quibble; it largely determined the way the green belt was set up. Since the emphasis was to be on containment rather than use, the program did not call for much outright purchase. What the planners wanted to achieve was absence of growth and under the Town and Country Act of 1947, they were given broad powers to freeze the green belt land against it. Proposed boundaries were enlarged and the green belt widened to between six and ten miles. On the next page is the Green Belt Plan as adopted in 1955.

The program called for a combination of zoning and compensation. The Minister of Housing and Local Government laid down the broad outlines of the green belt; the county planning authorities were to draw up the precise boundaries for their segments. Once these were laid down,

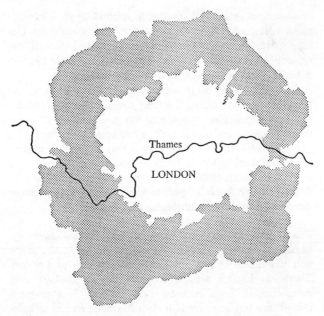

anyone within the green belt who wanted to build would have to apply for planning permission. Since the whole point of the green belt was to curb building, there would have to be very compelling reasons for it and the changes would have to be compatible with the green belt. If a man wanted to add some farm buildings, for example, he was likely to get permission; if he wanted to put up some tract housing, he would not.

The government intended to use police powers to the fullest, but it recognized that there would have to be compensation as well. If a landowner was refused permission to build, he could file a claim for the "development rights" that were being stripped from his land. Funds for this compensation were to be paid by the national government and a sum of some 300 million pounds was set aside for this purpose.

It was to prove an enormously complicated process, in-

volving considerable difficulties in estimating the development charge for specific properties, and eventually this
aspect was to prove somewhat unworkable. For all the
difficulties, however, by 1959 the green belt had become
a reality, and some 840 square miles secured.

In 1955, when the government urged extension of the
principle to other cities, it strongly reaffirmed the containment principle. The purposes of the green belt, the Minister of Housing and Local Government declared, should be
"(1) to check further growth of urban areas, (2) to prevent neighboring towns from merging, and (3) to preserve the special character of towns." Recreational use of
the green belt land by people was not listed as a major
purpose, though it was noted as desirable.

Has it worked? In some ways, it has worked superbly.
Measured against its primary purpose, however, the green
belt has failed. It has not halted the growth of London.
There has been a greater concentration of business and
commerce in London than ever before. The outward
growth has not been contained; it has been forced to leap-
frog over the green belt.

So far there has not been too much encroachment on the
green belt itself, but the pressures are becoming extremely intense. People who have coveted green belt land
are now openly calling for development of certain sections
of it, and even some of the staunchest green belt advocates have been discussing ways of adjusting to these
pressures lest the whole thing cave in.

It does not follow that the green belt was a bad idea—
many fine accomplishments have been pushed through for
the wrong reasons, and the English will probably underpin
it with a more workable rationale. But the experience does
illustrate that the negative containment concept is a faulty
one. Growth can, indeed, be contained; but it cannot
be contained by a vacuum.

The only way open land can be maintained against
growth pressures is function, and it is in this respect that
the green belt is wanting. Absence of development is not

a function. The space must be usable to people, and not just a few people, but the people of the metropolis. They must be able to use the land for recreation, to see it, and to enjoy it.

Lack of access is the trouble with the London green belt. There are parklands within it, but they are only a fraction of the total, and much of this parkland is relatively difficult for Londoners to get to. Because development has been frozen, the English do have a reserve of land that could later be purchased for recreation. Because so little has been purchased to date, however, the green belt has become all the more vulnerable to pressures for other uses.

Nor is there much visual access. From a plane circling London, the green belt is highly visible and immensely pleasing; and one senses some of the order and symmetry apparent on the planner's map. On the ground, however, the green belt is not so easy to see. There are many lovely stretches of countryside within it, such as the Downs and parts of the New Forest, and throughout the green belt if you take a car and poke down the byroads you will find many an enchanting view.

But most people don't poke down the byroads and the main routes that they do travel tend to be the less comely. Take a bus along some of the main routes to suburbia and you will scarcely see the green belt; it is close at hand, but you see only tantalizing glimpses of it, for most of it is screened by temporary housing structures, weedy growths, and dilapidated farm buildings. Some of the spaces that are open, furthermore, are of a nondescript kind that look worse than development. The planners could say what should not be done with the land: they could not say what should be done. Sometimes very little has been done. Many areas constitute a no man's land— they are forbidden to development but no longer serve any useful function. Literally, they have gone to seed.

There is, in short, too much vacuum. Where land has been purchased for public recreation there is little danger of encroachment. Where it has not been, which is to say in most of the green belt, the pressures for conversion to other uses are becoming increasingly difficult to stave off. The problem is not the easy one of commercial blight versus open space. Competition comes from other good uses, housing especially, and in the clash of causes the tangible has a strong edge over the intangible.

Thus the vulnerability of containment. When you put a green belt athwart the path of development, your defenses had better be impregnable. In choosing land for containment, you have at one and the same time chosen land that is well-located for housing. As time goes on and the pressure for more housing grows, the need for an offsetting function becomes critical. The abstract case for open space that early seemed so strong is no longer sufficient. What is it to be, as the question is so often put: people or space?

This poses a dilemma for planners and it is a particularly excruciating one when the planners are responsible for both open space and for housing. This is the case with the English Minister of Housing and Development. To its discomfiture, it recently felt compelled to grant permission for the city of Birmingham to use 1540 acres of its proposed green belt for housing. City officials were discomfited too; they would have liked to have left the green belt alone, they said, but there was no more building space available. They would not stay long in office, one of them remarked, if they "left 100,000 people in Birmingham to rot in slums for the sake of possessing the green belt principle."

English planners now acknowledge that the concept of the green belt needs a great deal of rethinking. It would have worked, they say, if population and business growth had been as static as they had expected. But these assumptions proved wrong; or, as the planners put it, were "falsified by events." Now the expectations are for even more growth to come. In its planning study for southeast England, the Ministry foresees another million more people in the area encircled by the belt by 1981 and almost as many in the outer ring. Something, it would seem, has got to give.

The green belt, possibly? The Ministry's planners cautiously raise the unthinkable, and with the felicity of expression that distinguishes English official papers from ours, the planners embrace heresies while seeming to attack them. The green belt must be maintained, the study asserts, but the best way to do it is yield a little. Some of the green belt land is not really ideal green belt land, it is noted, and might make "a most valuable contribution toward meeting the land shortage"—that is, be used for building.

The planners warn against drawing a green belt with too broad a brush. They suggest that the proposed extensions to the green belt—which would add some 1200 square miles—ought to be critically re-examined. If it gets too big it will defeat itself. "The danger of spreading the green belt extensions too far afield, and of drawing them tightly round existing development is that, in the long run, population pressures will make it impossible to hold the line. If the green belt is to be strongly maintained, and if it is to enjoy popular support and respect, its boundaries must be such that they can withstand all foreseeable pressures." Just because space is open, they warn, is not reason enough for green belting it; "in the areas at some distance from London, a positive reason should be shown if it is intended to bring land into the rigidity of the green belt system."

Positive is now the word. While the dream of containing London has by no means been abandoned, there is a swing back to the earlier idea that the green belt's main function should be amenity. The emphasis now is on seeking landscape and recreational values, of securing more parkland, of finding ways to make the green belt more accessible to people, the people of the inner city especially.

The planners see great possibilities in the sterile areas. The worked-out gravel pits that disfigure the river valleys, for example, could be used to help solve the problem of solid-waste disposal, and when filled, could be landscaped into recreational areas. (The English have always been very good with rubble; the famed Backs at Cambridge were built out of medieval rubbish dumps; more lately, rubble from the Blitz was used to create a vast expanse of football fields on London marshland.) The most exciting scheme is that for Lea Valley. This is a strip of derelict landscape that runs from the countryside into the heart of London's East End. The Civic Trust has worked up a very imaginative plan to show how this strip could be rehabilitated into a linear playground for Londoners.

If an entirely new start could be made and a green belt were to be fashioned on the principles now being stressed, the result would be a plan very much like that drafted by Unwin; the green belt land would be much more closely tailored to the topography, the primary emphasis would be put on recreation and landscape values, and the open space would penetrate into the pattern of development rather than be laid across it.

Reading between the lines of recent government papers, one gets the strong inference that the planners wish they could start afresh. With what seems to be very much like approval, they discuss the unthinkable by commenting on certain "radical proposals" put forth by other people. One was for junking the green belt in its present form and refashioning it into a more tightly planned and functional one. Instead of being constricted by a girdle, development would grow along the main lines of communication with the open space in between. The planners comment that this pattern would have two great advantages: It would bring town and country closer together and would be much more flexible than the present green belt in coping with the outward push of development. "The main difficulty about this idea," they comment, "is that it has come too late. If the green belt had first been defined at a time when the facts of population and employment growth in London were fully known, this might have been the chosen pattern."

If they had it to do over again, in short, they would have done it quite differently.* Since we in the U.S. have yet to take the initial steps, we ought to consider doing it differently too. Despite the clear lessons of the British experience, however, many of our metropolitan planning efforts seem to be seizing on precisely those elements of the British experiment which have not worked out.

Too many of our plans are insisting that negative containment must be the primary function of open space and, if anything, with more dogmatism than ever did the Eng-

---

* In assessing the lessons, let it be noted, the planners remain obdurate about London. They still do not want it to grow. They do concede its increasing magnetism as a managerial and professional center. They note that it is the growth sections of the economy that have been most attracted to the area. They even concede that the shift has not been exactly unplanned. It is the cumulative result of countless decisions by individual firms made in full knowledge of the high costs of a central location. The firms have chosen London, the planners acknowledge, because it happens to be the most favorable place for them.

One conclusion to be drawn from all this is that perhaps the continued growth of London is not a bad thing. It may even be vital. This kind of managerial and technical clustering is a universal phenomenon, and it yields important efficiencies. If England is to compete with a more unified Europe, the visitor might conclude, it is going to have to abandon the idea of a pastoral dispersal and the gelding of London.

The planners do not draw this conclusion, however. They propose a second try. This time they hope to do it by beefing up existing centers beyond the London area and by more new towns. These are to be made much bigger than the first new towns, for the planners feel that if they are bigger they will be more efficient. The same logic, however, is not applied to London. Further expansion is looked on as something to be deferred, and the terms used to describe it, like "overgrowth" and "cancer," carry their own argument. The problem, to quote the Southeast Study, "is to break the vicious cycle of growth generating more growth. . . ."

It is just possible, though, that the planners are once again fighting the last war; several years from now growth might seem a rather good problem to have to worry about.

lish. Too many of our plans are emphasizing general, abstract open spaces and gross acreage; the lines that are being laid down are too often arbitrary and drawn with little or no reference to the topography. There is not the same bias against growth that marks English planning, but the plans are essentially decentralist and antiurban.

Worst of all, these most grandiose plans are unaccompanied by any hard thinking as to just how they are to be carried out. The English were consistent. They recognized that the containment concept of open space called for new tools and vast amounts of money, and they followed through the logic of their concept with a governmental program of admirable boldness. They put their idea to the test. We should heed what they learned thereby.

The fundamental lesson, to summarize, is that open space has to have a positive function. It will not remain open if it does not. People must be able to do things on it or with it—at the very least, to be able to look at it. Containment is negative, and it does not work—a conclusion the Japanese came to in 1965 when they abandoned a proposed London-type green belt to contain Tokyo.

The open spaces must be tightly drawn. The arbitrary boundaries that look so tidy on a map are extremely difficult to hold on the ground. The kind that work follow the idiosyncrasies of the land; the ridges and valleys, and especially the streams and rivers. Here is the line to hold. Surely there will be attacks on the open space, and some on behalf of good causes, worse yet. We must fight on the best possible ground and with the maximum number of allies. Many people must know the land and have enjoyed it. It is not enough that they have a stake in the fight; they must be aware that they do, and before it starts.

To repeat, use it or lose it.

10. Linkage

➤➤

To point out the dangers in the broad-brush approach to open space is not to argue for small spaces instead of big spaces. Both kinds are needed, and we certainly should try to get as many big open spaces as we can. I do not know of any local government that has acquired too much open space, and the danger that any will acquire too much seems rather remote.

The danger is that we will not get the smaller spaces that we ought to get now. Time is not on the side of the broad-brush approach. There is just so much land, and with more people to be housed on it, more plants to be built, willy-nilly we are going to have a tougher time saving any kind of open space. The kind we should save first is the kind that is most useful to people—the spaces that are closest to them. If some of them are big, so much the better, but in most cases what is left are the smaller spaces, the irregular ones, and the maligned bits and pieces.

Weaving these together is a far tougher challenge than setting aside large chunks somewhere else, but it can be done. There are all sorts of opportunities to link separate spaces together and while plenty of money is needed to do it, ingenuity can accomplish a great deal. Our metropolitan areas are crisscrossed with connective strips. Many are no longer used, or only slightly used for their original purpose and they are so ugly it is hard to visualize their being transformed into an amenity. But they are there if only we will look.

Traditional recreation standards tend to obscure such opportunities. They have their uses but the emphasis is on *how much* open space, ideally, an area ought to have. For park space the most commonly accepted formula is 10 acres in cities for each 1000 people, 15 acres in suburbs, and 65 acres in state parks. Just how these figures were arrived at no one knows: The National Recreation and Park Association, which has found them helpful in spurring communities to raise their sights, is frank to say that they were set many years ago by someone whose name has been forgotten. Another approach is to compute the amount of space that ought to be provided per person for particular activities. For trails, for example, the Bureau of Outdoor Recreation suggests that for each 50,000 people there ought to be 25 miles of trails for hiking, 25 miles of trails for cycling, 5 miles for horseback riding. Wisconsin planners specify 3.6 acres of water for each fisherman, 8 acres for each fishing boat, 1 mile of stream or ¼ mile of river per fisherman, 40 acres of water per waterskier. While some of the formulas seem unduly precise, there are just enough communities that come close to meeting the standards to indicate that the standards are not unreasonably high, and they can be applied to good effect elsewhere to dramatize how woefully deficient the areas are and that something should be done.

Unfortunately, a by-product of the formula approach is the notion, now firmly embedded in planning dogma, that there is a hierarchy of spaces—small spaces for neighborhoods, bigger spaces for towns and cities, and so on up to very, very big spaces for regions. State park officials, for example, take it as axiomatic that a park to serve a region must be at least 500 acres, and some don't want to look at anything under 1000 acres. In bespeaking the form-giving qualities of space, planners are even more expansive. If you want to think regional, they believe, you must think big. In the Year 2000 Plan for Washington, the wedges qualify as regional spaces since they are gigantic; however, Rock Creek Park, which cuts across the Northwest section from Georgetown to the Maryland border and beyond, does not qualify; it is not deemed big enough in acreage to be regional in scale.

Such distinctions are utterly unrealistic. A big space may have regional significance; it may not. A small space may be only a local space; it may be much more. It depends. Acreage is a factor, but only one, and not necessarily the most important. The significance of a space depends on where the space is, what it is like—range, hill, woodland, marsh—what the surroundings are, how many people use the space or see it, and when.

Viewed from this eye-level perspective, many small spaces prove to be eminently regional in scale. Rock Creek Park happens to be an outstanding example. On a 1:20,000 map of the region this green strip may seem thin; to the people, however, it gives a very strong sense of structure, and on several scales. For the city people it is at once a major boundary and a heavily used recreation area. It also is a major avenue from suburbia to the city for hundreds of thousands of suburbanites, and is one of the major elements in their perception of the region. Similar examples abound: Philadelphia's Wissahickon Drive, Boston's Charles River, the Westchester County parkways: a good open space can work at several levels and the fact it is so obviously useful as a local space does not prevent it from being important for the people of the larger area as well.

We are dealing with two kinds of reality. One is the physical open space; the other is open space as it is used and perceived by people. Of the two, the latter is the more important—it is, after all, the payoff of open-space action. But this reality is not charted. It is too subjective, it can be argued; and if you did arrive at such a map, it would diverge wildly from reality—like the joke maps showing the New Yorker's eye-view of the U.S.

This is why the attempt should be made. The divergences are important; and to find them out, planners would do well to try to construct maps of the open spaces of the region as people think them to be. It would be a formidable exercise in technique, including many interviews and a wide cross-section of people, but even a modest sampling might yield valuable clues. In any event, the result would be undoubtedly a highly skewed vision of the region; some spaces would loom disproportionately large or small and some would not show up at all; people's impressions would vary considerably according to where they lived, where they worked, and how much money they made.

But there probably would be a unity of sorts. Kevin Lynch, in his work on people's image of the city, has found that while the images differ according to occupation, means, and residence, they do overlap on the key elements. So it would likely be with the open spaces of the region; as a guess, I would venture that such maps would consistently show that people are aware of only a fraction of the open space that exists; that relatively small spaces would rank high among those they most vividly recall, and that they would grossly exaggerate the size of them.*

For park acquisition, the traditional hierarchy of spaces does make some sense. All other things being equal, a state park that is supposed to serve the people of a large region ought to be larger than a park that is to serve a

---

* New Englanders can test the proposition by asking people to estimate the number of acres in the town commons they know of. The chances are that the guesses be double or triple the actual size. When I did a reconnaissance of town greens I was surprised to find that the greens that seemed two and three acres were often as small as $7/10$ths of an acre. I also found that the residents themselves made similar overestimates.

city, and a city park ought to be larger than a neighbor-hood playground. But all things are rarely equal, and acreage can sometimes be a poor yardstick. What counts is *effective* acreage. Just as many small spaces loom dis-proportionately large in the mind's eye, many large spaces hardly register at all. People don't know about them, and if they do, they often don't know how to use them. Along the Eastern Seaboard, there are many large forests and state parks quite close to the major cities. Ask people to tell you about them, however, and you will find that for many they simply do not exist. Where the spaces are known, furthermore, the use tends to be concentrated in a few accessible spots and along the roadsides.

Underuse of big spaces is certainly a very good problem to have. In time, as the population moves closer to them and as they are developed with trails and facilities, they will become far more effective than they are now. Most such spaces, however, are the legacy of another era; they were set aside when there were big tracts to set aside, when prices were a fraction of today's. Many were as-sembled by wealthy people and given as gifts. A few such opportunities remain, but not many. As far as future ac-quisition is concerned, the emphasis will have to be on smaller spaces, spaces that are closer to the city, and on a very high intensity of use.

But there is a strong impulse to look in the other direc-tion. State park officials, some of whom do double duty as the state's foresters, retain an understandable bias to-ward rural areas. Being administrators, they also have a bias toward large, manageable spaces, and have long argued that small spaces cost more to maintain and op-erate than an equivalent acreage in large tracts.

Lately they have begun to pay more attention to the cities. They have had to. In order to get money from the federal Land and Water Conservation Fund, state officials must submit a statewide plan that considers the needs of the cities, and they must pass on a fair share of the money to them in direct grants. But it is still not very much. A study by the Conservation Foundation indicates that of

$200 million in federal grants for open-space and recreation development through 1966, less than a fifth was spent in densely populated areas.

The old ways die hard. For their state's own acquisition programs, state officials still tend to think of big spaces and they are scandalized at the thought of what they would have to pay for big spaces in metropolitan areas. Rather than scale down the specifications to fit, many would prefer to look further away and spend the funds where they could fetch more acreage. I remember the reaction of one state park director to a proposal for a linear park that would traverse a valley in a fast-urbanizing area. He thought it was an excellent proposal, but said he just couldn't see spending his department's money where land cost so much. "Why should I pay $2000 an acre for 400 acres," he asked, "when thirty miles away I can pick up 4000 acres at $80 to $120 an acre?"

There are lots of reasons. The high-cost land is close to people; the low-cost land is not. If you figure how many people will use the close-in land, and how frequently, and then compare these benefits with the costs, it may turn out that on a per-person basis the land with the seemingly outrageous price may be a better bargain than the cheap land. People will use the close-in land much more often, and they will use it much more regularly, day in, day out, throughout the year. Overhead costs, as a consequence, can be far less per visit than in the larger but more cyclical parks farther away. Strangely enough, however, there has been little effort to compute the costs and benefits in parkland acquisition.

Highway engineers are way ahead on this score. Long ago they discovered that the rural bypass was no way to meet the traffic problem; by comparing potential benefits to costs they found that high cost land in the path where traffic wanted to go was the most economic. This is one of the reasons the engineers have become the major shapers of the urban landscape. Praise them or malign them, they go to the thick of things. Park officials should do the same.

In looking for urban land, park officials have a great

advantage to exploit. While it is true that land close-in costs more than comparable land elsewhere, it does not have to cost quite so much as average land prices would suggest. Land that is best for parks tends to be land with slopes and streams and woods; and this kind of land is so much trouble for developers to grade and fill that the going market price is usually much less than the average for the area.

There is a surprising amount of this kind of land left in our urban areas, and because of the vagaries of water, it has the fine characteristic of being intertwined throughout the built-up sections. For the same reason, however, it does not fit the large-acreage approach; indeed, if you are bent on the big picture you won't even see it. The land is not massed in one or two big tracts; it is a series of elements, irregular, sometimes disconnected, and thus dismissible as bits and pieces of only local significance.

Orthodox space standards obscure opportunities; sometimes they rule them out. When the federal and state open-space grant programs were being drafted several years ago, many planners were fearful that the grants might encourage local governments to act hastily and to take the small view; since there was not much regional planning yet, planners thought that the governments might be inclined to spend the funds on bits and pieces and "tot lots." To prevent this, requirements were drafted that the open space had to be so many acres in size to warrant a grant—fifty acres in New York's program. Some of the programs also stipulate that the land had to be predominantly open land.

As it turned out, the restrictions proved unworkable. The minimum-acreage requirement was not too difficult for suburban communities to meet; it was very tough for the cities, though, and barred the way to a number of highly strategic acquisitions. The cities were quick to complain. A fifty-acre purchase for them could be extremely expensive even with matching sums; and while they might be able to afford thirty-five acres of an expensive tract, it had to be all or nothing. Some of the best situated tracts, furthermore, would be considerably less than fifty acres. The requirement that land had to be predominantly open was similarly troublesome; it effectively ruled out a number of imaginative projects for clearing shanties and old buildings from semi-derelict land and rehabilitating the tract as a park. Commercial operators who had other ideas for the land were quick to call attention to the "predominantly open" clause and threatened court action. Fortunately, the stipulations about minimums and openness have now been liberalized or dropped entirely.*

Another reason advanced for seeking big spaces is to separate communities so they won't fuse into one great glop of housing. The English have been especially keen on this kind of open space. In building their new towns they try to keep a clear line between town and country: where the town stops, the country begins. They have also gone to great lengths to keep existing towns from oozing together—this is perhaps the most successful aspect of the green belt program.

---

* The record of the Connecticut's excellently administered open-space-grant program, which never had such stipulations to begin with, shows how important in the aggregate small spaces can be and how average figures can be misleading. The 77 tracts that local governments acquired under the first phase of the program ranged from 3½ acres to 387, with an average of 62 acres. But few tracts came close to the average; the acquisition tended to bunch at either end of the scale: about thirty percent were big—100 acres or over—such as golf courses and large estates acquired for parks. Sixty percent of the acquisitions were under 40 acres and considerable portions of those under five acres. Were they bits and pieces? Some were acquired to round out other holdings but most are quite functional in their own right: a strip along the river, a steep slope for skiing, a beach or a pond, a site for a dam for swimming, a narrow gorge with a waterfall, a wooded hill bordering the city. There need be no invidious comparisons between big and small spaces. From what I have been able to see of them, both kinds are excellent. It is clear, however, that qualitatively the acres in the small spaces in some cases are as important for regional as well as local parks.

very adroitly. But the linear concept is even more relevant today. It provides us a way of securing the most highly usable spaces in urban areas where land is hard to come by, and, in time, a way of linking these spaces together.

The potential is great. Throughout our metropolitan area there is a reserve of linear strips awaiting rediscovering. The same changes in transportation that have made it so difficult for people to find a place to walk or cycle have made obsolete many old rights-of-way—aqueducts, canals, railroads, interurban trolley lines. Some have been obliterated but a tremendous amount of mileage lies unused and weedy that with not too much expense could be rehabilitated into a system of trails and walkways. Along the Hudson River corridor, for example, there are 350 miles of abandoned railroad lines, 190 miles of abandoned canals, and 60 miles of aqueduct rights-of-way through which water has long since ceased to flow.

The Croton Aqueduct is a good example of the kind of riches to be found. Back in 1837 the city of New York bought a sixty-six-foot-wide strip and buried a pipe in it to carry water from a reservoir in Westchester County to the city. By the 1930s it had become almost obsolete and bits and pieces of the right-of-way were made available as parklets. But though the aqueduct was public land, most of the public never knew it. The city had been giving permits to abutting landowners and the right-of-way became interrupted with parking lots, dump heaps, and chain-link fences. By 1955 it had been more or less abandoned as an aqueduct but because of legal complications it continued to lie in limbo.

In 1965 the Hudson River Valley Commission held up the aqueduct as a classic example of access and urged that the whole length be transformed into a linear park. New York City had already turned over the city park to its park department and in 1966 the state bought the rest of the aqueduct from the city. It is going to be made into a regional park.

The exciting thing about a project like this is that it can be made ready in fairly short order. It will take time to clear out some of the encroachments but the bulk of it will soon be available to the public, and in several years it will provide a reasonably continuous walkway all the way from the Bronx to northern Westchester County.

Railroad rights-of-way are another great asset. The railroads have been abandoning service on them at a rapid clip—some 10,000 miles have been abandoned in the past decade—and as there are more mergers a lot more mileage will become available. These rights-of-way make excellent bridle trails and walkways; they usually range from 50 to 150 feet wide, and since the railroads usually sell off the tracks and ties, there is not a great deal of work to be done. Communities can get money for buying the rights-of-way through the federal and state open-space acts and the job of developing the paths and facilities is the kind that can command the enthusiasm of many organizations and volunteer groups.

One such project is the Prairie Path, a stretch in Illinois along the route of the old Chicago, Aurora and Elgin interurban trolley line. In 1965 DuPage County acquired 27 miles of the right-of-way and then leased it for 12 years to the group which had sparked the project, Illinois Prairie Path, Inc. This group has taken out liability insurance to cover accidents along the trail—a not unimportant consideration in such undertakings—and is overseeing the development of the right-of-way into a trail system for walking, riding and cycling. It is parceling out the job, and the subsequent maintenance, to a host of local groups. It has also worked up an excellent trail guide which, mile by mile, tells people the different points of interest they ought to look out for on their left or right. It has to warn them about several detours, but there are not too many of these and before long the trail should be fairly continuous.

If such opportunities are to be seized, they must be seized quickly. The old rights-of-way are also attractive to utilities, highway departments, and sewerage authorities. Communities that have not seen the light tend to regard them as useful for parking lots and dumps. Actually, the rights-of-way can support a lot of uses and still be good walkways—an underground transmission line or pipeline, for example, does not hurt the scenery at all and it can help the economics. But if the multiple uses are to be satisfactorily joined, there must be an over-all unifying plan and many heads will have to be brought together to work it out. It is a rare right-of-way which does not have an incredibly complicated legal and political history behind it, and unsnarling questions of title and jurisdiction is difficult under the best of circumstances. It takes a hard core of screwballs to see this kind of project through.

Rights-of-way that have been mapped for future expressways are another possibility, unlikely as it may seem. Usually it is the other way around, with other kinds of rights-of-ways being pre-empted or bisected by the road builders. In one instance, however, there has been a turnabout, and it may be a forerunner of more to come. New York City is taking the rights-of-way for a proposed expressway away from the road builders and is going to make it into a linear park. The land is a four-mile stretch along a wooded escarpment on Staten Island. It was here, happily, Frederick Law Olmsted made his home in the 1870s. He thought that the ridge would make a beautiful linear park, and in his recommendation to the city noted that the land was, "totally unsuited, not to say impracticable, for rapid travel."

Twentieth-century road builders did not agree. In the 1950s it was mapped as Section 1 of the proposed Richmond Parkway. There were protests by park and recreation groups, but the road builder in charge was Robert Moses and that seemed to be that. With the election of Mayor John Lindsay, however, the park proposal got a new hearing.

In 1966, the Mayor called for an alternate route that would bypass the ridges and had the right-of-way demapped so that it could be used as a park trailway. (Just about this time, work was finished on a brand new interchange to connect up with the pathway. This may be the first relic of its kind.) *

Canals are another asset. The most celebrated, thanks to the itinerant Justice Douglas and his annual hikes, is the Chesapeake and Ohio Canal bordering the Potomac. This is a particularly entrancing stretch and one of the longest —some 185 miles between Washington and Cumberland, Maryland. But there are many others across the country which have almost as great a potential, and the cost of rehabilitating them as pathways need not be too great.

Stream valleys are the best connectors of all; they are usually good looking to begin with, but a humdrum water course, even one that is dry most of the time, can be the makings of an excellent facility. The concrete-lined ditches that run through many metropolitan areas in the West and Southwest are an example. They are not much to look at, and nominally they are rivers, and people are not supposed to trespass on them. But water flows in them only a few days a year, and a number of communities have begun to use them as cycling paths.

Arroyos that the engineers have not gotten around to can also be useful. Ordinarily these dry creeks are thought of as nuisances: they make steep ravines, and are often choked with thickets of brush. But there is much that can be done with them. In Santa Barbara, California, for example, the arroyos provide a natural framework by which the open spaces of new developments can be linked together. The county has been allowing developers to reduce lot size somewhat if they will dedicate the ravine

* At this writing, the issue is still in doubt. In 1967 the Bureau of Public Roads said that the alternate route proposed by the Mayor is unacceptable to it; the route would be longer and would cost more. This is the standard approach the Bureau has been taking in such controversies. Lately, however, it has begun to talk as though it favored a more flexible approach, in principle, at any rate. The resolution of this fracas might give it an opportunity to reconcile precept and practice.

portions as permanent open space. Since the ravines cannot be built on anyway, the developers have been glad to cooperate.

Can all of these different kinds of spaces be linked together? This is the great opportunity. These connective strips are worthwhile in their own right, but they become even more functional when they are tied in with other strips of open space—with community parks, school sites and with the open spaces of cluster developments. The total acreage is not a significant figure—it probably would not be much more than the sum of the spaces that might be provided in any event. What can make the acreage so effective is the fact of linkage, and a few relatively small spaces can often make the difference.

Europe is way ahead of us in this respect. Many of their cities started years ago to fashion open-space networks and since they have had few of the qualms about municipal land ownership that we have suffered, their systems are fairly complete. The complex around Stockholm is a superb example, but for the U.S. possibly the most relevant is the open-space network in the Ruhr Valley. Early in the 1920s, the Ruhr Valley Authority was set up and given an adequate budget, based on local tax assessments, for its work. By combination of direct purchase and grants to communities for local spaces and development, the Authority has fashioned a magnificent network of forest and recreation areas throughout this highly industrialized area.

We are starting late but even in areas that seem hopelessly ravaged by development there are many more opportunities for linking together a network than might appear. Santa Clara County in California is a good example. Its flat valley floor, as I noted in an earlier chapter, has been so splattered with subdivisions as to be the prime example of urban sprawl in all the United States, and at first glance one would think that any kind of coherent open-space system was out of the question. Yet the valley is crisscrossed with connective elements and through a program initiated by planner Karl Belser, they are being pulled together into a system of "greenways."

The drainage network, as in almost every area, is the key. Running down from the mountains to San Francisco Bay are a series of creek courses and these provide the sinews of the system. The land along the creeks is under a variety of ownerships—golf courses, county parks, town parks, utilities, and state commissions. The problem is not so much to bring them under one ownership but to get a joint action for protecting them. There are missing links and interruptions here and there, but eventually there should be a fairly continuous chain. As time goes on, cluster developments can contribute a sort of tributary network with their open spaces feeding into the system.

Utility rights-of-way furnish another set of connectors. Along much the same axis as the creeks, rights-of-way for high-tension lines and waterways cross the valley. They average between sixty and one hundred feet in width and total some 1000 acres. Usually, such rights-of-way are regarded as wasteland but under the Santa Clara Greenway Program they are to be landscaped into an 8-mile network of trails, with "nodules" of open space provided by eighteen school sites.* Several municipalities have already taken action and have developed vest-pocket parks in the rights-of-way. County park officials, however, have not yet demonstrated any great enthusiasm for the greenway idea.

In New York's Westchester County officials are enthusiastic. The men who ran it back in the 1920s sewed up the stream valleys in the southern parts. Now Park Commissioner Charles Pound is pushing a program to provide for the stream valleys in the northern portion and to tie these to road rights-of-way, utility rights-of-way, and the Croton Aqueduct. When completed, the network will total some 700 miles.

---

* Another use for rights-of-way is gardening. At Reston, Virginia, portions of a right-of-way for a natural-gas pipeline were divided into individual garden plots and leased to residents for $15 a year.

By linking open spaces, as these examples demonstrate, we can achieve a whole that is better than the sum of the parts. But it is important to remember that the parts come first. Each has to be functional in its own right; it must already exist and if it doesn't there must be a very good reason for it. There is no point in forcing a complete and continuous system just for the sake of having a system. For one thing, filling in all the missing links would lead to impossible cost situations. Many of the pieces would be extremely dear to buy up and unless there were other more compelling reasons for the acquisitions, it would be very hard to justify the expense on the basis that continuity demands it.

Highway interruptions are another problem. Almost any linear strip of open space that extends for any distance in an urban area is bound to be severed in one or more places by highway construction—and even those strips that are part of the right-of-way itself are cut up by cloverleafs. In some cases pedestrian overpasses or tunnels are the answers, but the recreational use must be intensive to warrant them for they are enormously expensive and if the highway is a six- or eight-lane affair, virtually prohibitive. The Croton Aqueduct, for example, is severed in a number of places by major streets and freeways. In some spots, pedestrian bridges are in order, but to make the pathway completely continuous would require prodigious expenditures. A bridge over one major expressway, for example, would cost almost as much as the facilities and landscaping for the rest of the twenty-six miles.

Full continuity is not so critical. Most people do not use open spaces that way. Even where there is an uninterrupted system, people do not necessarily use it as a system. They use the parts. I do not know of any origin-destination studies of recreational spaces comparable to those done for highways, but a check would probably indicate that at any one point along the way the use will be predominately local. Cyclists and horseback riders seek fairly long stretches and so do some hikers. Save for a few hearty souls, however, the beaten path does not go very

far. Most people will gravitate to the same spots time and
again, and few would ever traverse the whole system or be
aware of its extent. In the aggregate, of course, this system
will be used heavily, and there is every reason to try to
link together such an amenity. The regionality of it, however, is not its essential characteristic. The best regional
networks are networks of locally useful spaces.

Planners who are intent on regional scale would dispute
this vigorously. Instead of putting together a patchwork of
spaces, they argue, the challenge is to design a truly regional system. But is one really possible? Bruce Howlett,
a regional planner for whose judgment I have great respect, says that the more he has worked at it, the less sure
he is that a system is especially important.

"When you start thinking of how best to bring people
and open space into contact," he says, "you find yourself
questioning some hallowed planning concepts. One is that
we should design an urban open-space system and that
the system should be large, integrated, and continuous. It
may be heresy, but I think a fresh approach is overdue in
planning. It is noteworthy that no workable concept has
been forthcoming of how such a system should be organized and paid for. Perhaps the problem is that the
scale is wrong. I would go even further: Perhaps we don't
need a regional open-space system at all.

"The highly useful kind of spaces that provide a maximum contact with people—the kind we get in cluster development—are much more appropriate to real needs. If
we couple these many kinds of spaces needed to serve
specific places, we will come up with a non-system of scattered spaces. This may not satisfy those who want to
design urban regions in the grand manner, but it has every
likelihood of success and more profound and useful ways."

And there would be a design. It would not be that of the
drafting table, with its order and symmetry. There is another design that is far better. It is the design that nature
has provided. As I will take up in the next chapter, the
most inventive planning being done in the U.S. today fol-

lows this approach and though the efforts are regarded as great innovations in technique, what they consist of, essentially, is looking at the ground.

It is pointless, and cheeky, to superimpose an abstract, man-made design on the region as though the canvas were blank. It isn't. Somebody has been there already. Thousands of years of rain and wind and tides have laid down a design. Here is our form and order. It is inherent in the land itself—in the pattern of the soil, the slopes, the woods, above all in the patterns of streams and rivers.

Within this framework many alternatives are open to us. The pattern of nature, of course, is not sacrosanct for being the natural one; sometimes we will have no choice except to cut across the grain of it. But the natural design is still the best place to start. If we look to it, we do not have to puzzle about priorities. Certain steps will be obvious. Whatever we may have in mind, satellites or rings or linear corridors, good sense will dictate that we secure the stream valleys and the wetlands as quickly as possible.

Where the water flows, the positive benefits of open space are the clearest. It will still be a tough job in the face of competing pressures, but along the drainage network we can invoke the maximum overlay of benefits, for the land is most necessary for flood control, and the conservation of water resources tends to be the land that is most suitable for recreation and that is the most beautiful.

There is another important characteristic of water. It runs downhill. If we follow this track in our open-space planning, we are at once securing the prime lands and the lands which give linkage and continuity—in a word, regional design.

11.   The Design of Nature

>>

Instead of laying down an arbitrary design for a region,
I have been arguing, it might be in order to find the plan
that nature has already laid down. One way would be to
chart all of the physical resources of the region—especially
its drainage network—and see what kind of picture
emerges. The approach sounds ridiculously simple, but in
the few instances where it has been tried, it has seemed
an almost revolutionary concept. City and regional planning commissions have been staffed primarily by people
concerned with physical design and development. The
people who think mostly about nature, such as the ecologists and biologists, have been operating on the fringes
of regional planning, literally as well as figuratively. So
have the landscape architects.

Now a change is in the air. One reason is Ian McHarg,
an immensely persuasive Scotsman who is the head of the
Department of Landscape Architecture and Regional Planning at the University of Pennsylvania. In a series of ex-

perimental studies, McHarg has been preaching the gospel of "physiographic determinism," which, roughly translated, means nature ought to come first.

McHarg points out that nature performs a number of valuable functions for man, and does it free. The forests of the "upland sponge," for example help moderate floods. Underground formations store water for us to drink. Prime soils produce food for us to eat. Marshes provide spawning grounds for fish and wildlife. But when men make their development plans, unfortunately, they pay little attention to these functions and they obliterate what they should protect. ". . . Marshes seem made to be filled," says McHarg, "streams to be culverted, rivers to be dammed, farms subdivided, forests felled, flood plains occupied, and wildlife eradicated."

This is a wicked thing to do, says McHarg, and stupid too. If we want a development plan that makes sense we should look to nature first. The aquifers, the slopes, the wetlands, and the other elements should be identified and mapped and the design that comes through should be the core of any plan.

Several years ago, McHarg was given an unusual opportunity to apply these principles to a particular place. A group of landowners in the Green Spring and Worthington Valleys northwest of Baltimore approached McHarg and planner David Wallace and asked them to figure out a way the area could be saved.

It is an unusually comely example of a countryside on the brink of suburbanization. It embraces about seventy square miles and topographically consists of several plateaus cut by three valleys—one of them, the Worthington, is the setting of the Maryland Hunt Cup. The valleys are only about one-half hour's drive from Baltimore, and they are bounded on two sides by expressways, yet they remain almost unspoiled. Most of the holdings are large estates and farms and the owners are well-to-do and in no unseemly haste to sell. Until recently, there was no great pressure on them to sell, for the valleys had not been sewered and developers were still working over the land closer to the city that had been.

But the pressures began to mount. Developers were pushing outward even though the valleys did not have sewers. Here and there a few septic tank subdivisions were put up on the edges and there were unmistakable signs that others might be on the way. The landowners became alarmed. They were not entirely unhappy about the prospect of higher land prices, and they were not contemplating setting aside the area as a nature reserve. What they were worried about was the likelihood that some landowners would sell prematurely and for the wrong type of building. They saw a good bit of development as inevitable, but they also wanted to keep the estate-country flavor and if they could not have the best of both worlds, they wanted some of each. To this end, a group of the principal landowners set up a planning council and retained McHarg and Wallace to see what kind of a plan could be worked out.

The plan that McHarg and Wallace came up with is a superb piece of work. It is still basically a plan, let it be noted, but the simplicity of the approach makes it eminently reproduceable. Even if the people of the particular area do not follow through on the ideas, people elsewhere are likely to. Much like architect Victor Gruen's plan for Fort Worth, which Fort Worth did not use but other cities did, the valley's plan is the kind that can be swiped to good effect.

It is universal because it is highly specific. It is about a real place and real alternatives. The close attention to reality is dictated in part by the needs of the original clients and the relatively small size of the region. But it is also inherent in the approach.

Common to almost every regional plan these days is a chart or map showing how the particular area will go to hell in a handbasket if the planners' recommendations are not followed. This is usually done in a very generalized way; there will be photographs of acres of rooftops with television aerials, clutter of roadside signs, gas stations, and

pizza stands, and so on.* The Plan for the Valleys, however, gets down to cases. It projects uncontrolled growth
in minute detail. Wallace figured where the subdivisions
would probably go and platted them, complete to street
layouts. And they are not bad subdivisions. They have
curvilinear streets, cul de sacs, and all the features of the
best standard layouts. It is all very plausible and therefore
horrifying.

The result is called The Specter. "Uncontrolled growth,"
says the plan, "occurring sporadically, spreading without
discrimination, will surely obliterate the valleys, inexorably
cover the landscape with its smear, irrevocably destroy
all that is beautiful or memorable. No matter how well-
designed each individual subdivision may be, no matter if
small parks are interfused with housing, the great landscape will be expunged and remain only as a receding
memory."

Unfortunately, uncontrolled growth could also make a
lot of money for people. By 1980, economic analysis indicates, uncontrolled growth would produce $35 million in
development value in the area. The problem, as McHarg
and Wallace saw it, was not simply to find a more amenable pattern but one that would make at least as much
money.

* There is a bad tendency to use photographs taken with
telephoto lenses. This foreshortens the perspective so that the
houses look all jammed together, and a mile of roadside signs
seem compressed into a few hundred yards. These scenes look
bad enough without being hoked up with this perspective. It
is misleading in another respect. The pictures seem to say that
it is awful the houses are so jammed together when in fact the
problem the planners will go on to analyze is that the houses
are not jammed together enough. In almost every case, the
planners will recommend that in the future the houses be clustered more tightly so that land can be used more effectively.
This is a good recommendation, but if you took a telephoto
shot of the houses in a cluster development, it would make the
houses in the horror shots extraordinarily spacious by comparison. For consistency's sake, it is hard to beat a lens of normal focal length.

To arrive at the possibilities, McHarg charted the area's underlying design with a series of analyses of the major natural elements, such as the water table and geological elements. One by one, each element was traced to determine where, all other things being equal, it would be best to build and where it would not. The result was a sort of accumulative plan, for as the charts of each element were overlaid on top of the others, a message began to come through. It was simple: Leave the valleys open, build on the plateaus.

It is quite possible that McHarg and Wallace were seized with this thought the first day they looked at the valleys. The point is that they did look—a step that is by no means automatic in planning. What, they ask, was the *genius loci*? What gives to the eye the sense of place that distinguishes the area? From the beginning, they thought this was very clear: The genius of the landscape lies in the great broad sweeping valleys and the wooded slopes which confined them.

One could argue that they might just as well have made their final recommendations then and there: Keep the valleys open, build on the plateaus. But this would have put the case largely on aesthetic grounds, and no study can stop at that. It would not seem right. What gives the study of the valleys its authority is the way McHarg and Wallace go on to demonstrate that rigorous inductive analysis of the physical and economic factors leads to the conclusions.

But there is a satisfying concurrence. A check of the water table, for example, revealed that the best ground-water source in the whole Baltimore region is a limestone deposit called Cockeysville marble and that the valleys lay right on top of it. Septic tanks would endanger this great aquifer. The plateau, however, is underlain with Wissahickon limestone. This kind of rock is not valuable as an aquifer and therefore development on top of it would not do any harm. Conclusion: sewer the plateau; don't sewer the valleys.

Increment by increment, the case built up. A study of the flow of surface water indicated that to prevent pollution, a strip 200 feet on either side of the streams should be kept open. Computations for a fifty-year flood indicated the flood plain areas that should be kept open, and these lie mainly in the valleys. A study of the soil maps showed the areas unsuitable for septic tanks; a chart of the gradients showed which slopes should be reforested to prevent erosion. So on down the list it went. Leave the valleys open; build on the plateaus.

Obviously, there is a bias. Just as some planners start with the premise that open space is primarily a tool with which to structure development, McHarg and Wallace see open space as a primary resource in itself, and viewpoints do tend to influence the way different facts are regarded. A planner of one persuasion might see the valleys as good corridors for development and he would probably not find the physiographic obstacles against it at all compelling. That Cockeysville marble, for example; if it was so important to protect it from contamination, he might argue, then sewers ought to be laid in the valleys forthwith.

But some biases are better than others and McHarg and Wallace are admirably explicit about theirs. The plan is really a sermon. McHarg is a Calvinist preacher at heart and in calling down the wrath of nature against the despoilers and uglifiers he shows a fine ability to couple physical planning with a higher morality. Like all good sermons, his offers redemption. Nature punishes those who abuse her; she rewards those who heed her. The enlightened way, it turns out, is also the most economic. In the case of the valleys, the plan maintains, landowners stand to make $7 million more if they hew to the nature plan instead of contravening it.

But how is this to be accomplished? McHarg and Wallace have an extraordinary proposal to make, but they take care to preface it with the first steps that can be taken now. They point out, for example, that cluster zoning can be used immediately, under current county regulations, and that the next step should be the upgrading of regulations to make cluster zoning mandatory. Consistent with their approach, they do not have a static final master plan. There is a series of gradual steps, each one leading to the next.

But there is one very difficult problem. In a plan like this, the people whose lands are marked for development stand to make a lot more money than those whose lands are marked as open space. Working with lawyer Ann Strong, McHarg and Wallace offered an ingenious way to resolve the problem. They suggested that the landowners join in a real-estate syndicate that would pool the development values of the area. The syndicate could acquire land, development rights to land, options, and could sell land for development or do the developing itself. The money made in selling the rights to development on one portion would go into a general kitty, and the shareholders whose lands were to be kept open would share equitably in it. There would be plenty to share. Intelligent development of the plateaus, for example, would provide more than enough to offset the money not made by developing the valleys.

This intriguing idea may or may not work. The kind of enlightened manorialism it calls for needs an unusually far-seeing and agreeable set of landowners, and they are hard to find in most areas, even in the valleys. But the basic planning techniques should be applicable anywhere. In most areas, the soil surveys and geological and hydrologic data are already available and the task of plotting everything to the same scale and putting it on transparent overlays can be done by a competent draftsman. Interpretation is more difficult. The patterns of nature are highly irregular in shape, and there has been some difficulty in the past trying to figure out how much acreage is encompassed by each element. McHarg has found that a photoelectric cell can do the job in a few minutes. On each map overlay, the particular element being charted is shown in black. When this is put against a white background, the cell, like a camera exposure meter, measures the reflected light and the reading can be immediately translated into acreage.

McHarg has applied his techniques to the routing of highways. Several years ago a number of New Jersey groups became alarmed at the prospect of a new Interstate Highway. They had strong ideas as to where it should not go, and since they assumed this is where the Highway Department would probably want to put it, they thought it would be a good idea to have a constructive counterproposal. They asked McHarg if he would work one up.

He would indeed. In his gallery of rogues and philistines and destroyers, highway engineers were the worst of the lot; their formulas asinine. As a first step, he would figure out a new formula; instead of basing it only on standard cost-benefit items, he would crank in things that measured *social* benefits.

He fastened on eight measures of "social value": urbanization, residential quality, historic value, agricultural value, recreation value, wildlife value, water values, and soil resistance to erosion. His hypothesis was that if you could determine where these values were most heavily concentrated you would be determining where highways should not go. At the same time you would be determining where the highways should go—through the areas where the values were least in evidence.

On transparent map overlays each of the measures was charted. They were shown in three tones. With land values, for example, areas where raw land prices averaged $3000 an acre and over were tinted dark gray; between $3000 and $1500 an acre, light gray. Areas beneath $1500 an acre were left clear. When all the separate overlays were put on top of each other, the shades of gray accumulated into a pattern. It was almost black and white. Here is what it looked like.

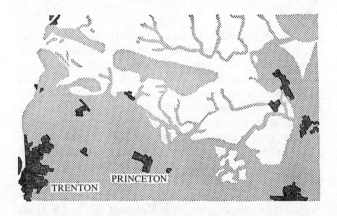

Since McHarg's measures of social value are fairly encompassing, more of the map shows up as dark than not. There is one band, however, that shows up fairly light. On this land there is not much in the way of resource values to damage or people to uproot, and land prices are

low. This would be the "minimum social-value area,"
and McHarg figured that it would also be the least expensive for acquisition and construction. He recommended that the alignment be within it.

McHarg's study did not appear to have any notable
effect on the highway people. Their engineering consult-

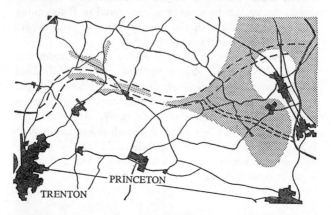

ants did hypothesize an unusual number of alignments—
34 in all—and in rating them they weighed some 23 factors, including the impact on open space and resource
values. But none of the alignments they studied followed
McHarg's minimum social value corridor. ("If the highway
is . . . so far from existing development that it cannot be
used efficiently," observed the engineers, "then the major
purpose of the expressway has not been attained.") The
final selection, approved by the Bureau of Public Roads in
February, 1968, was the route as shown on the facing
page.

A victory for the philistines? No. The engineers' formulas
are open to criticism, but so is McHarg's. To arrive at his
composite he lays many measures on top of one another,
but, as he cautions himself, he does not weight them for
relative importance. The resistance of stone formations to
erosion, for example, is given as much importance as the
amount of urban development. He has also built into his

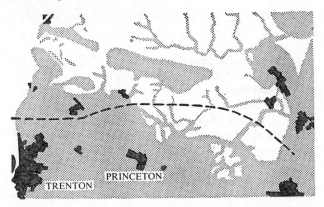

formula the assumption that people are best served when highways are located away from people. Highway engineers generally believe the opposite, and with some justification.

It can be further argued that in defining social values McHarg takes a rather patrician view. One of his criteria rates social values on the basis of the worth of the houses—the higher the price of homes in the area, the higher the social value. Some planners vigorously dispute this; as one puts it, the formula amounts to saying that highways should not only be away from people, but wealthy people most of all. But the social value of a $5000 house is apt to be the same as that of a $75,000 house—and the man with the $5000 house might suffer more from relocation.

But whatever the shortcomings of McHarg's formula, it does put the matter of social values out in the open and it attempts to give some objective basis for widening the range of the values to be considered. Such values, of course, are always considered—they are prime topics in public hearings—but they are too often considered after the fact, with great but futile passion. Because the values have not been presented in measurable terms, the people who raise the cry are dismissed as nature lovers, bird watchers, do gooders and worse. You need a formula to beat a formula. McHarg's may not be it, but it is a step in a good direction.

Another inventive landscape architect, Philip Lewis, has been applying the same kind of analysis to the landscape of an entire state. Several years ago he worked out a technique for analyzing the landscape and resources of small areas. A number of people in Wisconsin thought it would be particularly relevant in the state's $50 million open-space and recreation program. The program offered all sorts of opportunities to save key stretches of the landscape and to create and re-create recreation areas. The question was: Where? The state asked Lewis to apply his techniques to the landscape of the state.

The working proposition of Lewis and his associates was that there are a few key elements that tie the landscape together: water, wetland, flood plains, sand soils, and slopes. County by county they proceeded to chart these elements. The pattern that resulted was anything but random; as each of these elements was overlaid, one over the other, a pattern emerged. The combined elements defined a series of natural corridors. Each of these corridors was not only a key resource element in itself; together they formed a system that linked the parts of the state.

"At the end of the first year of inventory," says Lewis, "it was apparent that the elements, and glacial action, through the ages, have etched linear patterns on the face of the Wisconsin landscape. The flat, rolling farmlands and the expansive forests have their share of beauty. But it is the stream valleys, the bluffs, ridges, roaring and quiet waters, mellow wetlands, and sandy soils that combine in elongated designs, tying the land together in regional and statewide corridors of outstanding landscape qualities."

Opposite is a typical corridor pattern.

To Lewis the most exciting finding was that in these corridors were to be found most of the natural and man-made features that people wanted to see saved. To iden-

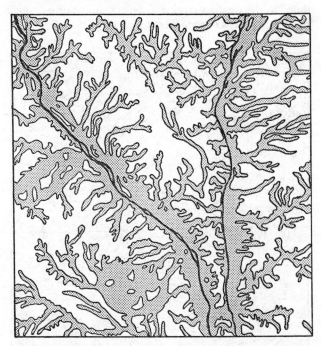

tify these features, Lewis and his associates made up an exhaustive list of elements—chasms, springs, caves, natural bridges, Indian mounds, historic buildings—in all, some 220 elements.* To find how they were distributed throughout the state, he turned to county agents and field people of the state and federal conservation agencies. Each was given a base map of his district and asked to locate all of the elements to be found there. The task was accomplished in a satisfyingly short time. These people know their areas

* Lewis has been finding additional things to add to the list —one is sunken ships. He has come upon maps of the Great Lakes showing the location of hundreds of sunken hulks, and has classified them as a basic resource of the skin-diving industry. He also has charted, as a tourism resource, the hundreds of empty log cabins scattered across the state.

down to the smallest creek and hillock and it usually took them only a week or so to fill out their maps.

When all of the separate maps were put together Lewis found that about ninety percent of all the features noted fell within the corridors, and often were concentrated in groups, or "nodes of interest." How they were distributed in the corridor previously shown may be seen above.

The findings have dramatized how much leverage power state efforts can have if they are concentrated in the corridors. There are practical implications for local planning as well. The corridors provide the values which attract people to an area, and if they are preserved, the local government can end up with a better tax base than if it permitted them to be blighted with the visual roadside clutter. If the corridors are protected, development can be encouraged to follow the fringe areas that parallel the corridors.

So far, the Wisconsin landscape inventory is the only one of its kind, and though it has generated strong interest in other states few are equipped to attempt this detailed kind of analysis. The big obstacle is lack of trained people. Until there are more of them, the best that can be done is to inventory the high-priority corridors along water courses and get around to other areas later. But Lewis has no doubt that the ecological approach is the coming thing in planning and he likes to vent his imagination on technical shortcuts to hasten the day. One possibility that fascinates him is the use of satellites or airborne sensors to take over the inventorying job. In time, he thinks, information from these could be fed into a data center that would keep planners constantly abreast of the minutest changes in land use.

Lewis and McHarg are such inventive fellows that some of their ideas can seem far out, rather literally in Lewis' case. But their basic approach is a simple one; so simple, indeed, that it is a wonder planners did not adopt it years ago. It does have a bias for the landscape built into it and the emphasis so far has been to show where man should forbear to trespass. Potentially, however, it is just as useful in showing him where he should go.

The message to come out of these demonstrations is a very encouraging one. What they show is that when you get down to hard cases it becomes apparent that a lot of the preservation-*versus*-growth debate is pointless. Some land should be left alone, some land should be developed, and there is enough of both kinds in any area that we do not have to make a hash of it.

Development

12. Cluster Development

>>>

We have been considering ways of saving open space.
Now let us turn to the question of how to develop it. There
is a conflict, to be sure, but you cannot grapple with one
problem and not the other. People have to live somewhere, as it is so often said, and if there is to be any hope
of having open space in the future, there is going to have
to be a more efficient pattern of building. The mathematics
is inexorable. The only way to house more people is either
to extend the present pattern of sprawl and cover vastly
more land, or, alternatively, to use less land and increase
the carrying capacity of it. The latter is by far the best
approach and at last we are beginning to pursue it. By
whatever name it is called—"planned unit development,"
"open-space development," "cluster development"—it signals a reversal of the land-wasting pattern that had come
to seem permanent.

In the great postwar building boom, developers froze on
a pattern that used five acres to do the work of one. They

had to, or they thought they had to. For one thing, it was a well-known fact that Americans had a deep psychic urge for a free-standing homestead on a large country plot, or as close a replica as possible. The assumption was self-proving, for it was built into the standards of the Federal Housing Administration and the major lending institutions. If a developer wanted mortgage money, he hewed to these standards or he did not get it.

Suburbs were similarly demanding. Most wanted no development at all, not in their area anyway, and they looked to large-lot zoning as their best defense. They reasoned that if they could force developers to provide large lots for each house, there would be fewer houses, and the grounds of those that did go up would conserve the open-space character of the community. Minimum lot sizes varied, but most suburbs pushed them as high as pride and wealth could enforce. The stiffer the minimum, they thought, the more likely the developers would be to leave them alone and go somewhere else.

The developers did go somewhere else, at first, but the respite did not help the suburbs, which soon found that they were not being penetrated so much as enveloped. Later the developers would come back; their first response to the barriers was to leap-frog over them and seek the open country where land was cheaper and the townships had not gotten around to zoning it.

So the best land was ruined first, and when developers got there, they sometimes found the locals had attended to the job already. While the gentry of the rural townships kept a wary eye out for the likes of Levitt, a motley of local builders and contractors would buy up frontage land from farmers and line it with a string of concrete bungalows on overblown lots. Very few people would be housed on a great deal of land, but since the land was along the road, the place would look filled up. The premature development also had the effect of sealing off many hundreds of acres from any kind of effective development pattern, and when the feared invasion did come, the chances for coping with it amenably were gone.

The suburbs farther back were coming under increasing pressure. Developers were filling in the spaces wherever they could and they were pressing relentlessly for variances. Where the minimums were as high as three or four acres, they attacked the ordinances themselves and complained to the courts that such minimums were not for the welfare of the public but to exclude the public that was not rich. Whatever developers' motives in saying so, this was the case, and in some instances the courts struck down ordinances as excessive and discriminatory.

The main problem, however, was not so much the relative size of lots as the uniformity with which they were laid out. With few exceptions, subdivisions homogenized the land with a pattern of curvilinear streets and equal-spaced lots that were everywhere the same, large lot or small, and in the denser areas, the pattern was compressed to the point of caricature. Even though lots were so small that houses would have only a few feet between them, the estate pattern was repeated, producing subdivisions that looked very much like toy villages with the scale out of whack.

These were the little boxes that so outraged people of sensibility and means. Photos of their rooftops and TV aerials, squeezed together—the telephoto lens again—became stock horror shots. But critics drew the wrong conclusions. What was wrong, they thought, was that the houses were too close together, when what was really wrong was that they were not close enough.

For years, planners had been arguing that if lots took up less of the land, subdivisions would be more economical to build and more pleasant to live in. Rather than divide all of a tract up into lots, they suggested, developers could group the houses in clusters, and leave the bulk of the land as open space. It was an ancient idea: It was the principle of the New England village and green, and its appeal had proved timeless. "Garden City" advocates had reapplied it in the planning of several prototype communities; most notably, Radburn, New Jersey, in the late twenties, the green belt towns of the New Deal, Baldwin Hills in Los Angeles during the late thirties.

Some of the utopian expectations with which these experiments were freighted were never fulfilled, but as individual communities, they were, and still are, quite successful. But they remained outside of the mainstream. Some of the features found their way into commercial developments, such as the superblock and cul-de-sac streets, but the basic cluster principle of the communities did not. Few developers even went to look at them.

By the early fifties however, the conventional pattern had been pushed close to the breaking point. It not only looked terrible, it was uneconomic, and for everybody concerned. Communities were forcing developers to chew up an enormous amount of land to house a given number of people and to provide an overblown network of roads and facilities to tie the sprawl together. This created havoc with the landscape, and saddled the community with a heavy servicing burden, the costs of which usually outran the tax returns.

For new residents, the open space was turning out to be a chimera. The woods and meadows that so attracted them disappeared as soon as developers got around to building on them, and if the residents wanted to find what other natural features would be next to go, they had only to check the names of the subdivisions being planned. When a developer puts a woods into the name, or a vale, heights, forest, creek, or stream, he is not conserving; he is memorializing. Subdivisions are named for that which they are about to destroy.

The open space of the resident's own lot was not much compensation. It was trouble to maintain but did not provide as much usable space as a small courtyard and nowhere near the privacy. (The open space between the houses strikes a particularly unhappy mean: big enough to mow, too small to use, and a perfect amplifier of sound.) Nor would there be much in the way of neighborhood open spaces. Most communities required developers to dedicate some part of the tract as open space, but it would be a very small space, and quite often a leftover the developer could not use for anything else.

The developers were being hurt more than anybody else. No matter how far and fast they pushed outward to the countryside, land prices kept soaring ahead of them. Contrary to public belief, most developers do not make money on land speculation; they do not have the capital to stockpile land for very long and they have to pay dearly to those who do. Such costs are usually passed on to the home buyers, but by the sixties developers were bumping up against a market ceiling.

The price that builders had to pay for land had risen far more than the price that people would pay for their houses. Between 1951 and 1966 the cost of raw land rose 234 percent. The sale price of the average house and lot, however, rose 87 percent and most of this increase was due to the larger size of the houses; per square foot, house prices rose only 21 percent. Even before tight money hit them, developers were in a bind. They could not mark up their finished product without pricing themselves out of the market, and they had to keep on paying exorbitant prices for their land to stay in the business.

There is one good thing about high land costs. They discipline choice. Since communities would not let developers squeeze more houses onto their tracts, developers had only one way to turn: they could try squeezing the houses they were allowed onto the most buildable parts of the tract and leave the rest alone—that is, cluster, just as planners had been suggesting. The National Association of Home Builders undertook a missionary campaign and began proselytizing builders and communities to try the cluster approach.

Here and there cluster developments began to go up. In several cases developers took the initiative; they retained land planners to prepare an advanced cluster plan and then went to work to sell the community on it. Sometimes it was the other way around, with the community doing the selling. Most typically, however, the genesis would be thoroughly mixed up, marked by plans and counterplans, false starts, and controversy.

To examine the pros and cons of cluster, let us follow such a case.

A medium-size builder has purchased a 112 acre farm in a well-to-do township on the outer edge of suburbia. The tract is pleasant, gently rolling land with a stream running through the middle and a stand of woods at one end. The site has some defects—a small marsh, for one— but it should make a fine subdivision. Mill Creek Woods, the developer will call it.

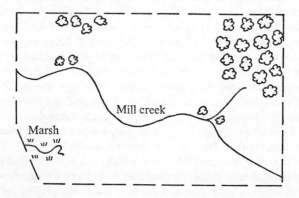

The township has zoned this area for half-acre lots. The developer explores the chances of getting it rezoned for quarter-acre lots, but finds that they are poor so he proceeds to work up a standard plan. This won't take long. He will probably work up the basic plan himself, possibly on the back of an envelope, and then later will turn it over to a civil engineer to be worked up in detail.

The plan almost draws itself. By rule of thumb, the developer knows he will have to subtract about twenty-two acres for roads. Another six acres he will have to dedicate for playgrounds. This leaves him only eighty-four acres for his half-acre lots and some of the acreage will require extensive land improvement. To squeeze in as many houses as regulations will allow, about 168, he figures to put the creek in a concrete culvert, level the wooded hill and saw down most of the trees. He would like to fill in the small marsh and develop it too, but finds the cost would be too great. He will dedicate the marsh as a park area.

Here is the tentative plan he submits:

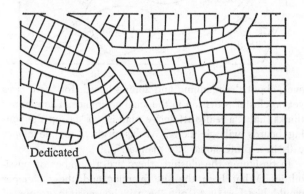

The county planner is very unhappy. He thinks it is a shame to ruin such a fine piece of land with a hack layout and he does not think it is necessary. He suggests that the developer start fresh, this time with a cluster approach. The developer is skeptical, but curious. The two go out to the tract and the planner makes a rough sketch of what could be done.

This way, the planner points out, the developer will be able to get up as many houses as before, possibly a few more, and his costs will be considerably less. Under the first plan, he would have had to spend about $4500 a lot for land improvement; under the cluster plan, he will pay about $3000. He will have to lay down only about half as much roadway, his utility runs will be shorter, and he will not have to cover the stream and chop down the wooded hill.

The developer's enthusiasm grows. He wonders, how-

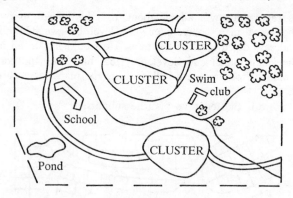

ever, about the planning and zoning board, for there is as
yet no cluster provision in the local ordinance. The planner
thinks that if a really attractive plan is worked up the zoning boards will go along. At his urging, the developer
calls in a professional site planner.

In designing the clusters, there are a number of possibilities. What both the site planner and the developer
would like best is to put the 168 houses into groups of
row houses and arrange them around common greens.
Here is how a cluster would look:

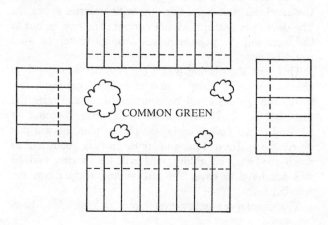

Such an economical layout would obviously be the most profitable of all for the developer. But it would also provide a very good buy for the homeowners. Dollar for dollar they would get the most house—whatever the price range—and one easy to maintain. There would be no private open space save the backyard patio, but this would be very usable space, and with the enclosed common green, would make a functional arrangement for families with children.

But the people in this particular township wouldn't swallow so dense a pattern, and they would be dead set against row houses. They would seem too much like a garden-apartment project, and there are very few forms of housing that can arouse so much resistance among suburbanites. After taking some more soundings of local opinion, the developer decides to settle on a modified cluster layout, grouping free-standing houses on quarter-acre plots.

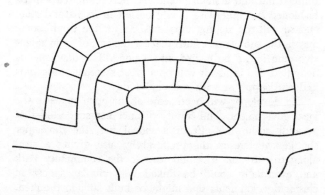

The developer will use stock builders' houses—ranchers and split levels that he has found successful in his other developments. This will sadden the site planner, who may be an architect also and who would like to see clean, advanced designs worthy of his site plan. The developer says he has stuck his neck out far enough as it is. He doesn't think architects know how to cost out a builder's house or design to the market, and he reasons that he is going to have enough trouble selling the cluster idea without saddling it with far-out architecture. (Developers tend to be much too timid on this score, but they do have some reason for their fears. Several of the best of the first cluster proposals were disapproved by local governments, and the deciding factor was not so much the newness of the cluster idea, but of the architecture of the houses.)

The over-all plan, however, remains relatively intact and it is a good one. Of the 112 acres, the house lots take 42, the streets 18, leaving some 52 acres open space to work with. In the center of each cluster there will be a common green and playground. Midway between the clusters there will be a swimming pool, tennis courts, and a clubhouse. The rest of the tract will be treated as countryside with a minimum of landscaping. Paths and bridle trails will be laid along the stream and a few willows planted. The woods will have some of the underbrush thinned out and a small picnic and barbecue area will be fashioned but otherwise it will be left in its natural state and so will the sloping meadows. As for the troublesome marsh, the site planner finds that for the cost of an inexpensive dam it can be turned into a pond. The developer is delighted. He thinks it will be a great merchandising plus and will supply it with a covey of ducks.

The developer will deed some of the open space to the local government. The county planner has suggested that in addition to the gift of a school site, the developer should sweeten up the proposal by also giving a strip along the stream. It would lead to the community park and eventually could be linked with similar spaces in cluster developments that might be built later in the area.

The bulk of the common open space, however, will be deeded to the people who buy the houses. If it were given to the community as a public park, the homeowners would have a legitimate complaint. They are the ones, after all, who will have paid for it. For though the developer will make a big point of his generosity in giving open space, he has already built the cost of it into the purchase price of the homes. The most equitable procedure is to give each person who buys a home an undivided interest in the common open space, and make this part of the basic deed.

To maintain the common areas, a homeowners association will be set up. Each home buyer automatically becomes a member and is obligated to pay his share of the costs of maintaining the open space and operating the recreational facilities. In a cluster development like this, the assessment will probably come to about $100 a year, with the cost rising when and if the homeowners decide to add more elaborate facilities.

Homeowners associations have a good record behind them. A number of them have been working since the twenties and thirties—at Radburn, for example, and the Country Club developments in Kansas City. Some date back much further—Boston's Louisburg Square has been run by a homeowners association since 1840, and New York's Gramercy Park since 1831. Today there are over 350 developments with homeowners associations and with very few exceptions, they are working out well. The key requirements, experience indicates, is that the association be set up at the very beginning and that membership be mandatory.

A question that will inevitably be raised by townspeople is the possibility of a sell-out. Suppose the homeowners later decide to cash in and sell off the common area for additional housing? The record is reassuring. In very few instances have such open spaces ever been converted. One of the green belt communities sold off land when the federal government relinquished ownership, but this happened only because there were no firm stipulations in the original deed. Where there are, it is virtually impossible for homeowners to divide up the common area. The local government, furthermore, can easily remove the temptations entirely. At the time the developer deeds the title to the homeowners, he can be required to deed an easement to the local government stipulating that the open space remain open.

Since the cluster subdivision will require a change in the
local zoning ordinance, a public hearing is scheduled. It
will be turbulent. Most of the members of the planning
board now favor the cluster proposal, but a number of
citizens do not. A vigorous antidevelopment group has
been formed ("Citizens for Open Space") and thanks to
its agitations and circulars, the hall is packed with non-
enthusiasts for cluster. They listen restively while the planner and the developer make presentations with flipflop
charts and slides. Then the questions start. If the developer
is so keen on this, what's the catch? If this new type development does not sell, won't we be left holding the
bag? Maybe it will sell too well, and then won't every
developer for miles be swarming over us? And what
kind of home buyers will be coming in? People who have
recently moved into the area will be especially zealous on
this point. Lower the bars, they will say, and we'll get a
new kind of element we've never had before. The meeting breaks up on a note of acrimony.

But the planning board has been won over and the fact
that there has been opposition gives it some extra bargaining power with the developer. It is suggested to him that
community resistance might be overcome if he will make
a few more concessions in the plan. The developer says
absolutely not. He is feeling very put upon by this time
and says he is going to chuck the whole thing and sell
the land. To a convent perhaps, he adds.

It is not entirely a bluff, but he has sunk too much
preliminary money into the project to give up now, and the
board knows it. He is persuaded to increase the size of the
school tract by two acres and to include the duck pond
in the park strip deeded to the township. To lay to rest
the fears expressed by the local Garden Club, he also
guarantees to preserve a line of sycamores bordering
the north part of the tract. The board reciprocates by letting him cut down slightly the width of one of the access
roads. A few more items are negotiated, and at length
the subdivision is approved.

These first, semicluster developments laid the ground-work for what was to follow. Now there were real-life examples to show skeptical planning boards and citizen groups on cluster tours. Soon a sort of critical mass had built up and by the mid sixties, cluster communities were going up in most areas. The Federal Housing Administration was now encouraging cluster design and had revised its standards to provide developers with incentives to try it. The leading barracks builder, the Defense Department, was beginning to apply the principle to multi-family housing at military bases.

The big question mark had been the attitude of the consumer and the answer was now at hand. If they had the choice, many people would choose cluster. Conventional, detached-house development still accounted for most new housing, as it still does and will continue to for some years to come. But the test of the marketplace had been met. Most cluster developments were selling as well as conventional developments in the same areas, and in a number of places, spectacularly better.

The best selling were the most compressed. These were the "townhouse" developments, and they caught on so well that the developers themselves were somewhat stunned. In the Los Angeles area one large town-house development sold out so quickly that developers all over the area junked plans for conventional subdivisions and so swamped the local FHA office with applications for townhouse developments that extra help had to be flown in from Washington to help with the paper work.

Townhouse developments have been such a market success that a standard all purpose layout is emerging. There are some regional variations. In the East, builders do them up as Williamsburg Squares or New England villages. In the West they are more eclectic, mixing colonial, contemporary, oriental, and the gingerbread known in the trade as Hansel and Gretel.

But the basic plans are much the same: groups of two-story row houses, the first floor featuring an open kitchen leading to a living room which in turn opens out through sliding glass doors onto a patio twenty feet square, with a cedar or redwood fence eight feet high, the gate opening onto a common area roughly 100 feet across to the patios of the next row of houses, a play yard at one end with swings, a large concrete turtle, and a sand pit. The area is lit with old-fashioned Baltimore gas street lamps.

The gimmicks are often laid on thick, especially in the lower-priced developments, and it is easy to look down one's nose at the whole because of these parts. Several corned-up but significant developments have been dismissed by architects and observers as of no consequence because of their banalities. But overemphasis on façade cuts two ways. For all the laid-on touches, these developments have fastened on a basic plan of commendable simplicity and serviceability. That is why people like them. They buy the houses not because of those gas street lamps, or diamond-shaped panes; they buy because they get more house for their monthly payment than they would elsewhere.

They also get services, and in some developments, a quite encompassing package of them. Townhouse developments not only relieve the homeowner of any mowing, they often take care of the outside of his house, including roof repairs and painting, and some throw in such services as daytime supervision of children's areas and corps of babysitters. ("The management of Pomeroy West cares for it all. The landscaping, the community center and pool, even your home. Whether it's weeding or watering, repainting or repairs, you have no maintenance worries. Everything is done for you. This gives you time for a weekend at the lake, or a month in the Orient, or just more relaxing moments in your own private gardens. There are no cares of home-ownership here, only the rewards.")

It is quite a package and is especially attractive to older couples who have done their time with a regular suburban homestead. With surprising vehemence, they will talk about the lawns they left behind, and how nice it is to be rid of such tyrannies. Young couples find the service package appealing too. Because they do not have to putter around and paint and fix up, they say, they have more time to be with their children.

Recreational facilities are elaborate, and becoming more so. Almost every cluster development save the very smallest will have tennis courts and a swimming pool, and the way competition is going, Olympic-size swimming pools are becoming standard. Usually there will be a clubhouse or community center and in some instances, a separate building for teen-agers.

Some of the larger developments, such as New Seabury on Cape Cod, make recreation their principal motif, and center each cluster around a particular activity—boating on one, for example, riding in another. In most large developments there will be an eighteen-hole golf course, sometimes two, and wherever there is any water, the most will be made of it. Developers will spend a great deal of money to create an artificial lake, as Robert Simon did at Reston, for these not only are good for boating and swimming—and scenery—but markedly increase the value of the encircling land. Where there is a waterway, developers will also invest heavily in marinas.

Big developments or small, recreation facilities take a lot of the developers' "front money" for they have found it vital to leave nothing to the imagination of the prospective home buyer. The first thing that most of them build, along with the model houses, is the swimming pool and the clubhouse, which will do double duty as reception center and sales office. Such complexes are often so artfully contrived that once prospects are inside the reception center, there is no way out except by following a labyrinthine trail through the models, and back through the sales cubicles.

At this stage, the developments can look oddly like a movie set. The townhouse façades have a two-dimensional quality and one almost feels surprised to find there is something real on the other side of the front door. Activity abounds. Few families may yet have moved into the development, but the swimming pool, snack bar, and cabana club appear to be going full tilt. (In one as yet

uninhabited development I visited, a troupe of happy
children could be seen cycling around the greens, hour
after hour after hour. They dressed up the scene so effectively, I thought they might have been hired as shills.
The developer said they certainly were not. But an interesting idea, he said, a very interesting idea.)

The packaging concept has been carried to its ultimate
in the retirement communities. For their monthly payment, couples get a small house or apartment unit and a
prodigious range of facilities and services—including,
among other things, complete medical care, golf courses,
minibus transportation, organized recreational and hobby
activities, craft shops, social rooms, library, and central
clubhouse. Whatever one may think of the concept of such
enclaves, physically they have been set up with great skill;
the land planning is generally of a very high order and so,
often, is the architecture. The Leisure Worlds of entrepreneur Ross Cortese are an outstanding example. Mr.
Cortese built so many communities so fast he ran ahead
of his market and further building has been stalled for
want of financing. The communities that are up, however,
furnish some of the best prototypes of cluster design in
the country.

Where to now? The cluster approach is opening up some
wonderful opportunities, but there are some pitfalls as well.
One is that developers will use cluster as a wedge for
achieving unreasonably high densities. What appeals most
to them is the cluster, not the open space; the doughnut
and not the hole. Where they have been allowed to get
away with it, some developers have compressed people to
the point of claustrophobia, with mean little spaces
labeled as commons largely given over to parking.

But compression is not the main problem. In the long
run, higher densities are inevitable, whatever kind of
layout, and the cluster approach is one of the best ways
of meeting the problem with grace. There will be efforts
to abuse it, but communities, not developers, lay down

the ground rules, and it is up to them to say this many people and no more.

The big danger is standardization. There is a strong possibility that cluster will congeal into a form as rigid and stereotyped as the conventional postwar layout it is replacing. This is already the case with townhouse developments. The basic designs of the first ones have been good, but not so good that they ought to be frozen. They have proved so marketable, however, that developers are copying their externals, gas lamps and all, no matter what the topography or the latitude or the surrounding neighborhood.

Cluster requires a fresh approach to house design. In too few cases do developers have architects design houses for the cluster layout—or, indeed, use architects at all. They use stock designs they have been used to. In outlying areas where lot sizes are relatively large, this is not too great a problem; there the conventional detached houses can work fairly well in a cluster arrangement— even the builder's stock ranchers. As lots are compressed, however, the houses and the layout begin to work at cross-purposes. The typical one-story house is designed for a wide suburban lot and throws everything into the façade on the front side, and puts it parallel to the street, which is just the wrong axis for a cluster layout. The windows on the side of the house not only lose their function but become a disadvantage; there is nothing to see except the neighbors' window shades. The vestigial strip of side yard becomes an echo chamber. The better-designed cluster houses solve the problem by doing away with side windows altogether—in the case of townhouses, by necessity.

Exteriors require different handling also. A cluster layout magnifies faults. When detached houses are laid out in conventional fashion, the contrived individuality of the stock models is mercifully separated by enough space to obscure the trumpery; a split-level colonial can be put on the next lot to a rancher without clashing too much, and with enough buffer space and greenery, Hansel and Gretel houses can be assimilated too. Move such houses close together, however, and the result can be a polychromatic mess—an out-of-scale toy village with all the visual defects of a conventional subdivision and no camouflage to hide them.

To go well with a cluster layout, houses should have an underlying unity. This is easiest come by in townhouse developments; even in the most hoked up examples, economic necessity forces the developer to keep the basic structure fairly clean. Variations or no, the houses will be unified by consistent roof lines and set-backs, and the recurrence of certain basic dimensions, as in the height and shape of windows. What makes stereotypes of them is not the uniformity, but the way developers tack them up to disguise the uniformity.

As with the houses, so with the land. There is still too much hack site planning. One of the most difficult things to find out in studying cluster developments is who, if anybody, was responsible for the final site plan. Small developers usually do the basic planning themselves and for professional assistance they tend to favor exsurveyors or engineers whose principal expertise is an ability to squeeze in the maximum number of lots the rules will allow. The larger and more successful developers do use trained land planners, and often very good ones; whatever the aesthetic impulses of the developers, they know that they will end up with a more economical layout if they do.

But the lesson comes hard to many developers. Often they will bring in a land planner only after it has become apparent that the original hack plan is not going to work very well. Of some sixty developments that I checked, in at least twenty cases the final site plan was drafted as a rescue job. (One of the most encouraging things about studying cluster development is to see the plans that *did not* get built.)

Site plans are getting better, but the unparalleled opportunities cluster opens up for imaginative treatment of the land are still relatively unexploited. Trees are an example. Since it virtually pays developers to leave as many standing as possible, they do not resort to the practice of sawing down all the trees and starting fresh with saplings. Cluster developments will have more trees around than conventional ones. But that is about it. In a few cases, trees will be used as an element in the architecture of the housing—in some cases, squares have been built around a particularly magnificent old tree, and with striking results. But this is the exception.

The way developers handle earth is similarly uninspired. Wonderful things can be done with the spoil from excavation, especially in prairie or desert areas where there is not a hillock in sight, but efforts are few and they are usually perfunctory. Occasionally a developer will proudly show you a big pile of dirt on which he has planted grass and talk to you about the creative use of overburden. It will look just like a pile of dirt on which grass has been planted—and a convenient justification for not carting the stuff away.

Where there are hills, the potential of cluster design is great but little exploited. As the flat valley floors are being filled up, developers have been turning to the hills, and they have been learning how to do things with rocks and slopes they never did before. They have been doing away with them. They have had to; under conventional zoning and building standards, they have to lay out their subdivisions as though the land were flat and then undertake extraordinary land-grading operations to reduce the topography to fit the subdivision.

The Los Angeles area is a particular case in point. One of the most horrifying sights in the U.S. is that of platoons of giant graders and scrapers chewing into the hills along the San Fernando Valley. Small hills the developers have simply leveled out of existence; the big ones they have chopped up so they look like the side of a pyramid; and on the building "pads" they have superimposed the same kind of ranchers with which they have covered the valley floor. The result is offensive to the eye, and as periodic slides and inundations have shown, is offensive to nature as well.

The desecration is so unnecessary. By applying the cluster principle developers can work with the slopes instead of obliterating them. This saves money. It also saves the terrain, for developers can concentrate the housing on the knolls and leave the rest undisturbed. The homeowner enjoys more privacy rather than less, and because of the successive changes of elevation, a finer view than he would have in the usual large-lot subdivision.

Where slopes are very steep or rocky, the cluster approach is even more relevant. Much can be done with the cantilever principle, and as Frank Lloyd Wright demonstrated so many years ago with "Falling Water," rocks can be used as structural elements with stunning effect. Unfortunately, this kind of imagination is still restricted to expensive custom homes and "second" homes in vacation areas. It has yet to be applied in any scale to developments.

One reason it has not been is the attitude of municipal engineers. They are a conservative lot, and for hillside plans they demand that developers lay down curbs and gutters and pavements almost as if they were working with a flat piece of land, and they generally insist on streets bigger than necessary. Developers are correct in protesting that the standards are overengineered, but then they have always been saying this about standards; steep slopes or gentle, they have habitually tried to get out of laying down curbs, gutters, and pavements so they can preserve the "character of the site"—and, at $5 a lineal foot, save a lot of money. Understandably, the engineers are skeptical, and many look on the cluster approach as another device of developers to cheat on the regulations. Planners have been arguing the developers' case, and since planners can talk about the public interest with more plausibility than developers, they have had some success in getting hillside standards liberalized. But there are many fights ahead.

Overengineered standards also help explain why streams are treated so insensitively in most developments. Developers are not against streams; they put them in culverts because the regulations force them to, and one reason they like cluster planning is that they can leave the streams.

But engineers like concrete. If there is the slightest danger that streams might overflow, they insist that the banks be "stabilized," and they usually mean by this that it be put in a concrete trough. Reston suffered from this: The master plan called for storm sewers in the high-density areas, but the bulk of the drainage was to be handled the way it always was, by the streams. Where banks had to be stabilized, it would be with ferns and trees. The county engineer objected strongly. He wanted concrete. After protracted negotiations, Reston won some of its streams, but it lost some.

The critical problem in cluster planning is the handling of the interior commons and the private spaces. One lesson is abundantly clear. The private space is far and away the most important. The space is usually quite small; in townhouse projects the patios average out to no more than about 20 feet by 20 feet, the dimensions being determined by the width of the houses. But these small spaces are extremely functional. They are fine places for parking infants, for naps in the sun, for the happy hour, and it is a rare one that doesn't have a well-used charcoal grill.

Patios and courtyards also have the great advantage of extending the apparent size of the inside of the house. Since the living room opens onto them through the sliding glass doors, there is a considerable visual sweep from the kitchen in the front of the house to the back of the patio. (In the perspective of developers' brochures, the expanse is so vast the patio is scarcely visible in the distance.)

The enclosed court or garden is especially suited to city living and it has been proved many times that people will pay a premium for dwellings that provide them; as a check of real estate ads for New York converted brownstones with south garden will demonstrate, the premiums sometimes reach the fantastic. But this kind of private space has generally been available only in rehabilitated housing. Until recently, designers of city developments were dead set against private spaces. They claimed they were uneconomic, raised maintenance problems, and cluttered up the picture. The projects provided plenty of open space to work with, but the designers preferred to mass the space into common areas and thereby give order and unity to the design.

Much criticism was leveled at these collectives and at length a few projects were put up that included duplex units and gardens. The mating of styles was not always felicitous and to some architects the trend seemed calamitous. I recall visiting a mixed project with one of the architects. We looked down from a tower, which he had designed, to a block of duplex houses with private gardens, which he had not. It was a warm afternoon in fall and the people were busy at one thing or another in their gardens. A pleasant scene, I ventured. A hideous compromise, he said, and with the intense moral indignation that architects can summon up in dismissing designs they do not like, explained that the gardens were an asocial, selfish use of space, and utterly ruinous to the over-all unity.

But the old brutalism has been giving way, albeit slowly. The trend in new urban projects is to have both towers and two- or three-story houses and to combine common open spaces with private patios and courts. In comparison to the stark projects of the past, these new ones do tend to look a bit messy, but this defect, if such it is, is apparent only when you are looking down at models. In actuality, the courtyards and gardens tend to enliven the scene for the people in the towers.

The trickiest problem is the relationship between the private spaces and the common ones. In most cases there is a fairly definite separation, with brick walls or high fences enclosing the private space. This method provides the maximum privacy but it does cut down the size of the interior commons and for this reason some architects prefer to treat both kinds of space as one. Save for a low hedge, or line of bricks, there is little to indicate where the private open space ends and the common space begins. This makes for a cleaner design and a roomier commons.

It also makes for ambiguity, and if architects had to

live in their developments they would not do it this way. In almost any development where people live close together there is usually a lot of neighborly contact. Where the houses focus on a commons, the amount of contact is at its greatest. There is more kaffeeklatsching, more visiting back and forth, and while this has its advantages, without fences it becomes mandatory. There is no avoiding it, and a good many people would like to avoid it.

But there is no redoubt, no place to draw the line. Wives complain that if they feel like stretching out on a beach chair to read or just plain rest, their siesta is sure to be interrupted. Then there is the entertaining problem. When couples do their *al fresco* entertaining in full sight of everyone, neighborly relationships can be put to a severe strain. (Will they understand it's an out-of-town couple we haven't seen in years? Shall we ask them to come over and join us just for cocktails? Will they leave before supper?) The poet's point about good fences and good neighbors is true. All in all, experience suggests, private open spaces should be private.

There need be no antithesis between common spaces and private ones. They complement each other; even in very high density developments there should be room for both. When there is a buffer zone of private gardens, interior commons do not have to be very large; the fact they are enclosed by buildings on three or four sides makes them look larger than they actually are.*

The usual commons consists of a rectangle of green lawn, some hedges and trees, and a play area at one end. The result is pleasant enough, but if you have seen one you have seen a great many. Occasionally there are fresh touches—an open air pavilion with a huge fireplace, for

* An old, but very excellent case in point is Macdougal Gardens in New York's Greenwich Village. This is a block of old houses in which the rear portions of the backyards were combined into a commons. It is an extremely pleasant place and because of the old trees and the adjoining gardens of the houses, the space seems quite large. But it isn't. The width of the commons itself is only thirty-five feet.

example—but in most cases the originalities are standard:
a piece or so of free form sculpture, perhaps, or a string
of those gas street lamps.

As Georgian architects knew so well, the great advantage of a tight housing layout is the opportunity it affords
to design the spaces for the buildings and the buildings
for the spaces—at one and the same time, and not seriatim.
But few aspects of cluster are so unexploited. If there is
to be an interior commons, for example, why not follow
through and design the buildings for real enclosure? Open
space is at its most inviting when it is approached through
a covered passageway, yet this ancient principle has been
little applied. Neither has the crescent or the arcade or
the circus.

There are many fresh approaches to explore. Do the
commons, for example, have to be green? There can be
too much and some of the most celebrated garden-city
communities suffer from the overemphasis. Without enclosure, or a striking foreground or background, expanses
of green can be quite dull, and sometimes they can be
downright oppressive. (Radburn, for example, is almost
smothered in foliage in summer, and to this observer, looks
best in spring.)

Punctuation and contrast are needed, and one of the
best ways to provide them is through the paved courtyard
or small plaza. It can provide an excellent common area,
and tends to heighten the effect of any greenery there is.
In few settings does a large tree seem so handsome. The
paved court also makes a nice transition between the private open space and the surrounding common areas, all
the more so if the housing clusters are surrounded by large
expanses of green. They are also the best of settings for
a fountain.

The paved court, however, still strikes many people as
much too revolutionary for the market. One of the best-
looking designs in the country was ditched because of
this bias. The site planner had set his clusters in the middle
of a golf course. Since there was to be green around them,
he planned the common space within each cluster as a

paved courtyard. The developer lost his nerve and asked a market consultant to give his judgment. The consultant said it was too radical, and recommended that the spaces be grass and look "pretty and soft."

Such timidity is unwarranted, even by commercial standards. The court has been given a pretty good consumer test for quite a few centuries, and where it has been tried anew it seems to work as well as ever. Charles Goodman's paved courts for the River Park development in southwest Washington are a fine example. Compared to architect Chloethiel Smith's grassy spaces in the neighboring Capitol Park development, Goodman's courts seem severe, but both projects sold well, and in both, the open spaces seem to work quite well—proving, once again, that different approaches can achieve satisfying results.

In rural areas where there is a lot of space to work with, there are many more things that can be done with common areas than have been tried. Grazing, for one thing. If fields and meadows are put to this kind of productive use they look much better than any formally landscaped scene. Sheep, for example, lend just the estate flavor that developers want to promote, and there is no better way to keep the grass cut. Instead of having to pay people to maintain the land, the homeowners can get it done virtually free, and sometimes even make a little. In one Colorado vacation development, the houses are clustered on the slopes, leaving three hundred acres of meadowland as the commons. The homeowners lease it out as pasture land for cattle.

Some people have suggested going so far as to have a complete working farm as the center of a commons; one such scheme has been proposed for the development of a small valley in upstate New York. One can only wish the proponents well, but the experience of subdivisions close to farms suggests that farm activity and its attendant smells is attractive to residents for about one day. After that they raise cain with the farmer for disturbing their peace —starting up his tractors at five A.M., using dangerous sprays, letting their children get into mischief, and such.

Another idea that is likely to come a cropper is the equestrian village centered around riding stables. This was proposed in the preliminary plan for Reston but was prudently dropped. There are stables, but they are located well away from any houses. People like to ride horses, developers have found, but they do not want to live near them.

While there are many more things that can be done with the spaces within developments, perhaps the greatest challenge is to find ways to link the spaces. Not much has been done to exploit this potential; by and large, the cluster developments are planned project by project, with little relation one to the other, or to the open spaces of the community. Very large developments, or "new towns," are planned on such a scale that they provide a community open-space system themselves, but while more of these are in the offing, the bulk of future residential growth will be an aggregation of small and medium-size developments.

Yet their open spaces do not have to be a miscellany. With the proper incentives, individual developers can be led to plan their open spaces so that they will eventually fit together in an over-all system. The key is for the local government to anticipate the development that is inevitable and to lay down in advance the skeleton of an open-space network to which each developer will contribute as the area is built up. This presupposes a very vigorous arm twisting of developers but there is a strong indication that if planning commissions were to take this kind of initiative, developers would go along.

Philadelphia has furnished an outstanding demonstration. In the 1950s, there still remained in its far northeast section a five thousand acre expanse of open land. It was mostly farm land, gently rolling and laced with a network of wooded creeks. It was also eminently buildable, and squarely in the path of row-house development. Mulling over the fate of this area, Philadelphia city planner Edmund Bacon, figured that there was no reason why the city should leave the basic land-use pattern for this area up to the speculative builders. The city, he felt, ought to lay down a master subdivision plan. Developers could fill in the details, but the open-space and housing patterns would be so strongly outlined that the end product would be the kind of unity that is usually possible only when one large developer is doing the whole thing.

With a cluster approach, Bacon figured, the total acreage could amenably house some 68,000 people. The area would be divided into a series of neighborhood groupings, and there would be an open space network based on the stream valleys. To obtain plat approval, a builder would have to dedicate these parts of his tract designated as green space to the city. Instead of the usual aggregation of bits and pieces, accordingly, there would be a continuous open-space system that would be highly functional for recreation, and would at once connect and define the neighborhoods. Here is the plan of one section of the area, with the public open spaces indicated by dark hatching:

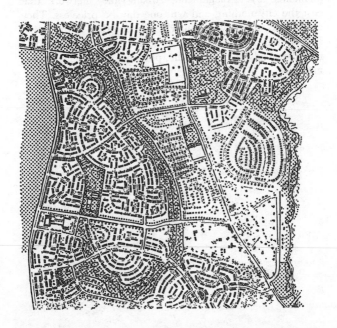

Builders took to the idea. The master plan did go quite far in telling them what to do, but it provided them excellent densities—about nine units per acre—and considerably less street and land improvement expenses than ordinarily they would have had to bear. The first builder started work in 1959. Since then other builders have joined suit and with few variations from the original plan.

The result is not a showpiece. For so advanced a plan, what one sees on the ground is disappointingly ordinary. The houses, which are in the $11,000–$13,000 range, are basically standard row houses with a few façade variations, and they do not always sit well in the circular groupings laid down by the planners. But the plan works, and one has only to look to the conventional row-house developments a few miles back toward the city to see what a difference it has made. The houses in the cluster neighborhoods have been just as profitable for the builders, no more expensive for the homeowners, yet they are complemented by a magnificent stream-valley network that cost the city nothing and will one day be priceless. They are indeed ordinary neighborhoods, but that is the point. If this kind of amenity can be achieved in middle-income neighborhoods in a city, the potential elsewhere is tremendous.

13.   The New Towns

>>

The next step, many people believe, should be the building of whole new towns. Better big subdivisions are not
enough, they say; what we should do is carry the cluster
concept to the ultimate; group not only homes, but industrial plants, hospitals, cultural centers, and create entirely new communities. These would not only be excellent
places in their own right; together, they would be the last
best chance of the metropolis.

It is a hope that at last seems nearer the threshold of
reality. Developers have been moving in this direction and
across the country a dozen large-scale communities have
been started, each of which is meant to have an eventual
population of 75,000 or more. In addition, there are some
two hundred "planned communities" being built which,
if smaller, claim the same basic approach. Big corporations
have been getting into the business. Gulf Oil financed the
start of Reston, outside of Washington, and has now taken
over the whole operation; the Connecticut General Life

Insurance Company is financing Columbia, outside of Baltimore. General Electric has set up a special division to assist the builders of new towns and a Rand-type of think center for the planning of them.

Some of these new communities have been having their troubles. Almost all builders have been hurt lately by tight money, but those who have launched the large scale developments have been particularly vulnerable. They have to borrow huge sums of money to get such operations going, and if house sales falter, they can quickly find themselves hard put to meet the interest payments. For want of enough cash flow, a number of developers have had to stop at phase one of their communities and several have gone bankrupt.

But this is the way things often go in the industry and new town advocates remain optimistic. The credit bind, they point out, does not prove that the new town idea is faulty; what it proves is that better financing arrangements are in order, and that the federal government should lend more of a hand. The administration has declared strongly in favor of new towns but the support it has been enabled to give so far has been largely moral. Through mortgage insurance and loans for land assembly, the Department of Housing and Urban Development has been offering some incentive for communities and developers to work together on new town projects. The enabling legislation is full of bugs, however.

The administration is now proposing as an aid the "federally guaranteed cash-flow debenture." This would provide developers of new towns the wherewithal to pay the interest charges on their borrowed capital until sales were rolling sufficiently to generate some real cash for them. In return for such underwriting, the developers would have to include in their plans some housing for low- and middle-income people. The administration is also proposing additional incentives for state and local government cooperation in new town projects. Congress has not been keen on subsidies for new towns—big city mayors don't want any at all—but as time goes on it will probably authorize more aid.

But this does not mean we will get a lot of new towns. Let me define terms. I am not taking up the pros and cons of better-planned suburban developments; and this essentially is what most of the new communities that appropriate the title of new town really are. What I want to explore is the validity of the ideal new town model, as planners see it. It is far more than a matter of degree. Philosophically as well as physically, the true new town is to be a *complete* community—so complete that it can exist independent of the old city, and, quite literally, help cut it down to size.

The specifications are remarkably similar to those laid down some half century ago in England by Ebenezer Howard. Like many generations of planners after him, Howard sought an antidote to the city. "There are in reality," he said, "not only, as is so constantly assumed, two alternatives—town life and country life—but a third alternative in which all the advantages of the most energetic and active town life, with all the beauty and delight of the country, may be secured in perfect combination."

He proposed a garden city in the countryside—a community of about a thousand acres set in a green belt of five thousand acres. The community would own the land and lease it to people who would build according to the plan. It would be a balanced community; in addition to residential development, there would be local industry, thriving agriculture, and in total there would be enough jobs for everyone in the town.

Howard saw this not only as good in itself but as a solution to the problems of the city. London, he thought, was monstrously big and unhealthy, and its land values inflated out of reason. If garden cities were built, they would prove so attractive that they would draw people from the city; this would depress the land values in London, thus making it possible to redevelop the city at a much lower density. The new towns, he prophesied, would "be the magnet which will produce the effect for which we are all striving—the spontaneous movement of the people from our crowded cities to the bosom of our kindly mother earth."

The language of this kindly utopian is not that of today's new town planners, but in their own more scientific way they are saying the same thing. They, too, are repelled by the city. New town proposals are generally prefaced with a sweeping indictment of the city as pretty much of a lost cause. We tried, the charge goes, but the city is a hopeless tangle. Medical analogies abound. The city is diseased, cancerous, and beyond palliatives. The future is not to be sought in it, but out beyond, where we can start afresh.

The possibility of working with a clean slate is what most excites planners and architects about new towns. Freed from the constraints of previous plans and buildings and people, the planners and architects can apply the whole range of new tools. With systems analysis, electronic data processing, game theory, and the like, it is hoped, a science of environmental design will be evolved and this will produce a far better kind of community than ever was possible before.

On the main specifications, however, there is already considerable agreement. First, the new town must be balanced. It must have people of all income groups and houses to match. Second, it must be self-contained; it will have its own industry and commerce and jobs enough for all who wish to work within the boundaries of the community. No one need commute to the city.

No one will need visit the city for culture either. The new town will be self-contained in this respect as well, with its own symphony orchestras, little theaters, junior colleges, and colleges, and the town center will have all the urbanity and services of the center city. Recreation will be built in, and close to every home will be green space, tennis courts, golf courses, hiking and riding trails.

To offer all this, a new town would really have to be a city, and lately proponents have been using the term "new city" in describing their communities. But these are not

to be like cities as we have known them. There is not to
be any dirty work in them. There are not to be any slums.
There are not to be any ethnic concentrations, or concentrations of any kind. Housing densities will be quite low.
There will be no crowded streets. Yet, it will be a city
—"a whole city," one developer puts it, "with all the texture
and fabric of the city." It will have everything the city has,
in short, except its faults.

This is an impossible vision. Certainly there are going to
be more and bigger new communities built and it is good
there will be. Architecturally and otherwise, some of the
ones that have been going up are excellent, and as I
will take up in the next chapter, they are providing
many important lessons in large-scale land assembly and
development.

But this is not the same thing as building self-contained
new cities, and it is the validity of this concept that I am
questioning: the pure, uncompromised vision—the community we would get if all the necessary legislation were
passed, all the funds needed were provided, and all of the
key specifications were followed.

It would not work. The reason it would not work does
not lie in the usual obstacles that are decried—fragmentation of local government, lack of trained design terms, and
so on. The substance of this critique is that the trouble is
in the idea itself.

As elements of the metropolis, new towns could not take
care of more than a fraction of our future population
growth, even under the best of circumstances; nor could
they significantly change the structure of the metropolis.
The English new towns have not; the Scandinavian new
towns were never meant to.

As a community, the self-contained new town is a contradiction in terms. You cannot isolate the successful elements of the city and package them in tidy communities
somewhere else. And if you could do it, would you be able
to have only the good and none of the bad? The goal is
so silly it seems profound.

I would further argue that the idea of getting people to stay put and work and live together in the same healthy place is somewhat retrogressive. Americans move too much to be thus beneficently contained. Their mobility does breed problems, but it is also a dynamic and in the oversight of this the self-contained community is irrelevant if not contradictory to the main sweep of American life.

American planners tend to overplan, even where the constraints of reality are great, and when they are given a clean slate to work with, the temptation to overplan can be irresistible. There are exceptions, but physically the most striking thing about plans for ideal new towns is their finality. Everything is in its place: There are no loose ends, no question marks, and it is this completeness of the vision, more than the particulars of it, that stirs recalcitrance. It is one thing to be beckoned down the road to a distant utopia, quite another to be shown utopia itself in metes and bounds and all of it at once.

This, the plans seem to say, is the way it jolly well is going to be. There is to be no zigging and zagging to adapt the plans to people. It is the people who are to do the adapting and if there is anything they cannot adapt to, it will be just too bad because there is no provision for changing the plans as time goes on. These designs are so ordered in their intricacy that if you changed just one element, the whole thing would be rendered inoperable.

As planners of more pragmatic learnings have noted, this fixation on the "end state" plan runs directly counter to the profession's favorite axioms about interaction, feedback, and planning as an ongoing process. "The planning is neat, rational, logical, and fixed," says one critic, Marshall Kaplan. "The range of alternatives given is quite limited. . . . That the community will change, will develop after 1980 is acknowledged by the planners but often denied by the plan. Every area is planned, with little flexibility provided in the design for unforeseen want. Obsolescence—either planned or unplanned—is not a considered input."

There is really only one plan. The kind of geometrics favored may differ, but whether linear or concentric or molecular, the plans end up looking so alike it is a wonder such large staffs are deemed necessary to draft them. Several graduate students steeped in current planning dogma could work up almost identical plans in a few weeks— they do it regularly as class projects, and how they do it is pretty close to the way the most elaborate plans are drafted. The plans come into being almost full-blown. They start with a visual concept. The approach is graphic, and for all the to-do about sociological and economic research, this is supporting documentation. The design comes first.

The designs all look the same because they spring from the same design philosophy. It is the design philosophy embedded in the standard redevelopment project, with its high-rise slabs and aseptic open space. Just at a time when it is finally being conceded that the design doesn't fit people too well ("I certainly don't agree with Jane Jacobs, but . . ."), the whole thing is about to be reincarnated in suburbia, only called something else and stretched even further.

The center of the new city is a vast expanse of mall surrounded by office and apartment towers and beyond these the various neighborhoods, or "villages," stretch off in the distance, each encircled by its own spaces. The sweep is awesome. The planners will have a great deal to say about human scale, and to make up for its absence in the plan, they supply it in the brochures with ground-level sketches of what life will be like. The sketches are now standard: people sitting at outdoor cafés, mothers with baby carriages looking at Paris-style kiosks or waiting for the monorail.*

* Planning brochures and promotional literature for new towns have become so standardized in their themes and illustrations that much effort could be spared if one all-purpose brochure were worked up. It would include the following: (a) aerial picture of farmland taken in 1945; (b) aerial picture of same area ten years later, covered with subdivisions; (c) photo

But it is the same old redevelopment project, magnified.
There is the same compartmentation of activities, the same
insistence on order and symmetry, the same distaste for
the street and its function, the same lack of interest in the
surroundings.

There are no surroundings. In birds-eye renderings of
urban redevelopment projects, the grubby details of neighboring streets and buildings are customarily airbrushed
away. People who sketch new towns have no such impedimenta to contend with, but even so, they give little
indication of what, if anything, might lie beyond the project. They don't seem particularly interested. The background is shown as a boundless tract of undifferentiated
space. It is almost as if the planners had come upon a
habitable planet unmarred by previous habitation. You see
no palimpsests of previous towns, factories, trailer villages,
or railroad tracks. Even the greenery is indeterminate; you
cannot tell whether it is farmland, forest, upland or low-
land, or some algaelike growth.

The treatment of space within the boundaries is similarly grandiloquent. New towns do not squander space the
way conventional large-lot subdivisions do, but this is not
saying very much. New towns have especial reason to
waste no space at all; the whole rationale of accompanying
wedges and green belts rests on this point; if planners are
to justify setting aside such vast acreages the better to

---

of massed rooftops and TV aerials; (d) photo of neon signs,
gas stations, and pizza stands on commercial highway; (e)
photo of cars in traffic jam; (f) sign at entrance to state park
saying "filled"; (g) bulldozer hacking at hillside. Next come
the good things: (a) photo of new town center at Stevenage
or Vallingby or Tapiola; (b) the Tivoli gardens in Copenhagen;
(c) impressionistic drawing of U.S. new town center, with a
group of children holding balloons; (d) picture of intelligent-
looking people around a table looking at a planner pointing to
a map; (e) flow chart of proper planning steps. Either at the
front or at the back there will be one or two mood pictures.
A special favorite is a photo of two children walking hand in
hand through a woods.

contain development, the development should be very contained indeed.

But it is not. The densest part, the core, seems extraordinarily expansive. The essence of a downtown is concentration and mixture, but the malls that are sketched in the plans are quite vast, even for a big city. Beyond the core, the densities decrease further, with the houses on the periphery set in half-acre and acre lots. This, too, begs the question of the green belts beyond. For whom are they functional? The people who live next to the green belts have already been provided with the most open space of their own. The majority of the people are put in the middle, in high-rise towers and garden apartments. These are the people who need the open space the most and yet they are the farthest away from it—in some plans, up to two miles away.

True, the people up high can always look out their windows at the green belt, and the distances are not so great that they couldn't walk there if they are of a mind to. However, if the pedestrian habits of present suburbanites are any index, even relatively short distances are a deterrent, and as these are increased, the use of open space falls off drastically.

In this best of both worlds there is to be bustle without noise, concentration without confusion, people without traffic, excitement without danger. What the planners mean to do, in short, is to isolate each of the good qualities of the city from its context and reconstitute it in suburbia without its companion disadvantages. In a word, urbanity without cities.

The good elements of the city and the bad elements, alas, are often different aspects of the same function. We should try to make the most of the good and the least of the bad, but separating them out is extraordinarily difficult. Where does the bad leave off and the good begin? One of the charms of the city, most people agree, is the cosmopolitanism of its small shops—the Irish bar, the German *Konditorei*, the Italian grocery which makes its own line of pasta, the street festivals on the saints' days. But this kind of cosmopolitanism goes hand in hand with ethnic concentrations and it is certainly not the kind of thing new town planners wish to perpetuate.

Conversely, among the obvious bad things about cities are the old, dilapidated loft buildings and the once-grand neighborhoods gone to seed. But the loft buildings are a haven for marginal enterprises and an incubator of new ones because they are dilapidated and inexpensive to rent. Similarly, slightly seedy neighborhoods are the makings of new bohemias, and eventually, as the advance guard moves on to another seedy neighborhood, high-rent areas.

It would be wonderful indeed if one could isolate the desirable qualities and export them without their context. Architects and planners have a gallery of urbane places they would like to borrow from: the hill towns of Italy and Provence, for example, are great favorites for exemplifying compact development; Venice, for the pedestrian's city. In citing the desiderata, however, the tendency is to slough over the not-so-good elements that make the good elements possible, and this is even more pronounced when planners consider what is worth copying from American cities.

Let us take the matter of urbanity. Almost all new town prospectuses make a big point of it. No typical suburban shopping center for them. Their centers are going to be highly urbane, with a full range of cultural activities, specialty shops, second-hand bookstores, craft shops, offbeat restaurants, sidewalk cafés, and a host of touches evoking the flavor of Greenwich Village and Georgetown, for which latter place a considerable number of new developments have been named.

But it never seems to work out that way. What middle-class suburbia gets are shopping centers for middle-class suburbia. The institutions that flourish here are those which do an excellent job of catering to the middle range—such as Sears Roebuck and Howard Johnson—and where there is a branch of a large downtown department store, the top and the bottom of the line are left out. The supermarket provides the same kind of choice; acres of goods lie before you but they are the same goods, and they will be the same in the other big supermarket. You can find every known brand of corn flakes, or tomato catsup, or processed cheese, but if it is something slightly special you want, like a good head of lettuce, you will roam the aisles in vain. Only small stores have this kind of variety.

Restaurants seem to be an especially vexing problem for developers. In most of the new postwar communities, the restaurants are rather bland, and residents will frequently complain quite strenuously about them. Developers never planned it that way; many of them have made special efforts to bring in a good specialty restaurant or at least a first rate operation. In one case, the developer offered generous lease terms in an unsuccessful effort to get an Italian family to set up a Greenwich Village-type restaurant in his new town center.

But the environment is not right. In the first place, the kind of restaurateur that is sought does not have the capital to wait out the lean years while the population builds up sufficiently to provide a reasonable market. Only chain operations usually have the capital for that. Secondly, well-capitalized or not, the operation must inevitably become an all-purpose one. It will be a service element—the place, for example, where the local groups will hold their meetings. The lunchtime clientele will be the people who work in the center and they are the blue-plate-special or club-sandwich crowd and not the two-martini people who provide the midday support for a city's French and Italian restaurants. The weekend business will be mainly prospective homebuyers with children in tow, and the restaurateur will have to put in a supply of high chairs. And whom does he get at nights? A few regulars in the bar, a smattering of residents, and a few visitors.

To survive, the operation will have to adapt to the median. From community to community you will find that even the best of the operations generally feature the all-American menu—shrimp cocktail, baked potato with sour cream and chives, steak, salad with roquefort dressing,

and selections from the dessert wagon. As staples go, these
can be pretty good fare; nevertheless, the residents will
complain that there is no decent place for eating out, and
even if the food were really good, they still might complain.

The image has been fixed. At nighttime the restaurateur
can put checkered cloths over the formica tables, dim the
lights, put out candles in fishnet containers and add a
pianist. But it just won't wash. To the residents, it is still a
community-service center and in their mind irrevocably
coupled with daytime shopping, children, and luncheon
meetings of women's groups.

In another respect, the new towns lack self-sufficiency.
There's to be no sin in them. Despite the claim that the
new towns are to have all of the attractions of the city,
there are no provisions for night clubs, bookie joints,
or any but the mildest of vices. The new towns are to
cater to the widest possible range of tastes, but there is not
to be any bad taste. There will be no raffishness, no garish
"strip," no honky-tonks. Some suggestions have been made
about filling the void with a "fun palace," an idea bruited
in England for a large factorylike structure in which, as in
a free play period, people could improvise all sorts of
activities. But the fun would be wholesome, and as with
a similar suggestion for a permanent carnival for the town
centers, one senses a monitoring and somewhat conde-
scending presence.

The bars are to be genteel, too: In the new towns of
England some of the pubs are so prim they look as though
they should be called alcohol dispensaries, and the ones
over here are not real bars but the cocktail lounges of
adjoining restaurants, the kind with Muzak. All this is understandable enough, and new towns are not to be scorned
for such wholesomeness: It's one of the reasons they would
be nice places to live in. But would you want to visit them?

The affinity of such communities for the middle range is
a universal phenomenon. When they planned the new
town of Vallingby, the Swedish planners, who are quite

city-minded, were especially anxious to have a highly urbane town center, and they went to considerable lengths to provide attractive plazas, fountains, and well-designed street furniture. But the urbane shops did not take root. To the disappointment of the planners, the shops that flourished were good average, but not much more.

The same thing is true of the English new towns. The planners have lavished fine statuary on the centers, elaborate water fountains, and so forth. Enterprises that have leased the shops, however, are of a more mundane style, some rather plebeian, and the effect of the whole is somewhat tacky. (The food in the restaurants is beyond description. It is so awful that even new town planners blanch; they much prefer to eat in old towns nearby, and will be sure to take a visitor there.)

There is not very much planners could do to change things. These centers lack the essential quality of the city —its location. Urbanity is not something that can be lacquered on; it is the quality produced by the great concentration of diverse functions and a huge market to support the diversity. The center needs a large hinterland to draw upon, but it cannot be in the hinterland; it must be in the center. This is the fundamental contradiction in the new town concept of self-containment.

The kind of self-containment that most excites new town proponents is the idea of everybody's working and living in the same place. It is not to be just another suburb. In the ideal new town the planners mean to provide as many jobs as there will be workers, and the jobs will cover the whole range of skills and occupations.

Some kinds of jobs, of course, won't be included. Plans do not call for dirty work and the kind of smoky, noisy plants that would pollute the environment. But the planners don't think there will be any imbalance, for they are sanguine that the industrial trends are going in their direction. What with automation, atomic power, computerization, they hold, industry is transforming itself into the kind of clean, white-collar, smokeless facilities for which new towns would be the ideal setting. Because of this affinity, they further argue, the new town will be a powerful vehicle for the decentralization of employment. The present pattern of industrial clusters close to the city will be loosened up, the components dispersed all over the region, and each encapsulated with its own resident work force.

The planners are misreading the trends. Suburbia is going to get more plants, just as it's going to get more people, but the two are not to be so neatly packaged together. As far as employment is concerned, I hope to demonstrate, the self-contained community is impossible to achieve and it is a very good thing that it is impossible to achieve.

To have any claim to self-containment, the new towns must provide something for export. Taking in each other's laundry can keep a lot of people busy, and almost any new community provides a considerable number of local jobs—store clerks, deliverymen, service-station attendants, doctors, lawyers, bankers. But there is a limit to the number of service jobs a community can provide, and vital as these are, they give the community no dynamic. The new town must have primary industry. It cannot have just one kind, either, for it would be simply a new version of the company town.

Significantly, the most notable communities built from scratch have been built around the industry of government—Washington, D.C., Canberra, Brasilia, Chandigarh, and Islambad. These capitals may have many admirable features but they are essentially one-function towns and they are anything but models of the complete community.

New town planners are very keen on having a "balanced" population, with a pretty complete spectrum of income, education, and skills. This is all very fine, but to match all these people with jobs would require that the planners create not only a miniature city but a miniature metropolis.

No new town comes close to these specifications. The English new towns, some of which are factory-worker communities, do provide a good number of jobs, but the range is not a broad one, and a sizable number of people journey into the towns or out of them to earn their living.

In practice, it is virtually impossible to tie jobs to homes. Even when a lot of jobs are provided in a community, the people who fill them will not necessarily be the people who live there. As a matter of fact, the chances are strong that a great many won't be. In a number of places where a large supply of close-to-home jobs has been provided, there has been a large amount of commutation and reverse commutation. Vallingby is a case in point. There are 9000 jobs there, but most of the people who work at them do not live in Vallingby. They commute to them, some 7000 people, and as they do, the bulk of the wage earners who do live in Vallingby—25,000 of 27,000—commute outward, mostly to the center of Stockholm. In varying degrees, this mixed commutation pattern is true of most new towns in any modern industrial society and it is hard to see how it could be otherwise.

The oneness concept of work and residence is at odds with our dominant growth trends. It is true enough that factories are moving outward and that certain expanding industries find outlying locations excellent for new facilities. To deduce from this that a massive decentralization of employment is taking place is quite wrong. As factories have been vacating their cramped, high-cost city locations, there has been a corresponding increase in managerial, professional, and service jobs in the center city. More, not less than before, the city is headquarters. The people who service it are basic to any balanced population; any new town that is to have its share of them is going to have a lot of people who must commute, just like any other suburb.

And what, it might be asked, is so therapeutic about working close to home? There is much to say for it, and it is a beguiling thought that one could take a five-minute walk along a footpath, or a short ride on a minibus, to a campuslike office in the woods, and even perhaps return home for lunch, like French businessmen used to do. But all this propinquity is not without price. The fact is that a lot of people rather like the separation of work and home. They enjoy having as neighbors people who are not the same people they have been working with all day; they even enjoy the geographic buffer between the work place and their wives, and many of the wives do too. The commute, furthermore, is not always the ordeal it is often pictured; for many people it is the only time they ever get to do any reading, and the ride back can serve as a decompression period.

But let us suppose, for the sake of argument, that in one case the new town planners achieve their dream. They do reproduce the metropolis in miniature; they attract a broad range of people—low income, high income, blue collar, white collar—and on a one-to-one ratio, for every kind of person they provide jobs to match.

Self-containment still wouldn't work. There would be no real choice. In the aggregate there might be a lot of jobs, but for any one person there would be only a few that were suitable, and the more educated and more skilled the person, the fewer. If you were, say, a certain kind of electrical engineer, there might likely be only one job slot in the whole area for you—the one you have. You are, in effect, in a company town. If you came to dislike the job, you would have no practical alternative within the community. If you did like it, you would be in a poor bargaining position with your employer. In the tacit negotiations for raises or advancement, or, simply, having your opinions prevail, your ability to get as good or better a job, and the employer's awareness of this, is crucial. Pleasant surroundings cannot compensate for a lack of choice.

Self-containment would hurt employers as well. When residence in a certain place is packaged with a job, the employer may have some good talking points about the good life and the non-job benefits. But for all this, he is under severe disadvantage in competing for people with specialized skills. Just as the worker needs access to a wide range of jobs, the employer needs access to a wide range of people, and the further he is out on the periphery, the tougher his position. In a more central location he can compete much more effectively for prospective employees, for he does not have to persuade them to pick up stakes and move to the new town as part of the deal.

Theoretically, the accessibility problem could be solved if the new towns were linked directly with each other with a circumferential rapid transit system. Then a man might live in New Town A and journey around the circle to work in New Town B, or C, or D. Ebenezer Howard suggested something like this in his original prospectus. He proposed a circular arrangement of municipal railways that would link the new towns in a system. Much the same idea has been advanced for tying together future new towns, with the inevitable monorail sketched as a possible means. Another suggestion is creation of an additional set of belt freeways around the outer ring.

This circumlocution would be very bad transportation planning. To be economic, mass-transportation routes must tap great concentrations of high-density traffic. We are having enough trouble in getting good mass-transit systems even when they go with the region's traffic flow, which is essentially radial, with the lines converging toward the center. The capital cost of another mass-transit system cutting across the grain would be prodigious.

Highways, of course, can go where mass transit cannot. The new beltways have created a great deal of suburb-to-suburb traffic and in some areas more commercial development is being built to tap these circumferential routes than the old city to suburb axes. But only so many circles can be built. Additional freeways across suburbia would consume inordinate amounts of expensive land, and would further aggrandize the role of the car, a prospect that should be anathema to planners. In the long run, such freeway systems would be economically unfeasible for the same reasons that a similar rapid-transit system would be; high-cost facilities to serve low-density traffic.

Theoretically, the only way you could generate enough traffic to justify these systems would be to force new town people *not* to work in their own new town or in the city but in another town along the ring. But this would be a refutation of the new town ideal, and the worst of both possible worlds—suburbias without a city, a vision truly peripheral.

As the major answer to the growth problems of the metropolis, the new town concept is not practical. For the New York metropolitan area the Regional Plan Association has figured that to take care of the expected population growth over the next two decades via the new town route, one hundred new towns of 100,000 each would have to be built. This would take some doing and even if it were possible, the Association does not think it would be desirable. The result would be an extremely inefficient pattern, for the dispersal would rule out any effective mass-transportation system.

The Regional Plan Association believes that the heart of the growth problem is employment. The RPA is trying to encourage a concentration of industry and business in a relatively small number of centers; some would be new, some would be built on existing centers. There would be residential development around these centers, to be sure, but job and residence would not be tied together.

Access to jobs, not propinquity, is what is important. "For the same reason that people prefer to live and work in large metropolitan areas," says Stanley Tankel, RPA's planning director, "they are willing to trade a walk to work in a self-contained new town with its limited choice of jobs for a somewhat longer trip to work to a center where job choices abound. A region with deep and well-greased channels of transporation provides security of choice whether you are seeking work or workers."

In the new town scheme of things, people not only won't have to leave the town to go to work; they won't have to leave ever. The new towns are to provide total environments so encompassing, so beneficent that they will to a large extent eliminate the rootlessness and mobility of urban life.

somewhere else is sheer escapism. Building new towns can greatly improve suburbia but as a means of saving the city the movement is somewhat off-center—rather like taking a mistress, Robert Herman has observed, to improve relations with your wife.

And is the tangle so hopeless? It is hopeless if the measuring stick is perfection; it is hopeless if we demand a solution. There is no solution to the city. It is full of circumstances; some of them are good, some of them are bad, and as soon as one bad one seems about licked, others will crop up. That is the way of cities, and of people.

14. The Project Look

>>>

I have been arguing that the building of self-contained new towns is not a very good way to expand the metropolis. This is not to argue against building more and better large-scale developments and "planned communities." We are going to get them in any event. The trend is unmistakably toward the large-scale approach in land assembly and development, and it is a good trend. It is a much more efficient way of using land than the usual miscellany of small subdivisions, and a far more efficient way of providing housing and community services. Dollar for dollar, the planned communities that have been going up recently offer the homebuyer far more than he can get in conventional subdivisions and most of them are a lot better looking.

In the large-scale approach, however, there are large pitfalls. I am not referring to the misadventures that befall particular enterprises—these are inevitable—but to the recurring institutionalism which is the denominator of so many big projects. Stronger financial support will not solve this problem. More government aid for land assembly, long range master-planning, the setting up of quasi-public development corporations—such measures can help: They can also further institutionalize what ought most to be avoided. In drafting new legislation, we should bend over backward to see that the result is not, as so often has been the case with housing legislation, a set of Procrustean formulas which will maximize the disadvantages of project building and minimize the advantages.

The point I am going to make is much the same as the one I made about green belt and open-space planning. As the area covered by a plan grows in size, there is a change in the character of the plans as well as in the scale of them. We tend to accept as axiomatic that a large-scale master plan produces a far better result than a host of small plans. In some respects it does, but in some respects it does not, and the more comprehensive, detailed, sophisticated, and generally enlightened the plan, the greater the pitfalls that beckon.

The first is quite visible. Big housing projects tend to look like big housing projects. It does not seem to matter when they were put up or where. The phenomenon is quite international. Anyone who has made the standard pilgrimages to Vallingby and the new communities of England and Europe ends up, halfway through the journey, with the feeling that he has seen them all somewhere else before. There are exceptions. Projects of the dour Finns, for example, are wonderfully punctuated with cheerful splashes of color, and there is one that is an utter delight. But most of the new communities have an institutional grayness to them, and some are quite grim. The Danes, of all people, have put up a series of housing barracks outside Copenhagen almost as forbidding as those constructed by New York City.

All in all, however, it is the sameness, not the differences, that impress one. Whether the projects are built by a speculative builder or by a government agency, whether

they are animated by social impulses or the desire for
money, the layouts and the arrangement of space—even
down to the fanciful statuary—has the same recurring patterns.

Like all itinerant observers, I have accumulated a large
collection of 35 mm. slides of projects on my travels. Once
I had the misfortune of having them dumped from their
boxes and all mixed up together. When I tried to reassemble them I had an unexpectedly difficult time in distin-
guishing which were of what and where—indeed, in which
continent they belonged. They all looked the same as if
they were part of one gigantic project. The thought occurred to me of staging a puzzle show. To a select group
of the most knowledgeable architects and planners, the
slides would be shown in helter-skelter order and the contestants asked to guess what kind of projects they were
and where they might be located. A middle-income cooperative in the Bronx? A housing estate of the London
County Council? Workers' flats in a new industrial town
in Poland? Married officers' quarters at a model U.S. military base? Contestants would have trouble telling which
was which.

Signs, of course, are a giveaway. What they reveal,
however, is much more than the name of the project and
the language of the country. The frequency of signs and
the tone of them, I have found, are an excellent index of
the size of a project. For some reason, small projects seem
to be able to get along with comparatively few signs, but
as projects get bigger, the net density of signs per acre
goes up at a terrific rate and in very big projects they are
all over the place. *No Parking Allowed. These Stalls for
Bicycle Parking Only. Velocipedes Not Allowed in Playground. This Commons for Use of Residents Only.* Even
if you do not know the language they are written in, you
will get the general idea: No.

The same correlation can be found in design. One would
think that the individual units of a big project—a row of
town houses, for example—would be just as imaginatively
designed as if they were units of a small project. Indeed,

it could be argued that they should be more so in the big projects since there is more room for the designer to play around with, and the best of them are more likely to be chosen. It should work out this way, but it usually does not. The most felicitous examples of house design—in almost any category—are more often than not to be found in relatively small projects. And it is not necessarily that the architects of one kind are better than the architects of another; sometimes they are the same people.

There is a kind of institutionalism in the large-scale project, and it affects all who are bound up in it. Sometimes it takes the form of rigid external pressures on the designer. Public housing is the most extreme example of this. Until rather recently the legislative and administrative ground rules have been so detailed—they practically fill a volume the size of a phone book—that the architect has had most of the key design decisions made for him before he puts a hand to paper.

But the important pressures are more subtle. In some of the largest-scale projects an effort has been made *not* to saddle the planners and architects with rigid physical specifications; quite the contrary, they are given wide latitude and exhorted to come up with entirely fresh solutions. And there is the rub. Despite the freedom, or perhaps because of it, there is a predestination to the design.

Large-scale projects have philosophy. Sometimes it is explicit, sometimes it isn't. But quite early in the game, almost before the preliminary phase, certain basic assumptions will have been made and agreed upon by the members of the team. They may have agreed, for example, that the ideal neighborhood is that served by one elementary school, that there will be rigid separation of pedestrian and vehicular traffic, and so on. Since these assumptions happen to be fairly standard assumptions—international, indeed—the physical translation of them will be fairly standard too.

The size of the site will have a lot to do with the standardization. If the designers have to work with a small or odd-shaped site, they have insufficient space to give full expression to the model concepts. Model communities need lots of space, preferably flat space. You will note that whenever the hypothetical dream community is sketched, the site will appear to be as flat as a pancake and unsullied by difficult topography or previous habitation. There are no impedimenta to the total vision.

That is the trouble. As in theory, so in practice. The broader and cleaner the canvas, the more rigid and doctrinaire the design is apt to be. Government cities are a particular case in point. Brasilia, for example, is a striking architectural expression, but by all accounts it might have been a more livable place for human beings if the architect and planner had not had such a blank site to work with. The same has been said of Chandigarh in India and of Islamabad in Pakistan, "an abstract diagrammatic order," according to one critique, "rigidly applied to the landscape." Such judgments may be a bit harsh. Cities that are raw and new are not seen to good advantage and in time they may shake down into something more mellow and amenable. If history is a guide, however, this will be accomplished in large part by people doing that which the plans did not expect or wish them to do.*

Make no little plans, it is said, they have not the power to stir men's minds. Maybe so, but the admonition to make big plans can sometimes stir too much. The city of the future is an awesome commission to dangle before architects and planners and it can tempt them beyond their

* Brasilia demonstrates the capacity people have for subverting utopia. The original plan provided, among other things, that people in the same government agency or specialty would be grouped together in the same apartment blocks. But people did not like this arrangement and have subsequently been unsorting themselves into a more miscellaneous pattern. They have also been confounding the purity of the building façades by sticking out air conditioners and TV antennas. The temporary shanty towns surrounding the city have become permanent and now house more people than the city itself. It is reported that chief planner, Lucio Costa, is so appalled that he does not wish to visit Brasilia anymore.

area of competence. Architects and planners are fine people, but they are not especially good social philosophers; some, in a Dr. Jekyll and Mr. Hyde sort of way, are quite atrocious if they are asked to be. They may have done very sensitive and imaginative work; they may be very dedicated to "human scale"; they may detest the uniformity of projects, and would never live in one themselves. But ask them what they would do if they had free rein to design the complete city and the way they will respond will make your hair stand on end. Out comes the pencil. Swiftly and vigorously, a circle is drawn, or a square, or a triangle, or an amoeba shape. This is the basic cellular unit. Another is drawn, and then another. Lines interconnect them. Now all is in equilibrium and the optimum population reached. A big circle encloses everything. This is it. This is *the* form for living, the only rational approach, the deliverance from our urban chaos.

I am not arguing ad hominem. It is not the fault of architects and planners that they lack the capacity to create out of whole cloth the intricate mix of relationships that is a city. No one has that ability, not even a team, and were there more humility on this score, there would be less insistence on the blank slate.

The very constraints that architects and planners deplore can be a virtue. Architects seem to do their best work when they are faced with impossible situations—eccentric sites, ornery topography, buildings from another era to be encircled, abandoned pits. The new town of Cumbernauld in Scotland is a striking departure from the blandness of most British new towns—to the point of brutality in some respects—but what seems best about it stems from the challenge of the site, a hogback ridge partly made of old mine workings.*

* The original site proposed would have been even more challenging. Recently I asked Ian McHarg what he, as a Scotsman and as a landscape architect, thought of Cumbernauld. Ah, he said, there was a story. It so happened that it was McHarg himself that had been given the task of finding a site for Cum-

If we are going to provide government aid for stimulating new communities, it would be a good idea to attach a special premium to the development of difficult sites. This would, for one thing, provide a needed counteremphasis. The advantages of the large, virgin site are obvious enough but the search for such sites forces developers and planners to look further out to the periphery, for this is the only place where this kind of land still can be found.

They should be stimulated to look in the other direction. Developing new communities in areas closer to the city is enormously difficult. In total, there is plenty of land left for building, but the sites are odd-shaped, crisscrossed by roads, and encumbered with previous developments. Much of the bypassed land has been bypassed because of near-impossible soil conditions or sharp gradings. There is not enough room for utopia; because of high land cost, densities must be higher than in the ideal new community. The difficulties of the sites preclude the clean slate approach.

---

bernauld. The one that was finally chosen was not his first choice, but his second. The first was a hill that was really a hill, and positively magnificent: a large open ridge to the southwest of Glasgow. It had everything—good access, a beautiful view over the estuary of the Clyde, and a southwest exposure that would catch what sun there was to be caught. The only trouble was the slope. It was much too steep for ordinary building.

Why not, thought McHarg, terrace the town; every man's roof would be the next man's terrace and so on up the ridge. The density would be high, yet each person would have his own private view. Engineering feasibility studies were made and they demonstrated that it would be quite economical. This was an example of the best kind of innovation—not an exercise in innovation but a response to a particular and demanding situation. But innovation it certainly was, and the official whose approval was needed was disturbed. "It is too revolutionary," he told McHarg. "Why they haven't even tried something so new in England."

That night McHarg decided to take up an offer he had had to go to the United States to head up the Landscape Architecture Department at the University of Pennsylvania.

So much the better. The communities would be much more accessible to the metropolis. They would probably be much more attractive. The very constraints would impel imagination.

Another problem with very large projects is that they are often designed all at once, even though the parts will not be built until later. There is one great matrix and all the components have been detailed in conformity with the initial premises. Variety can be introduced later, but only the kind of variety that will fit.

The great disadvantage of the all-at-once design is that people must freeze on the concepts and assumptions of the particular moment. There is no space in time to acquire experience, to test various approaches, no provision for second thoughts, no opportunity to follow through on the happy accidents that always occur. Large-scale financing for large-scale projects will not be a boon if it encourages the all-at-once plan; if there is to be government support, it should deliberately encourage the messier, more accumulative kind of planning.

The stage-by-stage approach, by being spread over time, has the great advantage of the market mechanism. The plan is constantly being tested against the market, and discipline makes for a far better end result than any total vision will. Of necessity, of course, certain major commitments must be made at the beginning: the basic circulation pattern, for example, the trunk-line sewers, the location of the shopping centers and the industrial park. Similarly, the planners will have to commit themselves quite flatly to their assumptions in detailing the first stage of the development, even though it may be several years in the building. Beyond these initial steps, however, detailed planning should be deferred.

As soon as people start moving into the project, the lessons will come thick and fast. Some assumptions will be borne out. Some will not, and inevitably there will be surprises—a feature that can prove to be surprisingly popular or a feature that was designed for one function and turns out to be quite useful for another.

At the Baldwin Hills development in Los Angeles, perhaps the pleasantest features are the small redwood fenced patios. They were not in the original plan. Some were added later and they proved so popular that they were eventually added to all the garden units. Children's play areas, as I will note in the next chapter, rarely work out the way they were intended. At Park Forest, a fenced compound built for small children turned out to be an excellent recreational feature for the parents, who used it for their Saturday night parties; and during the week by the teen-agers, who used it to keep the young children out.

Another great advantage of the accumulative approach is that it enables planners to profit from a poor market. During the early years of most big projects, there comes a time when demand goes a bit soft. Temporarily the market for the entire area is saturated. This can be distressing financially, but it is at just such times that the most valuable lessons are learned.

As long as there are more customers than there are houses or apartments, anything goes, and all the assumptions of the developers and designers seem borne out. But there has been no real test. People have had no alternative, and their apparent preferences during a housing shortage can be very misleading. If the waiting list for a particular kind of unit gets too long, people who prefer that kind of unit will not bother to put themselves on the list but will choose the kind of unit they do not particularly like for the simple reason that they can get it, thereby giving proof to designers so inclined that this is what people want. Let the market go soft, however, and the situation can change very rapidly. The decline in demand does not have to be great; all that is needed is a margin of unsold units, for then choice becomes possible.

Speaking of his experience in the building of English new towns, Sir Frederic Osborn makes the point of how important it can be for good planning to be chastened by a temporary oversupply of dwellings. "Without such a margin," he says, "there can be no free market choices— either by renters or buyers. In our experience as estate developers, we recall two short periods when our production of dwellings locally outpaced demand, giving us a sharp lesson in the true preferences of homeseekers, which had a salutary influence on the types of dwellings we subsequently built."

The all-at-once design prevents planners from taking advantage of lessons even when they become apparent. For one thing, the lessons come too late. Secondly, even if they are not too late, the builders and the planners are sometimes so committed that they can't see the lessons when they stare them in the face. Some years ago, a large life-insurance housing development was completed in the San Francisco area. It consisted of groups of high-rise towers, supplemented by two-story duplex apartments arranged around interior patios. Despite the fact that there was a housing shortage in the area at the time, there was an extremely sharp difference in the demand for the two kinds of units. Most people did not want the tower units, and for over a year, several towers stood almost vacant. But the patio units, which, incidentally, were cheaper to build than the tower units, were a tremendous success. People lined up for them at such a rate that there was a waiting list at one time of at least a year.

The consumers could not have spoken more clearly about their preferences, but the company was not able to heed the lesson. It was convinced that the basic plan was right and it could not have shifted the balance to more patio units if it had wanted to. The whole thing had been built almost at once; not only that, the company was completing a virtually identical development in Los Angeles. The institutional momentum of a large project can be unstoppable.

Lack of market discipline is one of the reasons public-housing design has remained so sterile. Demand is assured. It is not merely that the housing projects are better than the slums they replace; there is nothing else in between. The consumers involved have no market sanctions to apply and thus all of those regulations for correct design are self-confirming. In actuality, as study after study has indicated, many of the design features work very poorly for people and have been working poorly for some decades. Still they are perpetuated.

The difficulties that developers have in getting adequate financing for large projects creates many problems. Most lending institutions are extremely conservative, and often insist on conventionality as a condition of their loans. I have seen several instances where the developer was willing to stick out his neck with a fresh and imaginative design but was forced to replace it with a hackneyed one to satisfy the lenders.

But the difficulty of getting money does have one good aspect. It restrains the developer from overplanning. Even those who have assembled a very large tract and are comparatively speaking well financed can rarely get hold of enough money to start the building of all the components, or even the planning of them. They will, of course, have a master plan and their promotional material is apt to give one the impression that it has been thought through down to the last detail; brochures for these projects are quite imaginative, and every element of the new experiment in total living will be attractively sketched. They tend to be somewhat more suggestive than descriptive, however.

The emphasis is on the *spirit* of the project and for good reason: Big projects are built on a pyramid of credit and the developer's ability to fill in the total blueprint depends on making a success of the first part of the project. This is where his chips are riding and he is not so committed to any final vision that he cannot zig and zag readily if things do not work out as expected. And they never do.*

* European developers seem less pragmatic on this score. Large projects, even when they are to be built in phases over a long period of time, tend to be planned in their entirety, and this is true of privately financed projects as well as government

The most instructive venture so far has been Reston, in Virginia's Fairfax County. Developer Robert Simon's concept for it had many aspirations and assumptions—some of them rather brave—but he wanted a master plan that would be flexible. Architect William Conklin sketched out a complex of seven villages, an industrial park, town center, and a network of open spaces. The first village center, to be built around an artificial lake, was planned in minute detail, but the outlines of the others were left blank. The hope was that each would have a distinctive quality, and together would offer a wide range of recreational facilities and styles of life.

To draw up exact plans for these later villages would take a good deal of money, however, and since there were enough questions for the marketplace as it was, Simon left the plan open-ended. As things turned out, it was good that he did.

---

ones. A conspicuous example is Paris Deux, a "nouvelle ville" being put up near Versailles. It is a source of much pleasurable indignation for many Frenchmen for at first glance it seems highly American. As with many American developments, the come-on facilities have been staged with great flair; a showy bazaar, "le drugstore," symbolizes the shops to come; the model units—condominium apartments—are artfully grouped around a swimming pool; in the sales pavilion scores of uniformed attendants channel the crowds and, much like the sales pattern in some of our senior citizen communities, the line of least resistance is toward the rows of "closing" cubicles.

But the plan is rigid. The down payments of the first customers are the leverage for financing the buildings to come, yet the developer has not hedged his bets by leaving any blanks in the plan. The number and proportion of the various type units offered have been set and all of the future buildings, of four stories and near-identical design, have been precisely sited. The market may bear him out, as it has done with similar projects on the outskirts of other European cities. To an American eye, however, this approach seems unnecessarily rigid; the result is bad aesthetically: It is also extremely vulnerable to any softening in demand. If it turns down, a lot of people may find themselves locked in some ghost new towns.

The first village, which was opened in 1965, is architecturally one of the most interesting new communities to be built anywhere. Simon is a man of taste, and strong convictions, but he is also an eclectic and while the plan has style and unity, it is also notable for its differences. There are, for example, three separate groups of town houses, each done by a different architect. One, by architect Chloethiel Smith, is homey and cheerful; another, by Charles Goodman, is urbane and severe. A third, by William Conklin and James Rossant, is midway in feeling; eminently contemporary, but reminiscent of a Mediterranean fishing port. A high-rise apartment tower serves as the focal point of the village.

An interesting innovation is the provision of two stories of apartment units over the shops of the village center. They were not put up because they seemed like a good market bet; it is a well-known fact in the business that apartments over stores do not rent well, and the experts told Simon he was out of his head to contemplate them. He still wanted them and the reason was aesthetic; looking at various shopping centers, he had noted that it is virtually impossible to have good architecture when the shopping buildings are only one story high. For the proper mass he wanted at least three stories, and apartments over the stores seemed to be the answer. They were a great market success.

Surrounding the village were lots for detached houses. Simon left the building of these up to the purchasers, but did set strict architectural controls. He also sold several tracts for development by local builders. The results were not entirely felicitous. The design of some of the houses were stringently conventional and greatly dismayed the architectural critics. One particular group of houses dismayed the village residents as well. In this section a local builder put up a group of overblown colonial mansions, locally referred to as the "Taras." This created a small ruckus. The townhouse people felt that many of the detached houses were not quite Reston and the "Taras" most definitely not. Such houses are indeed somewhat out of tune, but even this kind of difference is not without merit. The danger in a model community like this is that it ends up in such excessively good taste that it does not look quite real. A touch of bad taste gives relief.

Simon got overextended, and at the worst possible time. The houses in the first village sold, but they did not sell fast enough to return the kind of cash flow that was needed to keep up the carrying charges on such a large enterprise. Simon's land holdings were going way up in value, but earlier he had had to put them up as security for loans, and the rise in paper values produced no cash.* The tightening of money in 1966 aggravated matters, and some of the local subdividers were so pinched they had to suspend operations.

Another problem was the relative inaccessibility of Reston. It should have been the easiest of places to get to. The new freeway to Dulles Airport runs right through the middle of the Reston tract, and it is nearly empty of traffic. The Federal Aviation Authority, however, refused to open up an access road. It may have to sometime in the future, but that is not the time Simon needed it. During the crucial

---

* One of the greatest problems the developers of very large tracts face is their inability to properly capitalize the rising value of their land. They profit best by holding on to each parcel until it is ready to develop, but heavy carrying charges force their hand. If a developer buys land at say $1000 an acre and a year later sells one of the acres at $1500, he has a cash return to show, and this is very important for keeping creditors satisfied. But if he has land that he wishes to hold for later development or sale, the bookkeeping does not work out so well. Several years later this land could be worth $10,000 an acre, but this future appreciation will not help very much in producing cash to pay interest and taxes. If he has enough money of his own to hold out until the property fully appreciates, he would be in very fine shape indeed. Not many developers do have the money and a number have been forced to liquidate land holdings of great potential value just as the game was beginning to get interesting.

first years, people had to beat their way to Reston by back roads.

In 1967, Gulf Oil, Simon's principal backer, moved in to protect its investment. They put their man in charge of Reston and pushed Simon out. The new man made it known that there would be a harder-nosed approach, and that while Gulf Oil was going to follow the general lines of the master plan, there was going to be much more attention to the marketplace and the styles it favored.

Simon came a cropper, some people now say, because he aimed too high, and they argue that all this proves that advanced architecture and townhouse cluster design won't go in suburbia. This is nonsense. Tight money, not good architecture hurt Reston. Certainly mistakes were made— if anything, Simon was not eclectic enough—but he has made a great and probably lasting contribution. One of the most fascinating things about the growth of any town or city is the way the design of its first component and the settlers it attracts, largely determines the character of the community's growth for generations to come. So, in all likelihood, will it be with Reston.

James Rouse's Columbia differs from Reston in several ways. Its location, astride a main Baltimore–Washington highway in Maryland's Howard County, is more central. It has stronger long-term financing and a more market-oriented approach to design. Rouse is a man of taste too, but he has a low opinion of most architects and places less emphasis on urbane flavor or architectural distinction for his housing. He is farming out most of the residential development to other builders. The core of his effort is industrial development and the construction of a regional commercial center. It will be a very big center and though a handsome one, frankly suburban. The villages will provide a captive market for it but Rouse aims to tap the whole surrounding region as well.

The master plan is a mixture of innovation and pragmatism. Like Reston's, it features a system of villages and weaves the open space into the villages as well as around

them. There is also an artificial lake. The villages, however, are to be unabashedly middle-class. Each will be
centered around an elementary school rather than a town
plaza. A system of minibuses operating on their own rights-
of-way will connect the villages and the main center. Save
for the first components, the plan is quite open ended. The
villages to be built later are only sketched in as zones on
the map.

Reston and Columbia are the vision of two unusual men,
and are not easily reproduced elsewhere. But for all the
singularities, and vicissitudes, they provide excellent prototypes for future community development. They are heralded as new towns, but the reason they have universality
is that they do not bear out the specifications of the ideal
new town. For one thing, they are not going to be self-
contained or independent, nor are they going to be life-
cycle communities. What they promise to be are first rate
communities in the suburbs.

Both are close to the city—Reston is sixteen miles from
Washington; Columbia, fourteen miles from Baltimore.
Both will in time provide many residence-based jobs, but
they are going to be commuter towns also. The moving
vans, furthermore, will be constantly in and out. The
capital area has an especially impermanent job structure,
and as long as we keep holding periodic elections, there
will be a lot of residence turnover, voluntary and otherwise.

It is because they are in the thick of the metropolis that
Reston and Columbia are so worth watching, and in the
trials of the stage-by-stage approach may lie the most
significant lessons. These projects are going to be a long
time abuilding and there will undoubtedly be many lean
periods and unexpected market changes to adapt to before
they ever come near their target populations.

The best demonstration of the eclectic approach is the
Finnish new town of Tapiola, six miles from Helsinki. It is
a stunning place, cheerful and lively—a project that does
not look like a project—and as is generally the case with
such anomalies, the reason is a man. The creator of Tapiola

is Heikki von Hertzen, a lawyer-banker who enjoys people
and who thinks the cardinal sin of new towns is conformity
and dullness. He had long agitated against the standard
barracks design planners had favored for housing projects,
and when he seized the opportunity to build Tapiola, he
was determined to try a fresh and flexible approach.

Tapiola was not designed all at once. The master plan,
by Aarne Ervi, allowed great leeway to architects in the
design of the components. Von Hertzen used many architects and he encouraged them to experiment. There is a
unity—everything seems to be white—but there are all
kinds of houses and apartment buildings, and for blue-
collar as well as white-collar people. The parts are nicely
tied together by a handsome town center, the focal point
of which is a sort of artificial "moon," a large illuminated
object atop the tallest building. Von Hertzen is also a
showman.

He is so persuasive an evangelist that it is easy to overlook some of Tapiola's limitations as a model for U.S. new
towns. Its density is unusually low (about twenty-six
people per acre). It has a self-imposed population limit of
twenty thousand people, and it is, for all its delights, essentially a suburb. But it is a splendid demonstration just
the same. What it proves most signally is that the flexible,
step-by-step, approach is absolutely vital if a place is to
have humanity and esprit, and perhaps a touch of humor.

Housing experts hope that Congress will provide massive
financing support so that new towns can be built here without having to suffer lengthy gestations. Such aid could be a
boon; it could also undercut the necessity for the flexible,
accumulative approach. The history of public housing and
urban redevelopment has demonstrated that there is
reason to be apprehensive on this score. The idealists who
pushed through the initial legislation did not want stereotyped design. They did not want a mass of regulations
built up that would make any fresh approach virtually
illegal. But that is the way it worked out for many long
years. The same thing could happen to a new town pro-

gram. Unless great care is taken to anticipate the pitfalls, it probably will happen.

Massive aid should not mean massive projects. It should be a condition of government grants or mortgage insurance for land assembly and planning that the master plans *not* be complete; that they deliberately leave blank spaces; that they hew to a stage-by-stage procedure; that they encourage the widest possible variety of design approaches and types of housing. It will also help if the incentives are not saddled with too much idealism. It does not institution-alize very well. Perhaps in time the new-town advocates will prove the rightness of self-containment, optimum populations, and the completely balanced community. I doubt it, but if there is to be a variety of approaches, they ought to have a crack at theirs. Let it not be the standard, however. The important task is encouraging better com-munity development in the here and now, and there are lessons aplenty in the here and now.

And in the past. Let me conclude by citing the develop-ment of eighteenth-century London. Some of the entre-preneurs who put up the residential squares we think so attractive today were jerry-builders and rascals but some were extremely gifted planners. Reading John Summerson's *Georgian London,* one is struck with how sophisticated they were in the handling of large projects. Samuel Pepys Cockerell, who supervised the subdivision of the Foundling Hospital's extensive holdings in the Bloomsbury area, is a good example. Here are the guidelines he laid down in 1790; the master plan should embrace housing units for all classes: The focal points should be the residential squares and their gardens; the projects should be planned so that their edges blend with the existing neighborhoods; the plan should be amenable to step-by-step development so "that each part may be complete in itself and not de-pendent for its success and a return of profit to the under-takers upon the execution of the others."

Those who would draft guidelines for modern project planning could hardly do better.

15. Play Areas and Small Spaces

>>

In visiting various housing developments, I have been puzzled by a curious fact about children's play areas. The children seem to play somewhere else. Developers and architects have repeatedly assured me that this could not be so. Often they have pointed to awards given for the excellence of the design; they have shown me stacks of house photos of the play areas, invariably jammed with children. Surely I must have visited at the wrong time of day.

Maybe some happenstance was involved, but I am persuaded by what I have seen, and in the majority of developments that I have studied, the formal play areas are comparatively unused, and this is true of middle-income projects as well as public housing. I arrived at this conclusion inadvertently, by trying to take pictures myself. I wanted pictures of the play areas being used. Time after time, however, it seemed to be the wrong time. Occasionally the areas would be full of children; but more often there would be barely a quorum, and sometimes no children at all. Infants, who have no free choice in the matter, might be there with their mothers; but to find the children, you do best to look somewhere else.

Look for them where they are not supposed to be. They go where things are going on—in the streets, in the alleys, in the parking courts. Here is where the deliverymen come to unload, where father washes the car on weekends, and where the children have the most room for wheeling around on their own vehicles.

This mixture of traffic is exactly what planners have sought most to avoid, and if there is a hallmark of modern project design, it is the separation of the children's play areas from the vehicular and adult traffic. The original Radburn design is still the most encompassing in this respect, but most of the new projects have the play areas tucked into the interior of the project, and through the use of fences and other separators, the play areas are carefully isolated from contact with the traffic stream, and frequently, from the surrounding neighborhood as well.

There is logic to this, but it is not necessarily the logic of the children. At Radburn, for example, the children do play in the large open commons, but their most intense activity seems to take place in the parking alleys, and spaces between the houses; a fact that drives some fathers crazy, particularly on weekends. ("I don't get it," one said to me. "Here is all this wonderful green space for them, and why do they have to make a racket here.") At Park Forest, two-story garden apartment units were grouped so that all the cars would be contained in interior parking courts, leaving the grassy areas on the front sides of the buildings free for the children. The design has worked well, but not quite as expected. The children do not use the safe grassy areas very much; they use the parking courts.

Children want the right-of-way, and they will get it. When they are on velocipedes and bicycles, they look for hard surfaces, and hard surfaces that go somewhere. A few projects do provide a fairly continuous cycle network, sometimes with Radburn style underpasses, but in most projects, the hard surfaces for cars provide the network and this is what the children use. They can be quite tyrannical about it too, as deliverymen know. If there are enough children, they will dominate the traffic.

Their patterns are worth following. We have elaborate techniques for measuring origins and destinations of people in cars, but children's vehicular traffic has received little attention. I have made no systematic study myself, but simple observation will demonstrate that this traffic tends to follow certain recurring patterns and that there are good reasons for it. (Why not a study of children's traffic by children? They see much that we do not.)

One clue to the pattern is the door of the house that is the real door. In many developments, the back door is the only one that is ever used; in others because of the placement of streets, the front door is the origin of the journeys. From project to project, the routes that children take vary a great deal, depending on such factors as the location of the school, the nearest store, the available short cuts, and the kaffeeklatsch itineraries of the mothers. Once these patterns are established, however, they tend to be quite regular, and they have a very strong bearing on how the open spaces and play facilities of the project are used. If the spaces and facilities are along these traffic routes, the children will use them quite heavily; as distance increases, the use falls off markedly.

This seems to be a fairly universal phenomenon. Several years ago, to cite an English example, children's playgrounds became quite a problem in Welwyn Garden City. The children were not playing where they were supposed to. In an uncommonly tolerant report, the local planners made this observation: "Children, being unaware of planning principles, continue to play happily wherever the mood or game of the moment takes them. Like dogs, the other source of complaint, they roam wherever the leader of the pack takes them. It so happens that both children and dogs leave the house by the front door, and children with their friends tend to wander off to some place visible or easily approached from the front of the house. It also happens that playgrounds or garage areas approached or seen from the main road are those most used. A piece of grass adjoining a road gets more use than an apparently better and more expensive piece of grass in the rear of the buildings—even if this is baited with swings and seesaws."

There is a need, of course, for informal play areas, but too many of them seem designed for a sort of all-purpose child. For one thing, they do not distinguish enough between the needs of the young and the very young. There doesn't have to be too many years of age difference to produce frictions. Children between six and twelve, for example, will push the others around if they don't have room for their games, and they usually don't. Most play areas tend to be too small for them; too large for the younger ones.

Fences are another anomaly. They are usually most evident where they are least needed. Most of the children in the fenced play areas are taken there by their mothers and if there is no play director around, there are always several adults. Fences do have their uses, but it is interesting how often they serve quite different uses than the designer had in mind.

In such uses, or misuses, are cues for future designs. But the designers rarely see them. They do not, as a practice, go back and study how children actually use their projects, or how adults do, for that matter.* If they do go back, they can suffer from a strong occupational capacity to see what they believe. I recall visiting a small project with the

---

* One exception is planner Clarence Stein. In revising his *New Town for America,* he has called attention to some of the ways people have used planned communities differently than he and his fellow planners expected them to. He thinks the people are usually right. In noting the use of Radburn's lanes as play areas, he says: "I have studied the reasons for this so that in the future we might keep children and autos apart to an even greater degree. We will never do so completely, nor do I think we should attempt to. The spirit of adventure should not be extinguished."

man who had designed it. He was especially proud of the
play area, which had been pictured in the leading architectural magazines. It was very good looking, and had an
elegant piece of free-form sculpture as its centerpiece. At
the time we were there, however, the play area was absolutely empty. Nearby, there was a tremendous hubbub in
an alley filled with old crates left behind by a contractor.
This is where the children were. But the designer was not
in the least discomfited. He was looking at his play area,
and in his mind's eye, I suspect, the children were clambering all over the free-form sculpture. Quite the best
thing he had done, he told me.

I am not arguing that non-planned places are better
than planned ones. But there are enough such instances
to make it clear that it is not simply for lack of an alternative that children so often use the non-planned places.
They actively seek them—in part out of sheer perversity,
being children, but for some quite sensible reasons as well.

Consider the maligned street. People are always talking
about taking children off the street, as though it were
self-evident that the street is the lowest form of recreation.
It is certainly true that one of the reasons children use
streets so much is that in many neighborhoods there is
not much else available. But the street has positive values.
As its foremost champion, Jane Jacobs, has pointed out,
the very congestion and mixture of activities that many
people deplore are important attractions for children.

They like the concentration. Fenced-in play streets get
extremely heavy play, even when there are playgrounds
nearby. So do streets that are not fenced. Their traffic
presents all sorts of dangers, but it is instructive to watch
how children respond to them. One thing that never ceases
to amaze me is the way kids play touch football on Third
Avenue on the Upper East Side of New York. The timing
is almost choreographic. They not only have the game to
think about, but through the corner of their eye they have
to watch the traffic lights and the rhythm of the oncoming
traffic. In one sense it is the scene of deprivation, and they
deserve better. But is there not something here of value?

Follow children and there are lessons to be learned. They like clutter, forbidden clutter best of all, and they show a marked antipathy to barriers and signs telling them what not to do. Planners cannot be too permissive about all this or there would be no peace for the adults. But the children's impulses are not wholly perverse, and a site plan that takes them into account can be quite effective.

One of the best public-housing projects in the country is Easter Hill, outside of San Francisco. The site was a rocky hillside, but rather than bulldoze it away, architects Vernon DeMars and Donald Hardison left the rocks pretty much as they were, and although they did provide some playground equipment, they conceived the hill site as something of a playground itself. Those who like the order of the standard project find it messy, but children love it. They roam all over—there are no chains—and the place has an amiable quality.

There are many other reasons why topography should be exploited much more than it has been. Aside from their attraction for children, rocks and hillocks make a much more interesting layout, and if nature doesn't provide them, the developer can. It is often more economic for him to do this than not to. It costs him money to haul the overburden away; with less expenditure he can make it into an asset; though, as I have noted, imagination is also required and not much has been shown. Central Park can still teach us lessons on this score. It seems like a vast expanse, but thanks to the way that Olmsted and Vaux worked with the terrain, at eye level it is a series of spaces, some of them quite intimate.

Places like Easter Hill are exceptional. In most housing projects, private as well as public, the play areas appear to be designed by administrators. Administrators who dislike children. Everything is geared for order and ease of maintenance, and signs and fences are clearly meant to keep the little beggars at bay. Some of the play areas look like small prison compounds, and not wholly by inadvertence.

Municipal and school playgrounds are marked by the

same institutional stamp. There is the inevitable expanse of asphalt: the cyclone fences, the standardized swings, and sliding boards and steel climbing bars. Another constant is the absence of trees. Children like trees, particularly the kind with branches low enough that they can climb. But trees mean hazard to the administrator and they require additional maintenance work. So there are no trees.

Nor is there dirt. One would think there would be lots of it. It is very cheap. It is highly malleable, and it cushions falls. Dirt is one of the reasons that vacant lots are so beguiling to children. There are so many things they can do with it. Digging, for example; when children have the earth to work with, it is amazing the foot pounds of energy they will expand in creating elaborate tunnels and caves and earthworks of various kinds. Yet this kind of recreation is rarely countenanced in park programs.

Children ought to have some "soft" parks and they ought to have areas that are purposely left undesigned and undeveloped. Philadelphia, which has one of the most imaginative city recreation programs in the country, provides a good example. In its plan for the far northeast area, the planners saved a whole series of wooded creek valleys that wind throughout the heart of the new developments. The planners and the recreation people are purposely leaving a good bit of this untouched. They are providing a full range of such facilities as tennis courts and baseball diamonds, but they are also making sure the children will have places that they can go explore on their own, and with no one around to blow whistles. The adults who first settled in the development were less permissive; being city-bred they tended to view woods as danger areas, and some forbade their children from playing in them. The children, of course, have been adapting to the environment on their own terms. They like these unkempt sanctuaries.

Perhaps the most celebrated examples of the open-end approach are to be found in the "adventure playgrounds" created in England. Most of these are on derelict areas, and they are very, very cluttered. In some, for example,

piles of lumber and old car hulks are provided, and it is
left entirely up to the children how to use them. In effect,
the children play by constructing their play facilities. By
all conventional standards, these areas should be extremely
unsafe. So far, however, the record indicates there are
fewer accidents in them than in the conventional playgrounds.

Now at last there is the beginning of a revolution in
playground design in this country. It is being fomented in
large part by a number of private groups and foundations.
In addition to badgering city governments into better
design, they have been providing seed money for prototype
projects and have given some top architects and landscape
architects a chance to show what can be done with
relatively small spaces.

Few of these areas are adventure playgrounds in the
unfettered English sense—adults do the designing here;
the children take over later—but in spirit as well as detail
they are a radical departure from the stereotyped playground. Instead of conventional equipment, they provide a
maze of forms—igloos made of stone, tunnels and pipes to
crawl through, tree houses and latticelike wooden forms.
Instead of grass and asphalt, they use combinations of
various kinds of textured paving, wood chips, and sand.
They also do wonderful things with water. In the usual
playground, there may be one spray area or wading pool
but that is about it. In the new ones, water really cir-
culates; it jets out of pipes or fountains, splashes down
walls, runs through labyrinthine sluiceways, and then back
again.

The basic design has great universality. It seems to work
for the clientele of one kind of neighborhood as well as
another, and the designers do not need a clean slate to
work with. Some of the best of the new play areas are
transformations of the institutional spaces of conventional
housing projects. The most notable example is the job
that has been done in the Jacob Riis public-housing project
on Manhattan's Lower East Side. Its central open space,
which has been one of the dreariest of such expanses, has

been refashioned by landscape architect M. Paul Friedberg and the architectural firm of Pomerance and Breines into four separate "outdoor rooms." One is a sunken amphitheater, which does double duty as a place for events, and in the summer, a gigantic spray area. The place is very attractive; it is, in fact, downright chic, and were it luxury housing the residents would consider themselves lucky to have such a commons. The people who live there, however, are low-income people, principally Negroes and Puerto Ricans, and they like it very much. Certainly the children do. They do not seem to mind good design.

In some playgrounds the design gets just a bit arty, and one or two have been flops. But most of them work extremely well. Children like the free-form equipment, for it becomes whatever they imagine it to be, and they imagine no end of things. It is fascinating to see the infinite variety of games and situations they contrive out of these objects and how much more drawn to them they are than to standard equipment. A nearby conventional playground may be nearly vacant, but in a new one children will be splashing, crawling, jumping, shouting, and in such concentration that you wonder why they aren't colliding and fighting more.

This jam-packedness is probably the most remarkable feature of these areas. Square foot for square foot, they handle an extraordinary number of children—far more so than most play areas—and so consistently as to suggest that the sheer density of the traffic is one of the reasons they work so well. Why, for example, aren't there more accidents? In spite of the sand and the soft surfaces, these places certainly *look* dangerous. There are numerous places to fall from, and with all the jostling and clambering about, children have to exercise a radarlike perception to keep from banging themselves up. Maybe this is why they don't bang themselves up much.

Apparent danger is a safety factor. In conventional playgrounds the equipment is full of built-in hazards—tumbles from the eight-foot top of a steel sliding board, clouts from the arc of a swing. Because of the conventionality, children tend to underestimate the hazards. Not so in the new play-grounds. The equipment poses obvious challenges, and it seems to put children on their mettle.

The smallness of the space is another safety factor. In conventional playgrounds, the large expanses of asphalt give children plenty of room to build up a full head of steam. In the adventure playgrounds, however, the spaces are so small, and so full of intervening objects, that the children are forced to decelerate before velocities get out of hand.

Some observers think that there has been too much emphasis on design, not enough on personnel. We have much, they say, still to learn from the Europeans on this score. Attractive as many of their playgrounds are, they concentrate less on equipment than on having good people show children how to get the most out of the equipment. Our park budgets are woefully short in providing for such people, or for any kind of people, for that matter.

Our park budgets are woefully short in almost every respect, of course, and while they are a matter for local government, the federal government has unwittingly con-tributed to the problem. Its grants-in-aid for parks are, like almost all its grants, for capital expenditures, not opera-tions. Since cities have to dig up matching money of their own to get the grants, they have that much less money for adequate supervision and maintenance. One of the best recommendations of the President's Task Force on Natural Beauty, made by Jane Jacobs, was that the federal govern-ment begin giving grants for park operations; in return, cities would set up programs for training young people in park and recreation work. The recommendation did not get anywhere. But its time will come.

The popularity of some of the new small play areas does not prove that smallness per se is an advantage; most of the spaces are small because there was not any more space available. They do prove, however, that we can wring a great deal more usefulness from limited areas than con-ventional recreation space standards suggest. And this is something we are going to have to do. More big parks should be sought, but the plain fact is that cities do not have the money for much of this kind of acquisition. If they are to provide more recreational facilities, the cities will have to turn increasingly to the so called "vest pocket" parks, and make much more effective use of vacant lots and odd-shaped spaces.

Old-line park officials do not think much of vest-pocket parks. They say that the spaces are too small to be useful, are extremely difficult to maintain, and are a prey to vandalism. But what is the alternative? Many small spaces do present more administrative problems than several big ones, but they can be made to work where officials want them to work. The principal lesson is that there has to be a sort of critical mass: the parks have to be distributed throughout the city, and there have to be enough of them in any one neighborhood so that a group can be serviced and maintained by one man. It is also important that the people of the neighborhood be thoroughly involved in the program. Where vest-pocket parks have failed, neither condition has been met; they have been isolated, and there has been no continuing neighborhood involvement in either the planning or the operation. Where there has been, as in Philadelphia's program, there are still plenty of maintenance problems, but by and large the parks have worked well for people.

Another kind of small space that is very much needed is the midtown parklet for office workers and shoppers. There is no lack of small open spaces in the heart of our cities, but almost all of them are used as parking lots. To use them for people instead would, of course, cost a great deal of money, but by the very fact of being located in the highest traffic areas, they could provide immense benefits. The best example is the small park donated by Samuel Paley for midtown New York—fashioned, appropriately enough, on a site previously occupied by a night club. The park is only 42 feet by 100 feet and cost over $1 million, but it is one of those wonderful amenities that is really without a price. Landscape architect Robert Zion,

who had long advocated just such an experiment, has cap-
italized on the surrounding buildings to create an outdoor
room with a comfortable sense of enclosure. The whole
rear wall of this room is a waterfall, and the sound of it,
which mutes the street noises and delights the ear, makes
the term "oasis" entirely appropriate. Another feature that
ought to be copied is the use of chairs—comfortable chairs,
the kind you can pick up and move.

To bespeak the importance of small parks is not to dep-
recate the importance of big ones. In their enthusiasm
for parklets, some people have suggested that it would
have been better for New York had the same amount of
land taken up by Central Park been parceled out in the
form of lots of small parks throughout the city. What we
should have had, of course, was both. (The civic leaders
who put through Central Park were eager for other park
areas, and had not the real-estate lobby intervened, today
there would have been some magnificent stretches of
woods and shoreline parks along the East River.) But the
mass of Central Park is vital to the city. We could never
fashion something like it again.

At the moment, however, more small spaces are what
cities need most. They are an achievable goal and through
reconstruction and clearance, and plenty of citizen support,
we can gain them. Hopefully, one of these days we might
have gained so many of them that people will begin to
suggest that the city would be better off if the same
amount of land had been purchased for a really big park.
But that is a bridge we do not have to cross yet.

Landscape Action

16. The Plan of the Landscape

>>

In the preceding chapters I have discussed two parts of the landscape—open space and developed space. Now I want to turn to the effect of the two together—the landscape as people perceive it. This is not to be comprehended by maps or models or tables of acreage figures. Open space, for example, and the effect of open space are not quite the same, and while the former is helpful for the latter, effect is more important. The landscape is a mass of perceptions, and it is this reality—the image in the retina of the eye—that we must comprehend. In large part, we are dealing with illusion and it is good that we are. If it is true that we cannot save vast swaths of pure countryside, we are going to have to get much more out of the smaller spaces and the bits and pieces that we can save.

To overstate the case, we must contrive the landscape. I am not going to argue that we should try and hoodwink people with false-front greenery or that we should prettify away the factories and refineries. An urban landscape should be urban. But there must be artifice in its construction, showmanship, and even some visual sleight of hand. Only now are we beginning to tackle the job, but if we attend to it well, the more crowded landscape of tomorrow can be made more pleasing, more expansive, more green, than the relatively more open one of today.

No technological breakthrough is necessary—the spade and the saw have been invented. What is necessary is a systematic effort by communities to look at their landscapes—as most people see them most of the time. Once this effort is started, a host of exciting opportunities will become apparent—for the landscape of suburbia and beyond, and for the approaches and riverfronts and downtowns of the city itself. Some of the opportunities require money, lots of it. But many are tremendous trifles—the brook by the side of the road you do not see for the second growth, the wall that hides the skyline. This is not the grand-sweep approach to regional design, but in the aggregate, it is the host of small pictures and the perception of them that is, for people, the true regional design.

The difference between open space and the effect of it was brought home to me in a tour I made of Connecticut. Earlier, I had worked up a proposal for a state grant program for local open-space acquisition; the legislature had passed it, and it had gotten off to a good start. I wanted to visit as many of the specific spaces as possible to see what had been accomplished.

It was satisfying to see how many fine tracts had been saved and to what good recreational use they were being put. Yet the tour was vaguely disappointing, and at first I could not figure out why. Then I began to realize that the trouble was visual. Unless you sought them out, you would not be aware many of the spaces existed. The spaces are certainly important, but saving them is not enough. They ought to be seen, and this calls for a kind of landscape-development approach we have never really attempted. Without such an effort, even a doubled acquisition program would only make a small dent on the appearance of the community and of the region and of the state.

Our countryside is becoming a hidden countryside. One problem, of course, is the way commercial and residential development and billboards have sealed off the countryside. But just as great a one is the greenery. There is too much of it. As farms are being abandoned, they are reverting to second growth, and in New England the process is so far advanced that there is more woodland today than there was in colonial times. Statistically, this makes the open-space equation very satisfactory, and it all looks fine from a plane. On the ground the effect is something else again. In the first place, the woodland is dull. Perhaps mine is too subjective an impression, but most of the new forest growth is oppressively green and monotonous to drive past, and the neat pine plantations that foresters like are downright hypnotic. You feel as though you are going through a tunnel, and no end is in sight.

More important is what the second growth hides. Many a view of a valley from a hillside has been walled off by a mass of nondescript greenery; open meadows of only a few years ago have disappeared, and many that still remain open have a sadly derelict appearance. There will be the carcasses of several abandoned cars, and here and there you will see the forerunners of reversion—scattered cypress, saplings, a patch of weeds.

If you poke down the side roads you can find plenty of good scenery left to enjoy, and the fortunate people who have farms and country estates enjoy it very much. For the great majority of people, however, the views simply do not exist.

On the edges of the cities there are still enclaves of countryside with great scenic potential that should be tremendously enjoyable but that are not because people do not see them. The most beautiful expanse of open space in New England is the Glastonbury Meadows, a natural expanse of parklike pasture land bordering the Connecticut River, complete with white steeples in the background. Here, only six miles from downtown Hartford, is the epitome of what the New England landscape should look like.

But a landscape is not beautiful if you do not see it. Few people know about the Meadows. You cannot see them from the river because of the tangle of thickets that have grown up along the banks, nor can the drivers on a nearby new freeway catch more than a glimpse. Even in Glastonbury, I found, many people have never seen the Meadows, let alone walk on them.

Such lack of visual access can have an important bearing on acquisition programs. The sight of open space is only one benefit, but with the competition for land so intense, it can be the critical one. The fact that people may not have enjoyed the view of a tract may help to keep it unspoiled; it also makes it very vulnerable. When commercial exploitation becomes imminent, there will be no base for public counteraction. In the case of Glastonbury, a fine conservation commission is at work drumming up interest; in many another area, however, such spaces are being lost by default. At two minutes to midnight estate owners and conservationists will sound the alarm. A save-the-such-and-such-place committee will be formed; there will be petitions, letters to the editor. But it will be too late. Most citizens will not have cared. And why should they? They did not know what they were losing.

Another thing that strikes you in a reconnaissance of the landscape is how a few elements in a scene can color the perception of the whole. In Connecticut there is a particularly pleasant scene from the Wilbur Cross Parkway as you slow down for the toll station at Wallingford. There is a pond by the side of the road and beyond it the buildings of Wallingford and a tall church steeple. It is a lovely pause, very reminiscent of a Constable painting.

The view does not bear close inspection. Most of the buildings are late nineteenth century commercial, the church is nondescript Gothic, and the pond is a slough of mud and weeds. But the driver does not make a close inspection. From his perspective the scene is handsome, one of those visual mileposts drivers look forward to and remember. A number of people who are now residents of Wallingford say they got the idea of moving there because of this sight of it.

Another example of effect is the Taconic Parkway running north from New York. Many people believe it is the most pleasant parkway in the East, and if you ask them why, they will tell you that it is because most of it runs through magnificent stretches of open farmland. But it does not. Only a small portion runs through farmland; the greater part is bordered by woodland, so tightly so along some stretches as to give the claustrophobic effect people complain of in other parkways. But the farmland makes a vivid impression. There is one particularly striking view as you emerge from a forested section and see before you a sweep of rolling meadowland with old farms and barns and silos. It is these intermittent Grandma Moses scenes that people remember; and though in total there are only a few miles of them, in the mind's eye they set the character of thirty or forty miles.

Conversely, just a little blight can make an area seem desecrated when in fact it is not. Roads along ridge lines are especially susceptible. They may afford a view of miles of unspoiled countryside, but it is apt to be punctuated by automobile graveyards, roadhouses and the kind of premature frontage development marked by concrete bungalows and plaster flamingos. For all the openness and beauty of 99 percent of the scene, the foreground is so obtrusive it becomes the 99 percent. Along such roads you can get less the feel of space than you do in many a more densely developed area of suburbia.

In these disproportions lie great opportunities. If relatively small elements of the scene have such a leverage effect, relatively small actions can too. A scenic clearing to open up a meadow, a row of sycamores planted along a river bank, a screen of signs removed at the crest of a hill: Individually, such projects seem trivial. In sum, they can have a major impact on the environment.

But these tremendous trifles fall in a no-man's land as far as government jurisdiction is concerned. Who is to attend to them? Talk about the possibilities with officials, and most will agree that such action would be a great idea. But their department does not have the franchise. And where is the money for the job? There are programs for acquiring land; there are programs for developing it for recreation. There are programs for getting farmers to plant trees. There is no program, however, for the landscape as a whole, and similar as the purposes might be, landscape projects fall between all of the other programs.

Nor is there machinery for unifying such projects. Planning agencies are the logical vehicle, but when it comes to the landscape most of them suffer an operational defect. They do not look at it. The view of the region is the bird's-eye view, the view of the model, of the aerial mosaic, and it is once or twice removed from the ultimate reality of the region as people see it. The same is true of the landscape of the city. Of all the tons of studies done of our cities, it is rare to find any that attempt to discern the city as most people see it. The perspective is from aloft. Characteristically, sketches of projects or park plans or bridges show what they would look like from a helicopter several thousand feet in the air. Most people are not up there.

Proponents of the bird's-eye view can argue that with the increase in plane travel the aerial perspective is becoming more a part of people's everyday experience. So it is, and at night the brilliantly lit shopping centers and cloverleafs and highways are strikingly visible and one can get a sense of metropolitan structure. For some reason, however, most regular plane travelers do not seem very interested. Save on landing and takeoff, they are buried in their papers or magazines. On transcontinental flights an unusually chatty captain may get tourists to the windows at the Mississippi and some other spots, if they are not watching the movie. The only time most regular travelers look out, however, is if the plane happens to be crossing over Yosemite Valley.

Planners and architects have their own kind of myopia. In seizing on the larger perspective, they see structure and form that most people do not. This is what they are supposed to do, but the corollary too often is that they overlook the smaller-scaled pictures that people do see.* As persons, planners are an observant lot by and large, and I know several who can analyze very sensitively the minutest aspects of the local scene, at human eye level. But this seems to be in too many cases an extra-curricular exercise; it is not part of the regular planning process.

Why not provide a carrot? In thinking over the unexplored potentials in Connecticut, it occurred to me that the state could provide the catalyst with a program of landscape-

* For a revealing account of how this lofty perspective can mislead the best of architects, let me quote from a paper by Harry Antoniades Anthony, "Le Corbusier: His Ideas for Cities." (*Journal of the American Institute of Planners,* September, 1966) Anthony speaks highly of Le Corbusier's work but thinks his urban open spaces—as at Chandigarh—are out of scale. As an insight to why they are, Anthony recalls an experience he had working in Le Corbusier's studio in 1946. "My first assignment was to draw a site plan with five slab apartment buildings, 'Unités d'Habitation,' for the French city of La Rochelle-Pallice. When I placed the buildings equidistant from one another in logical and orderly fashion, following some of what I thought were his ideas, he looked at my drawing and said: 'Mais non, mon vieux, ce n'est comme ça! Les espaces, il faut que ça joue de la musique.' Spaces should play music! And he proceeded to relocate the buildings to achieve harmonious proportions between the open spaces. Although this incident indicates the sincere concern for the beauty of open space which he had, there is also a fallacy inherent in this approach to the design of open space which seems to disregard human scale. Is it an esthetic of the airplane view alone? Can the human being standing on his own two feet perceive at eye level these proportions of the open elements of the plan when translated to life-size scale? He cannot: The street views and the containment of space as seen from pedestrian level are what create the esthetic of the urban environment."

townscape grants for cities and towns. As a supplement to its open-space program the state would offer to match 50-50 the costs of getting a community landscape program under way. The idea would not be to get a given number of trees planted, amenable as this would be, but to get communities to take a fresh look at themselves and to make the process a regular part of their planning program. The cost would not be great. Once such programs were launched, communities would find ways to tie in many already funded public programs and to generate private enthusiasms. I suggested the state start things off with $1 million in seed money. State officials were interested, but they felt that they had enough new programs already to digest and that the moment was not right for legislation.

About this time President Johnson decided to have a task force on natural beauty, and I had the fortune to be included on it. The President, it quickly became apparent, might be quite receptive to such suggestions. When we first met with him he defined natural beauty by talking about the cypress trees in the Pedernales country. The trees weren't much, he said, but they were beautiful to him, and he would like to see all Americans have the same enjoyment from the kind of trees and country they had where they lived. He asked us to give him ideas for action and added, with some emphasis, that we should not worry ourselves about political feasibility or legislative timing. That was his line of work.

Given such auspices, it seemed an excellent idea to elevate the landscape-townscape program into a federal program. My colleagues liked the idea, and since I was stuck with the job of drafting the task force report, the landscape-townscape program was made the first recommendation. Which agency would best handle the program we did not venture to say, but we did suggest that $25 million a year would be a good sum to start it with.

The President responded strongly. He embodied most of the key recommendations of the report in his natural beauty message to Congress and had the landscape-townscape proposal worked up as a provision of the Housing Act of 1965, with authorization requested for $50 million for the first two years. The measure got strong support in Congress and passed handily.

It ended up more townscape than landscape. The administering agency is the new Department of Housing and Urban Development, and though its concern is with the whole of our metropolitan regions, the focus of the program is on the built-up areas. It is titled, badly, "Urban Beautification." In brief, the program provides 50 percent matching grants for landscaping and beautification efforts that communities undertake over and above what they have already been doing. As with the federal open-space program, with which it is administratively coupled, grants are not channeled through the states but go directly to local governments. The principal condition is that the landscaping program must be part of the community's comprehensive planning effort, and not be a miscellany of *ad hoc* projects. The program applies only to work on public open spaces, an unfortunate limitation in my view, but is flexible as to the kind of work that can be done. There is also a dandy provision for 90 percent demonstration grants to communities that want to do some real experimenting.

But there still is no program for the rural landscape. States can fill the vacuum with incentive programs of their own, but a comparable federal program would be a great stimulus. Many of the elements needed already exist. The Land and Water Conservation Fund administered by the Bureau of Outdoor Recreation provides grants to the states for recreation development and they can apply this to landscape work. Another source is the Department of Agriculture. Its small watershed program has already been amended to encourage recreational development around the reservoir areas. Its cropland retirement program also has great possibilities for landscape action, and there is even more immediate potential in its tree-planting program for farmers. When it was originally set up, soil conservation was the rationale and planting for aesthetic purposes was specifically ruled out. It would help if Congress changed a word or two, but even now the statutes need not be confining. Much of the planting has been aesthetic, whatever the purpose—in many of the flat valleys of California, for example, the landscape is virtually made by the rows of trees planted as windbreaks.

Other programs could be cited. The point is that they are not being pulled together in any kind of joint effort. On the ground, of course, they can be, but the burden falls on the groups least equipped for the job: the local governments. Leaf through a handbook listing federal grants-in-aid and you will see what a bewildering set of questions come up for local officials. Do these qualify under Section 122b? If they get a grant from Agriculture, will this nullify their chances for one from HUD? If the state will provide 50 percent of the non-federal share of the project, and the federal government will give 50 percent, does that mean they will provide 25 percent?

In a small valley in the East, a local planner saw a great chance for a demonstration of what could be accomplished if all these many programs were pulled together in one spot. It was an ideal situation; a new interchange was about to open up the valley to residential and industrial growth, but it was still unspoiled, had moderately thriving agriculture, an excellent stream network, and a number of landowners eager for a conservation and landscape effort. The planner went to Washington and toured the various agencies. He suggested that they set up an informal task force and work out a program for the valley as a model of what could be done elsewhere. All thought it a fine idea, but explained they had no specific authorization. Perhaps some other time.

Opportunities like this will continue to go by the board unless machinery and money are provided for the job. A federal landscape program could do it, and no great sums would be necessary. There should be grants-in-aid, but one of the chief purposes of the program would be to show local governments how to use the other tools already available.

Eventually, the effort should encompass both city and

countryside. In the next three chapters I will take up specific opportunities for action, and for convenience's sake I will compartmentalize a bit, starting with rural roadsides, and the farm landscape, then progressing through suburbia to the city. But it is the continuities that should be stressed, for on the ground it is often impossible to draw the line between what is townscape and what is landscape. They are all mixed up, and should be; perhaps the most important view of the city is not what you see within it but from afar.

There ought to be action programs for treating the urban landscape as a whole and I will offer some suggestions along this line. The fact that there are no such programs, however, is no reason for not pushing ahead with projects, *ad hoc*, microview, or otherwise. This is another case where action is preceding planning, and it may be good that it is. Urban design is fraught with pretensions; perhaps we had best approach it a step at a time.

17. Scenic Roads

>>

Since the landscape, for all practical purposes, is what we see from the road, it would seem to be good that the government has been considering a multibillion dollar program for a vast new system of scenic roads and parkways. Whether or not it will be passed is highly conjectural at the moment, and other programs that have recently passed are of more immediate consequence. Before taking these up, however, a hard look at the scenic-roads proposal is in order. Something is wrong with it, and in trying to figure out what it is, we may gain a better idea of how we should be using the tools and money we have now and what more we should ask for.

The movement for a scenic-roads program started, ironically enough, as a movement to stop highway engineers from building new roads. When the California State Highway Department began pondering the reconstruction of the famous Route 1 along the Big Sur coastline to freeway standards, conservationists in the area became alarmed.

The old road was indeed a twisty one, but it was also a spectacularly magnificent drive, and a four or eight lane highway could cut and fill a great deal of the magnificence away. Led by State Senator Fred Farr, the group got the legislature to authorize a scenic-roads study.

This in turn led to legislation for a scenic-roads program, the gist of which was cooperative effort by the state and local governments to designate and protect scenic corridors on roads that are scenic.

This sparked nationwide interest and many people began pressing for a federal program. In 1965 President Johnson proposed a scenic-roads program as part of the Highway Beautification Act. It proved to be premature. The scenic roads would not be financed with new money but would be a subtraction from the funds otherwise available to the states for their secondary roads. The states objected strongly. It was also pointed out that a special task force set up by the administration was at work studying the requirements for an ideal scenic-roads program. Congress, which felt it had enough to swallow in the rest of the act, said it would be better to wait until the study was done. The provision was struck out.

The task force, headed by the Bureau of Public Roads' David Levin, tackled its assignment with a vigor and dispatch not characteristic of most study groups. It asked each state highway department, to the consternation of quite a few, to do a crash research job. They were given a manual listing the basic specifications of different kinds of scenic roads and were asked to come up with concrete proposals listing specific routes, the priority they should receive, and the money they would cost. Federal agencies were asked to nominate national parkways.

When all the returns were in, some 136,500 miles at an estimated cost of $18.7 billion had been nominated. Levin and his group analyzed the proposals backward and forward and pruned them down to a minimum program. It was published in March 1967.

The minimum was a whopper. The report proposed a ten-year program for 55 thousand miles of scenic roads at a total cost of $4 billion. The bulk of the mileage would be based on old roads; the bulk of the money, however, would go for entirely new roads. New roads would account for 21 percent of the mileage, 67 percent of the cost.

Left to their own public works, highway departments would probably not spend money quite this way, and in part their new concern for scenic roads has been induced. As time goes on, however, they are likely to warm to the idea. So long as scenic roads threatened to be a diversion to the building of the Interstate System, the highway people resisted. But now completion is in sight. Even with the inevitable stretch-outs, it looks as though the Interstate System should be largely completed within about six years. What next? Highway people need a new rationale. The Interstate System was originally sold on the basis that it was needed for military movements. Why not another new system, this time for natural beauty and recreation?

If we need more new roads, let us build them. But not on this rationale. Implicit in the assignment given the task force was the notion of a new system. In detailing it, the task force commendably stuck out its neck; the boldness of its proposals forces us to the basic issues, and in many of the recommendations lie the elements of an excellent program. What is at question is the premise of the assignment. Should there be two systems of roads—regular ones and scenic ones?

I am going to argue that (1) we should put our money on enhancing the scenic corridor of every kind of road; (2) except for a limited number of new roads in outstanding areas, we should put the bulk of our efforts on existing rights-of-way, not the building of new ones; (3) road standards should not be so high they obliterate the values the roads are supposed to provide; (4) a more flexible concept is needed of what a scenic corridor should be, in urban areas especially; (5) the urban parkway was a great idea, forty years ago; now it is anachronistic; (6) by reversing the priorities in the scenic roads proposal we can

fashion a program that will be more effective than a
$4 billion system, and at a fraction of the cost.

The nub of the problem is whether the emphasis should
be on existing roads or new ones. State highway departments put it on new ones. In their proposals, they spoke
warmly of the attractions of secondary roads and rural by-
ways that already exist. When it came to figuring how
much money was needed and where it ought to go, however, it was on new roads they concentrated. In part, this
was a playback of what they thought the Bureau of Public
Roads wanted to hear, and they did not wish to under-
state the sums they could handle.

But people who build highways like to build highways.
Given the money, they find it easier to break fresh ground
across the countryside than to rework existing routes. They
can design to better standards. They can bypass settled
areas and their pockets of citizen resistance. They do not
have to pay as much per acre for the land they need;
there are fewer vested landowner interests to contend
with, and no billboards or junkyards or roadside detritus
to clean up; no crossroads, stores, and gas stations to buy
out. The slate is clean.

And that is the problem. Building new roads is unques-
tionably the most efficient way to serve heavy traffic, but
is it the most efficient way of providing *scenic* roads? In
certain circumstances the answer is Yes. New rights-of-
way are clearly in order where they can provide badly
needed access to a recreation facility, or open up access
to areas of outstanding scenic beauty, if, in the process
they do not destroy the beauty. The Blue Ridge Parkway
and the Great River Road along the Mississippi are excellent examples.

Except in such special cases, however, a new route is
probably the least efficient way of providing scenic roads.
They are extremely expensive. A road built to parkway
standards costs up to $1 million a mile; even a two-lane
scenic road in a purely rural area will cost as much as
$200,000 a mile. (Improvement of existing roads: $30,-

000–$100,000 a mile.) The question is not simply whether the new road would be desirable, but what could be done if the same amount of money were spent on existing roads. Highway-department proposals are extremely unbalanced in this respect. In many cases the top-priority route proposed would cost two to three times as much as the landscaping program for all the other roads combined.

But the most important reason for not building new rights-of-way is aesthetic. As far as scenic roads are concerned, the creation of entirely new rights-of-way works at cross-purposes with the very qualities the roads were supposed to provide. They are dull.

This is not because the highway departments do a poor landscaping job. The problem is in the landscape itself. New routes tend to be dull because they cut across the grain of it. There is a parallel here with what is wrong with so much of the urban redevelopment. The clean-sweep approach that obliterates the former street pattern can also obliterate the fabric of the city and some of its most precious elements. Much the same thing can happen with the fabric of the landscape.

A landscape is built up by people, accumulatively, over a long period of time and it is around roads that they build it. The elements that give the landscape its life—the farmhouses, the silos, the barns, the tree-lined lanes, the villages, the crossroads church—are either on the road or very close to it. It is true enough that much of this frontage, even along the most rural routes, has been hurt by poor development; and that much of it has been abandoned to second growth. But it is along these roads that the opportunities lie. They cannot be grasped by creating new roads without frontages.

A landscape has a front side and it has a back side. New rights-of-way, generally, are on the back side. The distance may not be very great—only a ridgeline away perhaps—but the perspective is far different, and much less satisfying. The farm-to-market countryside is still there, but we are in defilade and do not see it.

For an example of this, drive along the new Interstate highway that parallels the old Route 40 through Maryland. It had to be built. The old route was whored up beyond redemption, the landscape was walled off by diners and gas stations and billboards, and the traffic was hideous and dangerous. From such desecration the new route is free. It is so virginal, however, that aesthetically it is almost as unsatisfactory. Driving along it you would hardly know that you are going through some of the richest farmland of the Piedmont. You are looking at it from the rear. There is one magnificent view as you cross the Susquehanna—a farm atop a hill with meadows going down to the river; but for most of the drive what you see of the countryside is woods. It is an admirably engineered landscape—green, undefiled, and monotonous.

Another example of the new versus old right-of-way is to be found on Cape Cod. Old Route 6 is one of the slowest roads along the whole Eastern Seaboard, and on a summer Sunday afternoon the traffic is almost stationary. The new mid-Cape highway can get clogged too on occasion, but it is an infinitely more efficient artery. But old Route 6 *is* the Cape, and the very things that make it slow—the succession of curves, the towns and the elms that compress the right-of-way—are what give it special quality. The mid-Cape highway is another road that had to be built, but it gives no real sense of place; save for one glimpse of a steeple near Barnstable, you might as well be driving through the pine barrens of New Jersey.

Some new rights-of-way, let it be acknowledged, provide a view of the landscape that did not exist before, especially when they run along an escarpment or a high ridge. Parts of the Pennsylvania Turnpike, for example, have opened up superb views of farm valleys. It should also be remembered that one or two magnificent views can so color our perception of a scene as to convince us the route is a succession of them when it is not.

In most cases, however, new rights-of-way do not show a settled countryside to best advantage, and they become downright monotonous when they poke into the less settled forest and mountain areas. Many highway engineers are partial to forests—the land is likely to be in public ownership—and a number of the proposed scenic roads are routed through state forests. Many of the forests are not very good forests; some consist of rows and rows of equally spaced conifers, than which there is no more artificial a landscape. Why contrive such routes? They would be oppressive in their greenness. No villages, no farms, no crossroads store. Not even a neon sign or a honky-tonk to relieve the tedium. Just landscaped turnoffs and picnic areas—and woods, mile after mile after mile.

The engineers' standards are too high. For some low-traffic scenic roads they specify modest dimensions, but the grade of road they most want to build calls for a lot of work on the topography. For new two-lane scenic roads, the engineers set a 40-mph-design speed with room in the 300 foot right-of-way for an additional two-lane road to be built later. Curves are to be kept at 5 percent and so are the gradients. Such standards may seem low compared to those for 70-mph freeways; applied to the reconstruction of old roads, however, they would obliterate most of the qualities that make the old road scenic.

What makes driving along back roads such a delight? It is more than the scenery; it is the tightness of its scale. You go around abrupt curves, up sudden crests, under a canopy of overhanging foliage. Sometimes the view opens up to distant hills; sometimes it narrows almost to a tunnel as you pass through woods. But always the edge of the landscape is close by—stone fences, a line of maples, a barn—so close by that we tarry where else we would speed.

This tightness of scale is what gets improved away. Curves are straightened, crests flattened, the trees and stone fences moved out of harm's way. The edge of the landscape gets moved back.

Such improvement provides greater traffic capacity and more safety. But there is a price. Wherever sections of rural parkways have been reconstructed to modern standards, the cars go faster and there is less danger of running into trees. But they are much less interesting to drive. The old, unimproved segments still have the roller-coaster effects engineers deplore, and one has to mind the edge of the road more. But they are fun to drive.

New freeways do not have to be dull. Some are very enjoyable indeed, and it is significant that these also tend to be the safest. In their *Man Made America,* Christopher Tunnard and Boris Pushkarev rated thirteen freeways on their aesthetic quality and then compared their fatality rates. The pleasantest to drive had low fatality rates; the most monotonous, the highest. In another study, the Rutgers Bureau of Economic Research compared a wide range of roads; on the basis of the correlations between injury rates and the aesthetic character of the road it was estimated that a highway that is scenic will have approximately eight less injuries a year per 10 million vehicle miles than nonscenic highways.

Back roads are not necessarily unsafe. It is true that per 100,000 vehicle miles there are less accidents on modern high-design freeways than on other types of roads. Because of this disparity it has been widely assumed that roads on the other end of the scale, the small back roads, are the unsafest of all. But this is not so. The Highway Safety Research Institute has found that when the accidents are cumulatively plotted on the map of a county, the pins will be clustered in a few high-risk spots on heavily traveled secondary roads. There will be few or no pins on the back roads.

Nor are trees as much a hazard as design specifications would indicate them to be. The iniquitous "30-foot rule" is a case in point. Recently a safety committee of highway engineers recommended, among other things, that there be no trees within thirty feet of the pavement on highways in rural areas. The Bureau of Public Roads urged state highway departments to take heed. And they are. Some highway engineers have taken the ruling so literally that they are scheduling the destruction of thousands of fine old trees on highways that are already built. For want of a qualifying line of fine print, a wholesale mutilation is imminent for some of the comeliest roadsides in the country.

The men who are for the rule see an open-and-shut case. The idea is to give vehicles that run off the road room to come to a stop without hitting something. (As the safety people put it: "Provide the greatest possibility of recovery of errant vehicles and the least possible spectrum of discontinuities incompatible with off-road moving vehicles.") By averaging out accident records, the engineers have figured that about 85 percent of errant vehicles would escape major harm if there were thirty unobstructed feet beyond the roadway. Trees are an obstruction. Ergo, remove the trees.

But this syllogism is based on a misreading, and when written into rigid and detailed specifications, it becomes needlessly tyrannical.* Trees do not attract errant cars. The path a car takes when it runs off the road is determined to a large degree by the topography and drainage pattern the engineers have followed. If the edge of the shoulder slopes down to a gulley, that is where the car is likely to go. If a tree is in this path, the car will probably hit it, and the tree is indeed a hazard. If there is a sharp

---

* The rule was proposed by the report of the special traffic safety committee set up by the American Association of State Highway Officials in cooperation with the Bureau of Public Roads. The report, issued in February of 1967, recommended: "To increase safety when vehicles leave the pavement, a clear recovery zone area, free of physical obstruction, should be provided along the roadway thirty feet or more from the edge of the traveled way in rural areas. Corrective programs should be undertaken at once. . . ." The report puts trees at the head of the list of hazardous objects.

But the committee's own research indicates trees should be near the end of the list. It cites a study of the objects struck in 507 vehicle accidents. In 130 of the accidents, ditches or banks were struck; in 326, highway structures of some kind or another. But trees were involved in only 13 accidents, or 2.2 percent of the total.

There is an urgent job of reconsideration to be done. If the Bureau of Public Roads does not do it, it ought not be in the scenic roads business.

upward slope, however, gravity will work the other way and the car will never reach any trees that might be at the top. But the rule says that there should be no trees thirty feet from the roadway. Down go the trees.

Obviously, some curves must be straightened, some trees must be removed. But the very constraints of the old routes are not without some safety benefits of their own. You drive more slowly; indeed, even at thirty miles per hour, you often get the feeling you are going quite fast because of the effect of the passing landscape on your peripheral vision. As studies of driver reactions have demonstrated, the closer the roadside, the more slowly you tend to drive and the more you see to the side. Conversely, as the right-of-way widens, the further ahead is your focus of attention and the faster you tend to drive.

There are two ways to take advantage of this psychological effect. One is to condition drivers to take it easy. In the late 30s, the landscape architect of the Texas Highway Department deliberately designed "visual bottlenecks" by periodically bringing the planting very close to the roadway. At such points the driver would instinctively ease up on the accelerator.

This approach is rare today. The need for high-capacity freeways has been so overriding that engineers have been concentrating on adapting the roadway to the traffic rather than the other way around. This makes sense for freeways. It does not for scenic roads. The quality of the experience should come foremost and this is diminished by conventional concepts of high-design standards. New or old, scenic roads need much more sensitive handling; without it, a good argument could be made that the best thing engineers could do for our scenic roads would be to leave them alone.

Let us assume the best about the standards. Another large problem remains. Where, and how uniformly should they be applied? Bureau of Public Roads people want system. They believe a scenic route should have consistent standards throughout, both in the design specifications of the road and in the landscaping standards to be applied to the corridor. They also want long routes.

The Bureau of Public Roads manual for the scenic-road study put strong emphasis on route continuity, and for old roads as well as new. To quote:

> "Existing highways in scenic corridors may be sug-
> gested as scenic routes when not less than 90 percent
> of their length is amenable to development to scenic-
> route standards, either by improvement along the exist-
> ing location or by relocation of short lengths to bypass
> highly developed or unsightly areas through which the
> existing location cannot be suitably developed econom-
> ically."

Length is also stressed. The minimum scenic route, the manual suggests, should be twenty-five miles, though in fringe areas it could be as short as five miles.

This emphasis on continuity could be restrictive. The man who directed the study, David Levin, had no inten-tions of setting procrustean standards and would very much like to see plenty of exceptions where the topography and circumstances call for them. Whether state highway de-partments would be as flexible is another matter. Once such criteria get established, they have a way of harden-ing very fast. In the case of scenic roads the consequences could be a set of standards that would make it almost impossible to do a satisfactory job where it most needs to be done.

It is no great problem to fashion long scenic routes out in the hinterland; it is extremely difficult to do so around cities. In what metropolitan area can you find a twenty-five-mile stretch of road relatively uninterrupted by blight? Even a five-mile stretch is hard to find. The good parts are intermittent. Here and there will be places where there is a happy configuration of public open spaces, key topo-graphical features, a handsome bridge, landscaped insti-tutional land, golf courses, and the like. Along such stretches, a relatively moderate expenditure for some additional buffer areas and landscaping could achieve a great deal. There will also be some not quite so good stretches that would require more effort and more money to reclaim but it would be well worth it. Other parts of the route, however, would be impossible to upgrade to minimum scenic standards except through a prodigious expenditure of money. Why spend it there? Formulas emphasizing continuity ill fit such urban situations; either we would have to do nothing at all, or spend most of the money where it would fetch the least amenity.

It would be far better to ride with the punch and concentrate available funds where they would have the greatest leverage. The result would be a series of contrasts. Many a pleasant stretch would be followed, quite abruptly, with stretches of developed land and business and factories. Some of these would be interesting to look at; some would be awful. But this is the nature of urban areas. We cannot apply rural standards of continuity to towns for if we do we would be forced to a lot of unnecessary effort to obscure this reality. As Kevin Lynch and Lawrence Halprin have been pointing out, a scenic corridor in an urban area should be urban—as Lynch puts it, "a succession of visual events." Some screening here and there, yes, but the true art is to enhance and reveal the city.

Even in rural areas we should be careful about requiring that roads be continuously scenic. Let me refer again to the Wisconsin Great River Road along the Mississippi. In acquiring scenic easements along the river, the Highway Department did not attempt to buy away full development rights on portions adjacent to towns or in the towns themselves. It concentrated its efforts on the rural areas. The reason was primarily economic. The cost of easements prohibiting the development near the town would be quite high, but quite low along the open-space stretches.

But good economics has been good aesthetics. When you drive along the Great River Road you do not feel you are driving on a manicured parkway; you are driving through a real-life countryside, punctuated with real-life towns with their characteristic spatterings of outlying houses. Most of the road is along the old rights-of-way that were there before. Had it been laid out as a highly landscaped new route and detoured around the villages, it would have been far more expensive, and far less enjoyable.

There are, of course, precedents for continuously scenic roads in urban areas. If it proves too difficult to upgrade old roads to scenic standards, we can build entirely new ones. In the form of urban parkways, we have built such roads before, and very successful they have been. Why not build more? There is, indeed, a case to be made for new parkways in certain areas. As a general proposition, however, I submit that the urban parkways are a retrogressive concept.

It was a concept admirably suited to the needs of a particular time. When the parkways were first conceived in the 1920s, the idea was to provide city people with a pleasure drive. The parkways were not to be for day-to-day traffic; they were to give the people a chance to get away from day-to-day traffic. The parkways were to be essentially long parks, and driving through them was itself to be a recreational experience. Commercial vehicles would be barred.

The first real parkway, the Bronx River Parkway, was part of a plan to turn a rubbish-laden open sewer into a strip park. Along its length would run a parkway. In the design, landscape architect Gilmore Clarke anticipated most of the principles of the modern freeway. The right-of-way was wide and beautifully landscaped; it followed the topography in sweeping curves rather than the conventional straight-away tangents; the parkway was separated from local roads by overpasses and underpasses. The result was not only a beautiful road but one that allowed people to drive faster than they could along conventional roads and with far greater safety. The success of the design led to the great system of parkways Robert Moses built in the

New York metropolitan area and to similar parkways in other cities.

The very efficiency of the design, however, made the parkways become something else. They were fine for leisurely Sunday driving. They were better yet for fast driving Monday through Saturday, and that is how they came to be used. They were the first modern expressways.

The parkway concept has not changed. But everything else has. Most urban parkways are now anything but recreational; they have long since become commuter highways and are the scene of some of the most horrendous of traffic jams. Advanced as their design once was, they are now so overwhelmed with non-pleasure traffic that the average speeds—and speed limits—are actually lower on many stretches than they used to be.

What is to be done with them? The hard choices that are posed illustrate the near impossibility of having two separate kinds of road systems. Obviously the old parkways cannot be left as they are. They are too dangerous. They have to be upgraded to modern standards. Segment by segment, this is being done, and it is making the parkways more efficient as transportation arteries. It is also making them more like any other new road. Gone are the sinuous curves that made the old parkways so chancy, and so attractive. Gone too, along many a stretch, are the rows of trees that confined, and enhanced the roadway.* The only prime differences that remain between parkways and

* From the New York *Times,* October 25, 1967: "Scarsdale, N.Y. Hundreds of stately shade trees have been felled, scenic vistas have been bulldozed and old stone bridges have been razed in the modernization of an original stretch here of the Bronx River Parkway . . . The old parkway here had four narrow, winding lanes, with only occasional turnouts for disabled cars and no center barrier except for a scenic island of trees and shrubberies for a short stretch. When redeveloped, the parkway will be moderately straight, have four broad lanes, continuous shoulders for disabled cars and center dividers of fences and islands. Humps in the road that gave to motorists the sensation of a rollercoaster ride will be eliminated."

expressways are the identifying signs and the continued exclusion of commercial traffic, which fact has attracted enough additional motorists to make up for the slack.

But roadbuilders still like the urban parkway idea. Among other things, it provides them an excellent reason for building highways where highways ought not to go. If a route is to take parkland, it can be presented as a project to enhance parkland. Add some extra landscaping, some scenic turnoffs and picnic areas and call the whole thing a parkway. But a six-lane highway is a six-lane highway no matter what it is called, and if it is recreation that we are seeking, surely there is no more expensive way to provide it, or, to be more accurate, to take it away.

In looking over old metropolitan area plans for parkways, one is struck by two thoughts: (1) how rosy were the assumptions that the parkways would be sylvan and uncrowded; (2) how good it is some of them were not built. The regional plan of the Philadelphia Tri-State District of 1932 is a case in point. At that time, recreational parkways seemed to be the coming thing, and the core of the open-space plan was to put parkways through the heart of the loveliest stream valleys of the countryside, the Brandywine for one. These were to be developed in a "naturalesque manner." They "would offer to the motorist many delightful circuit routes, free from the annoyance of the crowded highways, so that he might drive from one park to another, passing at frequent intervals local recreational parks, any of which he may choose for his occasional outing."

The parkways never got built. Subsequently, highway engineers used some of the valley areas for freeways—not because the land was beautiful but because it was open and cheap. But most of the stream valleys have yet to be so improved, and access to them is still through the secondary and county roads. The opportunities for preserving them may yet be squandered, but the opportunities are still there.

To justify a new recreational roads program, much has been made of the finding of the Outdoor Recreation

Resources Review Commission that driving for pleasure is
the most frequent form of recreation for Americans. Few
statistics have been so widely quoted or so misinterpreted.
If Americans find driving their most important recreation,
the reasoning goes, and if more Americans are going to be
doing more driving, then the best way to provide people
with more recreation is to provide them with more recreational roads.

It does not follow. The ORRRC finding was significant
as far as it went, but it should be extrapolated no further.
What it boils down to is that when a sample of Americans
were shown a list of twenty-three activities, they said
"driving for pleasure" was the activity they did the most of.
They did not say it was the most important. They did not
say why they did it, or when, or what kind of roads.

For a scenic-road program such qualitative questions
have to be answered. How many times is the driving itself
the recreation; how many times a means of getting to
recreation? There can be quite a difference. Driving to
the beach on a hot Sunday afternoon, for example. Is this
pleasure? Some drives are clearly recreational—a vacation
trip through the Rockies, a leisurely tour along the Blue
Ridge Parkway. Some drives are clearly for everyday
business. But pleasure is mixed up in both kinds. For many
an American the most enjoyable driving may be part of a
business trip; even a stint on the boring Jersey Turnpike
may afford recreating surcease. Conversely, the most
nerve-wracking and unenjoyable driving may be for recreation—such as driving the wife and children to a summer
place. Conflicting examples abound. The point is that driving is so much a part of our lives that we cannot isolate
that which is enjoyable about it and encapsulate it physically in special-purpose facilities.

Looking ahead, can we be so certain that the automobile
is going to be the prime vehicle for recreation in the
future?* It is true that all projections point to many more

* A follow-up survey by the Bureau of Outdoor Recreation
would seem to indicate that driving for pleasure is losing some
of its relative popularity. In a report issued in April of 1967,

people using many more cars; it is also true that estimates of future traffic have usually been under rather than over the mark. We should be wary, however, of projecting all this too many decades hence. It is well we keep in mind that various forms of transportation have reached their zenith of attention, and polish and detail, just about the time they are to be supplemented by a new form. The clipper ships, the Twentieth Century Limited, the interurban trolleys, the transatlantic express liners—it is not utterly inconceivable that the automobile might follow in this progression. I am not suggesting that the automobile is about to become extinct or that we have not got at least several decades of roadwork cut out for us. But it is late in the game to be gearing a recreation program for future generations to the driving of automobiles.

BOR said that between 1960 and 1965 the amount of pleasure driving in summer increased only about 8 percent—just barely in line with the population increase. In the meantime, walking for pleasure and swimming jumped prodigiously—82 percent and 44 percent respectively—and are now in first and second place ahead of driving as summertime activities. For the year as a whole, driving is still ranked first, but the BOR projections show walking for pleasure gaining on it rapidly.

There is some question, however, as to whether this rather remarkable shift is in people's behavior or in the way their behavior has been studied. The ORRRC figures were based on four quarterly surveys. The BOR survey was of one summer—during which balmy months Americans might well be expected to do considerably more walking and swimming. BOR, which did not have the funds for a year-round study, had to extrapolate its figures to arrive at annual estimates. This is a difficult statistical exercise, and it is possible that some of the extra walking may have been in the calculators. It is hard to believe that the American way of life has become that much more salubrious in just five years. Are we really walking almost twice as much?

These statistics do not prove much about recreational driving one way or the other. They do prove something about the advisability of basing major policy decisions on questionnaire responses.

We come back to the basic question: Should we concentrate on making a new system of scenic roads—or on
making more scenic the roads we have? For aesthetic
reasons alone, the latter course seems by far the best;
indeed, even if Congress were willing to provide the bil-
lions necessary for a new scenic road system, we might be
better off if they were not spent. But the limiting fact is
that Congress is not going to vote that kind of money. In
view of its niggardliness in providing sufficient money to
back up the 1965 Highway Beautification Act, Congress is
hardly likely to fund a far more costly program. Nor is
there likely to be public clamor for one. Road builders
might press for it, but conservation and recreational groups
have indicated enough misgivings about the preliminary
proposal to suggest that their support would not be
enthusiastic.

But the discipline of economics is a good one. As David
Levin has taken care to point out, by far and away the
most important part of the program is for corridor enhancement, and this is the part that takes the least money. Of
the 4 billion dollars, only 4 percent is for corridor protection; 3.8 percent for landscaping, and 7.2 percent for
roadside facilities. All the rest, 85 percent, goes for right-
of-way acquisition and construction.

Why not turn the emphasis upside down? We don't
need the huge sums for construction. What we need are
moderate sums for work on existing roads. A budget of
$150 million a year should be extremely effective, and it
is a reasonable enough figure that Congress just might vote
it, or something nearby.

It would be essentially a grant-in-aid program. Some of
the money would be allocated for work on national parkways, but the bulk would go to the states. Emphasis would
be on improving the scenic corridors, but this would include some new acquisition and construction. The program would supplement the landscaping grants already
available for federal-aid highways, but would embrace all
kinds of roads. The states would probably want to spend
most of the money on their own primary and secondary

roads, but they should be required to pass on some of the money to local governments for enhancement of town and county roads. Such roads usually get hardly enough for bare maintenance, yet some of them are potentially the best scenic roads of all.

Such a program ought not to be run solely by highway people. They would have the primary operating responsibility, but the basic planning should be done by a joint board that would include the state's recreation, conservation and planning agencies. And local governments affected ought to have some say too.

There should be less emphasis on system and uniformity of standards. A national effort, yes, but this is not the same thing as a national system, let alone a system of single purpose roads. Save for a few parkways directly administered by the federal government, most of the roads that are scenic in this country are everyday roads and they are essentially local in character. That is what makes them scenic. The kind of federal program that will help best is one that will stimulate state and local action on the scenic corridors of all kinds of roads.

And we do not have to await a new program to have more scenic roads. New legislation and new money will help greatly, but there are many things that can be done with the tools at hand that are not being done and should be. One modest step, for example, is to identify the best of the rural back roads; give them identifying markers, work up "shunpike" routes and let people know about them. Several states have done this—Texas with its "Texas Trails," for one—but most have done little. Yet the cost would be nominal.

For work on the scenic corridor there are many programs to be tapped; the various federal and state open-space grant programs, the federal urban beautification program, the Agriculture Department's cropland-retirement and soil-conservation programs. It would be tidier if these were brought together more through an over-all program, but this is no prerequisite for effective action. The separate elements already exist and the opportunities they open up are immediate.

18. Roadsides

>>>

The first thing is to get rid of billboards. There is no need to take up the various subsidiary arguments against them. They are a desecration to the landscape and that is reason to be done with them. What is of moment is that Americans have been coming around to this elemental view, and so have the courts. For years the courts used to advance all sorts of reasons but the basic one to uphold billboard regulations. Now the courts are frank. In the wake of several key decisions they have been holding that billboards are not primarily a use of private land, but of the highway; the public paid for this and it can properly use its police power to prevent a trespass upon it. Whether it will use it, of course, is another matter and state and local legislative bodies are of several minds on this. But while much fighting remains to be done, a cardinal point of law has been established and the strategy should be clear.

So it would seem. The Highway Beautification Act of 1965, however, has temporarily muddied the issue. The act is both good and bad—two titles forward, one back. As the administration originally proposed, the act calls for regulation of billboards by the state, within 660 feet on either side of the highway. It also provides that the states that do not adopt satisfactory regulations will be penalized by having some of their highway funds withheld. While Congress was marking up the bill, however, two monkey wrenches were thrown in. One was a clause permitting states to exempt commercial and industrial areas from the regulations. This was an important concession for the billboard people, who went to work getting state legislatures to pass statutes of such generous terminology as to make almost any stretch commercial or industrial if someone wants to make it commercial or industrial. In Wyoming, for example, "commercial" includes all agricultural land; in Montana, any property within ten miles of a town or five miles of an intersection.

The other clause said that "fair compensation" should be paid for the removal of billboards, with the federal government footing seventy-five percent of the bill. This was the real kicker. It would, for one thing, call for a mammoth ransom fund. To buy the 899,000 billboards subject to removal would require some $558 million, and this quite clearly was more money than Congress would ever appropriate. The billboard people, needless to say, were not after the compensation; they wanted to keep the billboards up. The beauty of the compensation clause for them was that it threatened to undermine laboriously won legislative and legal precedents for using the police power to regulate billboards.

The provision is so outrageous that it may fall of its own weight. It beggars common sense. There is no reason to pay people to give up a right that they should not have had in the first place, and they certainly should not have it along the newly created interstate roads. The case is less clear, let it be admitted, along the older roads of the primary system, where in a form of adverse possession, sign rights have been established by long usage. It was concern over these older commercial strips and the fate of their small entrepreneurs, many Congressmen said, that prompted them to vote for the compensation provision.

But there are ways to deal with such problems other than by paying huge sums of money. It is within the legal powers of the states to accomplish regulation without compensation and they should be required to do so. A number of states, indeed, a number of counties, already have regulations far stiffer than those in the Highway Beautification Act, and they have worked. They do not pay money to prevent new billboards nor do they pay to retire old ones. In California, for example, when an area is zoned against billboards, the state does not attempt to eliminate by fiat all existing billboards overnight. It grants a reasonable amortization period for nonconforming billboards. The owners get a fair shake and at the end of the period there is no cause to reward them with payment.

The people who cry loudest against such regulations are the worst offenders—the roadside operators and the motel people. They say that they would almost have to go out of business without their big signs to help motorists find them, and they are busy putting up bigger and bigger "spectaculars," huge things stuck up on stilts. But if they were all in the same boat—on premises signs only—it is quite probable that motorists would still use motels, and the motels could use the money they spend on signs for more amenable kinds of promotion.

Vermont may prove the point. Scenery is virtually its prime industry and to save it from being advertised out of existence the legislature recently passed the stiffest measure proposed anywhere. All billboards are to be prohibited, save on premises signs, and the shape and size of these would be strictly regulated. Surprisingly, most of the motel and ski resort operators supported the measure. The sign competition between them had gotten out of hand and aside from what it was doing to the view, it was costing too much money. Under the act, they will all be in the same boat. The state highway department will set up sign clusters at informational centers at various spots on the main routes. Commercial listings can be included at an initial cost of $50, and subsequent maintenance fee at $10–$25 a year. Some existing billboards will be allowed to stay up for a limited amortization period, but most will have to start coming down. Penalties for not taking them down, or putting up unauthorized ones, can include jail sentences of up to thirty days—and each day an illegal sign remains up will be judged a separate violation.

Such toughness could be contagious. As a hopeful guess, one can hazard that after a lot of legislative hauling and pushing, more and more states will be applying their police powers as strictly as the courts will let them and that compensation for billboard removal will not be mandatory.* Local governments will be tightening up their regulations too. A trend like this tends to build on itself. As more people see for themselves the roadsides some states are providing, the more push there is for action in the others.

One thing that would speed the process up is a national roadside council. So far the brunt of the fight for effective legislation has been carried by the individual state roadside councils. They have done a remarkable job. They like to think of themselves as underdogs fighting against enormous odds, but they are every bit as canny in legislative and legal maneuvering as their opponents. They have nowhere as much money, but their zealotry makes them quite effective and the best of the state programs have been pushed through because of them.

But there is no national roadside council and for lack of one the roadside people have been less effective in Washington, D.C. Helen Reynolds, the soft-spoken battler who heads the California Roadside Council, has had her organization pinch-hit as a clearing house for various state groups. The indomitable Hilda Fox of the Pennsylvania Roadside Council has done the same. But there is still no permanent machinery for bringing all the groups together

---

* One precedent is the "Collier-Z'berg" Act passed in 1967 by the California legislature. It authorizes local governments to adopt billboard regulations stricter than those called for by the federal program, and it provides the state a possible means of avoiding compensation for billboard removal.

in a common front. For lack of it, the construction and billboard people have had a clearer field and what happened to the Beautification Act is one result. A stronger counterlobby is very much needed. The small amount of money it would take to set it up could make hundreds of millions of difference in the spending of highway funds.*

Necessary as it may be, billboard control is negative. The best way to enhance the view from the road is to widen the scenic corridor, either through buying additional land beyond the rights-of-way or easements on it. A happy by-product of this is the prevention of billboards, but it is not just for this boon that compensation is paid, much as the billboard people would like to construe it that way. A wider corridor is essentially a positive move; it is a way of keeping a living landscape and for providing room for trails, scenic turnoffs, rest stops and the like. In this respect, the Highway Beautification Act of 1965 marks a breakthrough. It authorizes money for the job; and provides it in such a way that the highway engineers cannot spend it for other purposes.

To understand the importance of the safeguard, a little history is in order. Back in 1940 Congress put an excellent provision in the highway code. This was Section 319,

* While I think the "extremist" position of the roadside councils is basically the right one, some people of sensibility can make a good case for a less combative view. J. B. Jackson, the editor of *Landscape,* who loves the countryside but likes to twit some of its more purist defenders, argues that signs on city approaches do have the virtue of acknowledging the motorist's presence and that the urban scene would be more unwelcome, and sterile, without them. Some observers go further. They say billboards are "pop art." Whatever the merits of this latter position, which are few, it is certainly true that one should not be too pristine in such matters. Billboards do have their uses. Nevertheless, on pragmatic grounds the extremist position still makes sense. No matter how intransigently the roadside councils wage their campaigns, there will be plenty enough billboards left to look at. If they get too conciliatory, the billboard people will win every time. For they are extremists.

which provided that of the federal highway funds available to the states, three percent could be used for widening, landscaping, and improving the scenic corridor. Three percent does not sound like much, but it would be a whale of a lot of money; with highway funds running between four and five billion dollars a year, over a ten-year period the three percent would amount to better than one billion. To make the provision more attractive, Congress stipulated that the states did not have to put up any matching money.

State highway directors universally hailed the provision. It was a logical next step to the "complete highway" they were preaching and at their annual meetings they regularly passed unanimous resolutions calling for more vigorous use of Section 319 funds.

And not a penny did they spend. They did not even apply. The trouble with Section 319 was that it was optional. The verb was "may include." The highway people could use the money for landscaping and easements or they could use it to keep on doing what they had been doing. That is what they did. They spent it on construction. Nor did the Bureau of Public Roads twist their arms unmercifully to do otherwise. Its top officials also praised Section 319—no bureau produces enlightened memoranda in such profusion—but somewhere down the administrative line the message got lost. The Bureau's engineers, like their counterparts in the states, were not enthusiastic about anything that would divert money from what they conceived was the real business at hand. They did not so much as prepare an application blank for the use of Section 319 funds by the states.

In its 1964 report, the President's Task Force on Natural Beauty was sharply critical of what it felt to be bureaucratic sabotage and strongly recommended that Section 319 be given more money and more muscle. At the very least, it recommended, the word "may" should be changed to "shall."

The formula finally adopted was Title III of the Beautification Act of 1965. It provides 100 percent grants to the states for widening and enhancing the scenic corridors.

The money is in addition to construction funds and cannot be used for any other purpose. Another provision, Title II, encourages the states to screen or remove auto junkyards along the rights-of-way of interstate and primary highways. Both the carrot and the stick are used. If the states do not act within a reasonable length of time, they will be docked 10 percent of their regular highway funds. More positively, the federal government gives grants for 75 percent of the cost of junkyard removal and screening.

These two provisions have been the least controversial of the program, and Congress voted enough money to get them started. It appropriated only $10 million a year for 1966 and 1967 for junkyard and billboard control, but some $60 million for Title III scenic grants.*

The first effects have been encouraging. Many states did not allow their highway departments to buy land in excess of right-of-way needs or to spend money on landscaping it; in order to get Title III money, the states have been revising the statutes to give the highway departments the necessary authority. States that were all set have been using the money to good effect; extensive easement programs, for example, have been launched in New Jersey, New York, Maryland, Florida, Illinois, Kentucky, Minnesota, California, Hawaii, and Washington. A number of states are following California's lead in setting up scenic-roads programs. The Washington state legislature has put through one and had designated twenty-five primary and secondary roads as the nucleus.

In almost every state, a concern for landscape values is getting cranked into the bureaucratic machinery in a way that it never was before. Landscape architects are in more

---

* Through August 1967, a total of $122 million has been spent under Title III for landscaping and scenic enhancement. About half was for roadside rest areas. The rest was divided between scenic easements and landscaping. Junkyard-control projects have received $9.2 million; advertising control, $2.5 million. For fiscal 1968 the Senate authorized $85 million for the three programs, and the House Public Works Committee recommended the same. The question is now up to the House.

demand, and not just to dress up the engineers' plans; they are beginning to have much more to say about what the plans should be.

Some of the most imaginative work is being done by local governments. The county that helped start the whole California movement, Monterey County, successfully nailed down the scenic corridor of coastal Highway I against commercial despoliations; this moved the state to name it as the first of its scenic roads, and thus it will also be protected from being upgraded into a freeway. The county is treating other roads in the same fashion. It designates conservation districts along the length of the roads, the width of the strip depending on the terrain. This does not rule out development—scenic easements are used where this is necessary—but it does give the county strong leverage in guiding the development that is going to take place. Gas stations and roadside service facilities, for example, are concentrated in a few spots rather than strung out helter-skelter. Where subdivisions are to be built in the corridors, the county encourages a cluster design and asks the developer to plan his open space so that there will be buffer zones along the corridor. This procedure is good for the subdivision as well as the roads, and developers have been cooperative. Monterey County has some things going for it that some counties do not; it is spectacularly scenic, and since it has had tough billboard zoning for years, it had a great deal of unspoiled roadside left to save. The basic techniques, however, work anywhere, and more and more local governments are applying them.

Valuable as they are, measures for revealing the landscape can only be supplemental. The nub of the matter is what is being revealed, and here we run into some quandaries. The beauty of our rural landscapes, by and large, has been created by farmers, and the problem, simply, is that they are not staying on the farm. The family farm is going, and with it the pastoral scenes we have so long taken for granted. The trend is to the one-product "factory" farm, and more intensive production on less land. Even the cows are disappearing from view. Instead of browsing on hillsides and meadows, they are eating on assembly lines; dairymen are finding that it is cheaper to import feed and store it in giant silos, which grouped together look very much like a chemical factory. There is still a lot of close-to-market farming in our metropolitan areas, but increasingly it is the highly specialized kind of operation, and aesthetically, it is no delight.

The best landscape program would be one that revivified the family farm. Some ecologists think that it would be a good idea in any event; one-crop mass-farming approach is bad for our soils, they hold, and on economic grounds alone a return to the family type of farm is in order. But there seems little likelihood that such a reversal is imminent. The government has been paying farmers to farm less of their land, and economic forces have been pushing them in the same direction.* For many years to come we can expect the farmland on the periphery of our urban areas to continue to diminish, with the prime land being converted for development, and the marginal land reverting to second growth.

What can be done about it? The answer is not very

* Our national policy is very inconsistent on this matter. The government spends a lot of money getting farmers to retire cropland, but it spends even more on water projects to create new cropland in the West. Some people think the policy would be better if turned inside out. In a blunt speech to a group of Westerners, Pennsylvania's Secretary of Forests and Waters, Dr. Maurice Goddard, had this to say: "It seems just plain ridiculous to us to keep placing Eastern farm land in the 'Soil Bank,' while continuing to bring additional marginal Western lands into production through subsidized water development. Instead, why not bring this Eastern land, where the people are, and where rainfall is plentiful, back into production? . . . You could put a lot of abandoned Eastern farm acreage back in production for the cost of furnishing water to one Western acre. . . . We have subsidized your dream long enough—far too many Western projects have been constructed with Eastern dollars, and we now need and want our rightful share. . . ."

much. As I have noted in the chapter on open-space assessment, farmers can be proferred low taxes to keep their land from being developed, but the bargain won't stick. The development will take place anyway, and all the public gets for its gift is a few years illusion that the open space is saved. Where the pressures for development become intense, the only way to keep the farm scene is to buy the farmland and use public money to see to it that it is farmed. This can work in special cases—school farms, experimental farms, nature centers for children, for example—and the investment can be well worthwhile. But the cases are special; the great bulk of the farmland on the fringe will stay open just so long as it is economic, and monies spent on freezing the scene will be wasted.

This is not to argue against subsidies. The English have kept their landscape by subsidy, and though agricultural benefits are the official justification, they know very well that it is landscape they are paying for. We should be equally frank. In maintaining the countryside farmers are providing something we want, and there are bargains to be struck.

As long as we are going to pay farmers for not farming land, we might as well get them to do something to make it look better as part of the deal. One partial move to this effect has been made by the Department of Agriculture. Under the new Cropland Adjustment Program, it can now pay farmers up to fifty percent of the cost of conservation work they do on unneeded cropland—such as the building of ponds, planting of grass, trees, and cover for wildlife. As a condition of aid, farmers sign agreements to keep up the work for a five- to ten-year period. Many also agree to allow public access for hunting, fishing, or hiking.

While the purpose is not better scenery, that can be the effect, and it would be if the measures were coordinated in area-wide landscape programs. Unfortunately, there are no such programs. Farm by farm, county agents do a good job, but it is not their business to draft area-wide landscape plans. It has not been made anybody else's business either; and most local governments have yet to realize what scenic opportunities the agriculture programs offer, and with monies already funded too.

Scenic clearing is one example. Farm conservation programs stress the planting of trees, but what many landscapes need most is selective cutting to keep the roadsides open. This is the kind of landscape action where a relatively small public investment could be extremely effective. The screen of brambles and poison ivy and miscellaneous trees that is choking off so many views has no great economic imperative behind it. These lands are truly marginal; along some stretches the land is just too poor to do anything with except leave it be, but in more cases than not it is close to a break-even proposition for the farmer to mow or graze the fields, and it would not take much to tip the scales.

There are a number of ways to do this. One would be for the public to buy strips of land along the roads and then lease them to farmers or give them use permits on terms favorable enough to encourage continued husbandry of the land. The National Park Service has used the latter technique successfully along some of its parkways. Another would be the acquisition of conservation easements stipulating that the land be kept free of second growth. A third possibility would be a novel subsidy; one for farming land. As a variant of the cropland adjustment program, payments would be made to farmers for keeping certain fields and hillsides open by mowing, grazing, or growing crops on them.

For volunteer work there are the part time, weekend, and summer farmers. Their numbers are growing and the farm look means a great deal to them—it is one of the main reasons they bought their properties. They show a special interest in having their meadows kept open, and some bravely start out trying to attend to the work themselves. This phase does not last very long. Most find they have neither the time nor the backs, and to get the job done they provide something of a subsidy program of their own. Characteristically, a summer farmer is only too glad to let a neighboring farmer have the hay on his land for the

mowing of it, and if this does not prove inducement
enough he will sometimes pay the farmer to have it done.
The problem is finding a neighboring farmer.

Another problem is lack of capital for machinery. There
are machines that mow fields with great efficiency, cutting the hay and baling it in one quick operation. They
cost a lot of money, but if many farms can be serviced,
the investment is worthwhile. In some areas landowners
have banded together to finance such a machine and have
set up a sort of community mowing operation. While their
purpose was primarily aesthetic, they have found that hay
economics are not so bad. For much the same reasons they
buy farms, people are taking to horseback riding in sharply
increasing numbers, and the demand for summer hay is
going up correspondingly.

There is a cue here for a public landscape program. A
county or community could underwrite the capital costs
of an efficient machine, and if the program was well conceived, the fees paid by landowners for the cutting service
would more than cover operating costs. And the fields
would be open.

Even better than machinery are animals; sheep in particular. Back in the 1940s planner Roland Greeley suggested to the State of Vermont that the best investment
it could make for keeping its countryside open would be
to subsidize sheep. At that time 85 percent of Vermont
was open; 15 percent in forest. Now, the proportions are
just about reversed, and the state is urgently searching for
ways to keep open what is left of its farm landscape.
Among other things, it is considering tax incentives to
farmers for keeping their roadside lands uncluttered.*

* An excellent report by Allen Fonoroff and Norman Williams, Jr., *Protecting Roadside Scenery in Vermont,* proposes
a wide range of devices, with strong emphasis on techniques
for unblocking the view. "The first step," they say, "which is
extraordinarily simple, may even be the most important of all.
On many Vermont highways, many of the finest views are now
blocked by a recent growth of trees—mostly poplar, cherry, and
other trees of no great value. Where these trees are within the

Sheep can still help. Quite aside from the pastoral touch they add, they are very efficient groundskeepers and have done an excellent job in many parks. A government aided program to put them to work on landscapes could prove quite economic. On a rotation basis, one flock could graze a very considerable area, and as with mowing machinery the costs might be more than met by the fees paid by landowners. In some cases, particularly where there are large public areas to be maintained, a municipal flock could be set up. One shudders to think of the bad jokes legislators would make of such a proposal but it could make a lot of sense.

Forests should be landscaped too. In their own way, many of them are becoming as choked as the fields. They have too many trees and often a dense understory that makes them dark and uninviting and sometimes impenetrable. Thinning is an expensive operation, but if it is concentrated at key spots along the public way—at stream crossings, for example—it can be transforming. Herbicides may also prove useful; recent experiments have indicated that by controlled spraying the undergrowth along the roadside could be thinned out at fairly low cost.

Another step would be to plan further reforestation with landscape values in mind. The conventional reforestation consists of one species, usually pine, laid down in precise rows, mile after mile, like a gigantic Christmas tree farm, and the effect is one of overpowering monotony. The regimentation does make maintenance and harvesting easier, but the timber value justification so often advanced is not very compelling. Other benefits, such as watershed protection, are more important, and in our urban states the recreational and aesthetic benefits are the most important of all. Forestry planning should reflect this. Along the

highway right-of-way, all that is needed is a chain saw. Where (as often) the roots of such trees are on private land, it should not be difficult to obtain permission to cut them, for a nominal sum or for free." A demonstration project to test the idea is underway.

edges and points of access of woods, if not in the interior, a variety of species should be planted, with both hardwoods and softwoods, and some spots should be deliberately kept unplanted and open. The result would be a forest more native to the region than the single species plantation, and if there is a well-contrived landscape plan, a scene far more natural.

Trail development, while financed as a recreational measure, should be part of the landscape plan. The forests close to our cities are, save for the edges, unknown country for most people. They have to be invited in much more forcefully, and artfully, for though the trails may be there the points of entry are not sufficiently known or dramatized. Riding trails have the greatest pulling power, and there are many opportunities to be seized for expanding them. Much of the forest land in the East, public and private, is crisscrossed with abandoned wood roads. At moderate cost, and with, perhaps, Job Corps help, hundreds of miles of these old roads could be opened up for riding.

As we move into suburbia toward the city the landscape becomes much more complex. The tree shaded streets of upper- and middle-income neighborhoods are self-tending and generally pleasant. Along the main commercial routes, however, the scene is disjointed. Here we find the detritus of suburbia, all the more jarring for the contrast—the junkyards, the sand and gravel pits, the rundown plants of the 1920s, patches of vacant land that speculators were sure would be developed but which never were.

Some judicious screening can help.* But the greater opportunity is reclamation. Many of these inelegant land uses are necessary. Quarries and sand and gravel pits, for

---

* A problem that especially warrants the cosmetic approach is the defacing of rocks and cliffs, which, thanks to the aerosol paint can, has become much easier for fraternity pledges and other people who like to do this sort of thing. Some park people spray fertilizer over the graffiti so that lichens will grow. Others recommend spraying paint remover.

example, are among the most recurring features of the urban landscape and because they must be located close to market, there will be more digging in the future. But there are advantages to be turned; eyesores they may be, but they can be made otherwise, and as anyone who has done his boyhood swimming in an old quarry knows, they can provide an amenity where none was before.

Until recently, beneficial reuse of quarries and pits was apt to be more happy accident than forethought. It costs a great deal of money to regrade old workings; the operators felt they could not afford to do it, and communities did not press them to. But now the operators themselves are getting religion. For one thing, they badly need better public relations. Community after community has been raising zoning barriers against them, and they cannot escape by merely pushing farther out. Meanwhile, as land prices have soared, some operators have found that the high cost of reclamation can be more than recouped by the residential development of remnant land, and with recreational areas as a sweetener for the community. The pits and quarries can be fashioned into lakes and with imaginative earth moving the "spoil" can provide a more interesting topography than what was there originally, especially so in predominantly flat land. (Even oil well operators are thinking along these lines; in Los Angeles economic pressures have been forcing them to clean up the derricks and turn to land development. By clustering their equipment into "drilling islands" and drilling from an angle they can free much of the intervening land.)

The key in reclamation is figuring the eventual landscape and reuse plan before excavation is begun. Since this is so patently to the self-interest of the operator, the community is in an excellent position to join in the planning. As with cluster development, the community has great leverage; whatever the commercial reuses may be, zoning changes will probably be required, and in exchange the community can suggest what portions should be dedicated for public use and how they can fit the overall landscape and recreation plant.

Sanitary land fill operations offer another opportunity for reuse planning. In too many cases the local government has no plan, and its refuse is dumped where it is most convenient for contractors to dump it; the "garbage gate" straddling the Bayshore Freeway south of San Francisco is a particularly noisome example. But refuse can create valuable community land. With its long range "garbage to park" plan San Diego has been putting its land fill into eroded gulleys to create public golf courses and recreational areas, and in one of them it has a city nursery to provide stock for landscaping other areas.

A particularly felicitous example of garbage economics is the recreation area being built in a forest preserve in Dupage County, twenty-five miles west of Chicago. The central feature is a "mountain" for skiing and tobogganing, which when finished will be 130 feet high and 39 acres at the base. The project is largely self-financing. The County has designated the spot as the point for garbage disposal in the County, and the contractors pay a fee for each load they dump. Next to this pile, the County is excavating a gravel pit. The sale of the gravel nets additional money; the clay in the pit furnishes a covering for each successive layer of garbage on the mountain, and when the digging is over, the pit will become a seventy-five-acre lake for boating and swimming and ice skating.

Where there is waste, there is opportunity, and this applies to almost every aspect of the urban landscape—the ever-burning pyres of rubbish, the town incinerators which do not incinerate very well, the lots piled with junked cars and stoves and refrigerators, the lots that are not used for anything. This combination of detritus and vacuum is especially characteristic of the gray area between the suburbs and the edge of the city—the kind of landscape for which the German word "dreck" is so appropriate. That we have so much of it is almost encouraging. It is the area of second chances.

19. Townscape

>>>

By now we should be approaching the entrance of the city. But where is it? The most frustrating part of U.S. cities is getting into them, or knowing when we have. Suburbia is behind us but the scene continues as before; used car lots, diners, borax furniture stores, gas stations, and gas stations, and gas stations. It is not just the blight but the interminability of it that is deadening, and this seems to be especially true of smaller cities, the approaches of which seem to stretch out in inverse ratio to the worth of what is being approached. Mile after mile they drag on, and the only indication that there is an entrance is the knot of signs saying where the Kiwanis and the Rotary meet.

A program to clean up the approaches should be a major part of a townscape effort, and it is the kind of high-visibility cause that can enlist widespread support. First priority should go to securing key open spaces; if there are any golf courses, estates, or farms along the approaches they should be secured forthwith. In most cases they are slated for eventual development; even institutions, whose landscaped grounds we tend to regard as a permanent part of the scenery, are often quite ready to sell out and relocate. Acquisition costs, whether in fee or by easements, may be very steep, but the location of these spaces gives them a benefit-cost ratio that well justifies the expense.

The commercial clutter can be greatly reduced, and action to do this can be good business as well as good aesthetics. New highway construction and improvement programs can provide parallel frontage roads for roadside business—as has been done on the Connecticut Turnpike at New Haven—and even if these are screened from the right-of-way, the ease of access, and of parking, makes such relocation quite profitable. Similarly, the various welcome and informational signs could be more effective if they were grouped in a service cluster at the edge of the city. One of the reasons airports are such excellent gateways is the way they concentrate these services and give the traveler a pause for rehabilitation. Road ports, on a smaller scale, could do the same. (And why not borrow the airport amenity of free direct-line phones to hotels and motels?)

In clearing away the clutter we reveal the city. The sight of it from afar can be compelling—Dallas across the cotton fields, Chicago from the Lake Shore Drive—and never more so than when first discovered at the crest of a hill or a sweeping turn of the road. And it is at just these spots that the clutter is often the densest; as a matter of fact, it is the job of billboard location scouts to find these key views so that they can be pre-empted with signs.

Many highways are so beyond redemption that it is best to start all over again, and the Federal highway program has provided a great second chance. Sometimes the new vistas are almost immediately expropriated—the sign-ridden Bayshore Freeway approaches to San Francisco, for example—but in more cases than not the thruways have opened up the view, and because of their scale and the speed at which we can travel on them, the experience of coming upon the city has been greatly heightened.

But so much more could be done. In many cases the engineers have failed to exploit the new vistas their works have created, and sometimes they seem to go out of their way to hide them. To this driver the most exasperating example is the New Jersey approach to the Lincoln Tunnel. It has all the elements of a great spectacle. First, there is a long drive up a hill in a submerged roadway, with a few glimpses of the Empire State Building to suggest what is to come; then, just after the crest, the road swings down to the tunnel and for a few seconds there is the river and the skyline of Lower Manhattan. If a late afternoon sun is picking out the towers it is almost too much to believe.

But for motorists driving out of the tunnel there is no view at all. The retaining wall of the ramp has been placed just high enough—by a few inches—to blot out the scene. The San Francisco Bay Bridge provides similar frustrations. From afar it is a great sight, but once on the bridge itself it is difficult to see anything because of the side railings and wires.*

One problem with the visual entries to the city is that the city often has no control over them. State engineers attend to the highway design, and the local governments which sit astride the approaches are usually bent on their exploitation. But as with water supply, however, the city does have extra-territorial rights, and it should assert them. It should also do more to inject itself into the design of the highway approaches. The best of the new freeways have come about as the result of a row being raised over the first, stock designs. Such rows should not stop at the city limits.

* One moral: take the bus. In most urban areas the extra few feet of elevation puts the passenger above the walls, fences, and other cars that wall in the motorist's vision. It makes a big difference.

Cities have a tremendous, and fleeting, opportunity to reclaim their waterfronts. Most are obsolete—a jumble of
rotting piers, old warehouses, scrapyards, and freight
tracks that shut off people from the water and yet no
longer serve an economic function. One or two modern
piers can handle the shipping that once required the whole
waterfront; the miles of freight tracks that once serviced
it are now little used; because of the efficiencies of pipelines, riverside locations for oil tank farms are less necessary than before.

The pressures for redevelopment have been building
up for a long time, and almost every waterfront is now on
the verge of a large-scale clearing and rebuilding program.
In some cases the rebuilding is well under way; in others,
the plans are still unresolved. For good or bad, however,
the die is soon going to be cast. The plans that are made,
or not made, in the next few years will determine the
character of our cities' waterfronts for decades to come.

What has been taking place so far is not very encouraging. Instead of opening up the waterfronts, many projects are resealing it more than ever. Housing projects for
riverside sites are designed like housing projects for any
site, insensitively, and the view from them does not make
up for the view of them. Riverside freeways are like other
freeways, and as with the Lincoln Tunnel approaches,
seem cunningly contrived to put the driver out of sight
of the river.

Too many projects are single purpose projects. Along a
stretch of the Hudson in New York City, for example, a
huge sewage disposal plant is to be built. As the sanitation
engineers planned it, the top would consist of several acres
of concrete, to be used for nothing. This would be an
inexcusable waste of space, and a truly monumental eyesore. It promised to be such an eyesore, fortunately, that
there was vigorous civic protest and the city reconsidered.
Architect Philip Johnson has redesigned it so the top will
provide a gigantic display of lights and fountains.

In many cases, it is too late for imagination. Not only
are the projects routinely conceived, they are planned

with little thought as to their relationship with other projects, the river, or the city in back. What is most needed is a unifying plan. The guiding principle should be access. There should be maximum visual access. There should be maximum physical access—and not just to the waterfront, but the water itself. While it takes believing, we should anticipate the day when the anti-pollution programs will have the rivers running clear again and people will be able to swim in them, even from downtown.

Every new waterfront project, public or private, should contribute to access, and the city should press the point early, and stubbornly. What will this particular arrangement of towers do to the view? Can people get to the shoreside park, or is there only a token footbridge? What is the angle of view from the roadway? If there must be a retaining wall, why this ugly one?

Cities should also cast a more imaginative look at the old structures along the waterfront. Before they tear them all down, redevelopment officials should take a trip to San Francisco. They should look first at the famous ferry tower and note how thoroughly the view of it has been botched up by an elevated highway. Then they should go to the north waterfront area. Here, without urban renewal aid, a number of architects and entrepreneurs have been rehabilitating old buildings and warehouses to excellent effect. The most notable example is Ghirardelli Square, an attractive complex of shops and restaurants fashioned out of an old chocolate factory. Such projects are rarely considered in conventional redevelopment planning, but they provide the offbeat charm that people will seek out, and just one or two can revitalize a whole area.

The Fisherman's Wharf idea is another that can be borrowed. Almost every city with a waterfront has a pier or shoreside structure that could be refashioned for restaurants and shops, and where this has been done they have proved a strong attraction. They are slightly fraudulent—the seafood is apt to be flown in from somewhere else and not very well prepared—but the view is good, and people do love the honky-tonk. Every waterfront should have some.

Small rivers and streams have their delights too, and with care and art, as San Antonio has demonstrated, they can be made into a great amenity for a city. But it takes fighting. Look at an old map of your city. Where are the streams of yesteryear? Underground, and that is where many that remain would go if some people had their way. There is a lot of federal money available to make water-courses floodproof and in the cause of "channel improvement" engineers have been burying many out of sight in big conduits. Failing this, they transform them into concrete troughs, and as a minimum measure they rip-rap the banks with bleak stretches of stone. Planners have argued that the banks could be stabilized by planting them with grass and shrubs and water thirsty trees, like sycamores and willows. The engineers have usually prevailed; much has been made of the maintenance and safety problem, and there is, of course, the pressure of all that money.

But now there is countervailing pressure—federal money for grass and trees—and streams and rivers may get a reprieve. As a major part of their new beautification programs, cities should launch stream bank improvement projects to save what has not been concreted or rip-rapped; they should also launch projects to bring back to life some of the stretches which have been concreted. Another possibility worth exploring is the unburying of streams.

The simplest kind of townscape action is to plant trees—big trees—and to plant thousands of them. It is the best kind of action. The streets of our cities are named after trees—walnut, spruce, poplar, maple—and it would be wonderful if someday soon these misnomers were planted with walnut, spruce, poplar, maple.

They well might be. Under the new federal beautification program, cities will be matched 50-50 for the additional efforts they will make over and above their regular tree planting programs. The response has been encouraging; many communities have been markedly stepping up their street tree programs, and in the process they have been stimulating a tremendous amount of matching work on the part of garden clubs, of block and neighborhood associations, downtown groups, and, not unimportantly, school children. Trees are contagious; as soon as one neighborhood or street is planted, citizen pressure builds up for action for the next street, and the next.

Various commercial interests can be stimulated too. Parking lot operators are an example. There may be no law that says they have to screen their lots or plant trees within them, but some cities have found that if pressure is properly applied, parking lot operators can be made to see the light. Owners of scrap yards and automobile graveyards can be similarly induced. Many cities require them to put up fences, but these are often as bad looking as what they hide; screening with trees makes far more sense, and the scrap people, now highly sensitive to the threat of more restrictive legislation, have often been quite ready to cooperate.

Developers can be persuaded too. As a matter of course they put saplings on the lots; shade trees along the streets they lay down would be a more important amenity, and cities should require this planting as a condition of plat approval. Airport authorities should also be pressed, and not just for what trees would do too for the looks of the airports but for the sound of them. Former FAA Administrator Neil Halaby has suggested that we start thinking of "hush parks" around all our airports.

We need more trees, we need bigger ones. We especially need bigger ones for downtown planting; saplings take a very long time to look like anything, and even after ten or fifteen years they are out of scale for their surroundings. Many a layman has wondered why we don't do the obvious and transplant grown trees from our woods instead of waiting so long. Our technology, we have been told, is not advanced enough for this. The transplanting would be much too expensive, nurserymen explain, the trees would be vulnerable to sun scald, and their root systems would be harmed.

But the English have tried it and it works. Some years ago the National Coal Board borrowed a technique developed in the United States at Chicago's Morton Arboretum and used it to save trees on lands to be strip-mined. The earthmoving equipment, also developed in the U.S., consists of a giant scoop which, in less than ten minutes, can dig up a tree and a large root ball and then transport it to a holding area. The trees can be stored for many months without harm, and when put back again, or transplanted to a new location, they do well. With this technique the English are now going directly to their woods for their street trees.

The English are surprised we have not done the same. We have a huge store of excellent hardwoods in our woods and forests, and quite close to most of our cities. Here are our tree banks, and with some initiative by the states they can be put to immediate use. Through their forest departments the states could initiate a grant-in-kind program for furnishing stock to local government. Cities which have extensive watershed lands in forest could set up their own tree bank operations. (Nurserymen should not raise a fuss over the competition; the new landscape and townscape programs should give them more business than they ever dreamed of.)

More must also be done to protect the trees we already have. One of the reasons so many of our downtowns are bare and monotonous is that the trees that were there have all been chopped down. My own home town was once famous for the maples and oaks that lined its shopping streets; now they are all gone. Merchants complained that they interfered with parking, buckled sidewalks, obscured their signs, and in a civic improvement campaign the trees were eliminated. Sometimes the crackpots and sentimentalists raise enough hell to stop this kind of thing, but similar improvement programs have been pushed through for many a downtown, and in some the merchants never allowed the trees to grow in the first place.

Some people just don't like trees. Many street departments have a predilection for chopping down trees in order to widen streets, and one gets the feeling that sometimes they widen the streets in order to chop down the trees. Most utility and telephone maintenance men prune with care, but some would be happier if there were no trees to contend with and see to it that there are none. And why is it that officials appointed as tree wardens so often are people who like to cut them down? Some wardens always seem to be finding obscure diseases in healthy looking old trees, and they like to operate, usually in winter, when there is not much other contract work around for the men who do this kind of thing.

It is good that there are so many vigilantes—were it not for the Garden Clubs many of our communities would long since have been denuded. But there should be much stricter governmental safeguards. In some cases the laws on the books are quite far reaching; in Massachusetts, for example, it is a criminal offense for a landowner to chop down a tree on property adjoining a public way. Similar legislation should be enacted everywhere, and it should be enforced. There should also be more on the books about tree cutting by public agencies and public utilities. They should be made to prove their case, before the cutting, and the full minutiae of bureaucratic procedure should be invoked for every application, with review by all other agencies, provisions for hearings, and all the time delays possible. This would make it a bit harder for officials to do necessary thinning and removal of truly diseased trees, but it would be a tolerable encumbrance. A chain saw biting into a tree has a very final sound.

There are many more opportunities to consider: better "street furniture," simpler and more attractive street signs, more variety of pavement textures, more imaginative treatment of subway spaces, the use of arcades and crescents and pedestrian malls—the agenda is as long as we wish to make it. But how are all the separate projects to be tied together? Who is to say which comes first? On what grounds? Most projects are worth doing in their own right, and many should be launched forthwith. Eventually, however, there must be a unifying plan, and if it is to mean anything there must be a rather thorough, and continuing, analysis of the visual assets and liabilities of the community.

This was the basic idea behind the new federal program of beautification grants. So far the results have been mildly encouraging. Instead of sporadic, one-shot community appearance studies, many cities have commanded long-range programs and have begun putting some real money into them. Cities which had already been doing a good job, such as Philadelphia, have displayed considerable imagination, and so have some county governments. Here and there interesting demonstration projects are underway: New York City is testing landscape architect M. Paul Friedberg's concept of "portable parks"; in the San Francisco Bay area, authorities are fashioning a 2.7 mile park strip under the elevated structure of the BART rapid transit system.

But the great bulk of the beautification programs are thoroughly conventional. About 70 percent of the grant money is going for what amounts to park renovation. The long range planning consists in most cases of adding up a shopping list of nice things to do. Few cities are developing techniques for analyzing the city as people see it, and until they do this as part of the regular planning process their beautification projects are bound to seize on the obvious. The lag is inevitable in any new program, of course, and there is much to be thankful for—all those new trees, especially. But the lack of imagination is dismaying nonetheless.

Beauty, of course, can be quite subjective. What is a Victorian monstrosity to some people may be a building of great appeal to others, and some of the most ferocious civic squabbles have been over proposed demolitions of beloved eyesores. Designs for monuments and public statuary often arouse similar passions. On the main elements of the landscape and townscape, however, people tend to have fairly similar reactions. When I was interviewing people in Connecticut to get opinions on what a state conservation program should include, I was surprised at how much the views of different kinds of people coincided. Whatever their income, occupation, place of residence, most cited the same objectives, and usually in much the same order (number one: save the "natural" countryside), and there was a great overlap in the particular sights they talked about as illustration. The only notable difference was that between long-time residents and newcomers, and that was of degree. The newcomers were more conscious of the landscape, and more zealous about protecting it.

Several interesting experimental studies have shown that the perceptions people have of a scene can be systematically charted, and that when this is done a strong correspondence is evident. In his work on the image of the city, Kevin Lynch has had cross-sections of people play back their impression of parts of the city and their walks through it. The reconstructions show that there is a great unity in their sense of place, with particular emphasis on "nodes" and the focal points and the edges. The work of such Englishmen as Gordon Cullen and Ian Nairn is also notable. Their approach is somewhat more impressionistic, but the substance of their work is that effects of landscape and townscape can be reduced to general principles that are applicable in any country, and, for that matter, in any century. By simple observation, the layman can test such propositions for himself. Sit on a park bench and observe the way people respond to space. Big city or small, East or West, they will gravitate to the enclosed spaces that cuddle them.

People are not all so much the same that there will not be disputes of taste in any landscape or townscape program. It would have to be pretty bland if people failed to get exercised over some of the parts. But a tougher problem than aesthetics will be costs and priorities. Even if everyone were to agree on every project, there will only be a given amount of money, and once past the obvious priorities—such as tree planting—some hard choices will be posed. Should there be lots of relatively low cost projects over a wide area? Or should the efforts be concentrated on the downtown business district? Is the money better spent on high traffic, high cost sites? By what yardsticks should they be judged?

The highway engineers have come in for a lot of abuse because of their preoccupation with quantitative data in arriving at their cost-benefit ratios. They have indeed emphasized too much the easily measurable, but at least they have made a major effort to assess choice on the basis of what would best serve the most people, and planners concerned with open space and recreation have some catching up to do. For years open-space acquisition has been planned with an eye mainly on costs, and this has unduly emphasized low price rural land. If benefits are given equal weight, the equations become more favorable for high cost land where people are. The same question of balance will be central to any landscape program.

Figuring the costs will be easy enough; it is the benefits that will need the work. The first step is an inventory of the looks of the area, not as a static set of scenes, but as a moving sequence, the way people experience the community driving and walking. One approach might be a series of stop-motion photographic records taken with a 16-mm. or 35-mm. movie camera; accompanying the frames, somewhat like a sound track, would be a running index of average traffic counts at particular spots, average vehicle speeds, and the like. The annotation is important. I once spent a lot of time taking eye-view movie inventory of the secondary roads in Chester County. It may be of some value as a record of what once was, but I have found that it is a bit misleading by not being related to how many other people traverse the view.

The work of Kevin Lynch, Donald Appleyard, and John Myer is highly suggestive. In *The View from the Road* they have charted a driver's-eye view of a freeway and have worked up a system of shorthand symbols by which one can score such visual experiences. Some of the methodology seems very complicated, but a lot of ingenuity is being applied, and the basic approach ought to be widely copied.

The other part of the benefit equation is the beholder. How many people see the view? At what time of day? Under what circumstances? Traffic counts are a help, but the fact that, say, 8000 people pass a given point a day doesn't tell us enough. Who are they? Each scene has a set of audiences: what the husband sees driving home in peak-hour traffic can be quite different from what a wife sees driving the same route to the supermarket in mid-morning, or the child on a bus ride to school. We must consider the great effect that speed has on scale. To return to my example of the Wallingford scene, if the toll station were eliminated and drivers did not have to slow down, the pastoral view would all but disappear.

The pedestrian's eye view is another rich field for inquiry. So far, there have been few studies comparable to the origin and destination checks highway people make of motorists, but several trial efforts suggest that there may be interesting patterns to look into. It would appear, for example, that people will take much longer walks if they can see the building they are headed to. It would also appear that pedestrian traffic and vehicular traffic are not quite so incompatible as it is axiomatically assumed. In downtown, it is the pedestrians who dominate. Similarly, the attractions of wide, uncongested sidewalks may be overrated. Pedestrians attract pedestrians, and they will often choose a narrow, crowded sidewalk despite the jostling and broken-field footwork it requires, or, perhaps, because it does require it.

No matter how well we chart the visual traffic, decisions on projects will always be a matter of judgment, and, inevitably, of politics. Nevertheless, a well-annotated inventory can be of great help in dealing with the critical choices. For one city I know of the most obvious project would be the improvement of a streamside drive on the outskirts, and there is much local agitation for it. It would be a worthwhile project, but it would primarily benefit the well-to-do whose suburbia adjoins it; nobody else in

the city has occasion to use it. A far more important opportunity is to be found in a less comely scene where two
secondary roads join at the entrance of the city. Potentially,
it is a magnificent gateway; there is a junkyard that
should be screened, a derelict gas station and a small
garage which obscure the view of a cove need to be removed, and nearby there is a fine old eighteenth-century
house which could be moved four hundred yards to great
effect. Since the area is zoned commercial, the costs could
be considerable. But the benefits would far outweigh them.
This is where the people go.

Is there not a danger that all this will be cosmetic? Yes,
there is. The danger is that people will be inhibited from
action for fear it will be cosmetic. Some worry that action
of such elemental and visual appeal will be a diversion
from the true urban task, and those who push for a program involving such mundane matters as tree planting
and roadside clearing must prepare themselves to be lec-
tured on the dangers of the small view. Prettification is not
the answer, goes the scolding, trees and flowers won't
solve the basic problems. True beauty is integral.

To be sure. To be sure. But where does that leave us?
Just because we cannot solve all the underlying problems
of urban growth with landscape programs is no reason
to scorn landscape programs. Nor is there need to be so
lofty about cosmetics—they do have their uses. Only in a
small part, furthermore, does a landscape program have
to be cosmetic, in the sense of covering a reality we would
like to hide. Certainly there are pitfalls in stress on the cosmetic, the picturesque and the antiquarian. But this is to
say there are pitfalls in bad design.

The cosmetic argument infers a conflict that does not
actually exist. To plant a beautiful tree by the side of a
road does not demand that we underrate the importance
of the design of the road itself; or that we be heedless
of the other elements of a good environment. More trees,
of course, will not solve the basic problems. They will
make no dent on racial discrimination. They will not halt

urban sprawl. One can go further; it is quite unproved that trees or other bits of nature have quite the uplifting influence on man that has so often been claimed for them.

Let us just say that trees are nice to have. The planting of them obtains no far-reaching solutions; neither does it prevent them. Auto junkyards, for example, have become a big problem because something has gone wrong with the scrap cycle, and any fundamental solution will have to be an economic one. Will it hurt, in the meantime, if we hide the worst eyesores with some trees? There should be no antithesis.

The usual anti-prettification critiques imply that those interested in visual beauty make up a separate category of people, and not a very hep one at that; such phrases as "well-meaning" crop up, and if "garden-club ladies" are cited, the reference is clearly pejorative. But is there this division? I have found that people who feel very strongly about their own landscape are more often than not the same people who are pushing for better comprehensive planning, water resources programs, and all the other components of the large view. But it is the landscape that commands their emotions.

There is a moral in the fact that threats to local landscapes arouse more passion than positive planning proposals. It is sometimes a shame that this is so; the passions are too often expended on lost causes, too often coupled with an exclusionist view of the larger community. But planning that becomes too abstract or scornful of this aspect will miss a vital motivating factor.

The landscape element of any long range regional plan will only be a small part of the total effort, but more than any other element it can enlist a personal involvement. People are stirred by what they can see. And they are right.

Design and Density

20. The Case for Crowding

>>

The net of what I have been saying about landscape action is that we are going to have to work with a much tighter pattern of spaces and development, and that our environment may be the better for it. This somewhat optimistic view rests on the premise that densities are going to increase and that it is not altogether a bad thing that they do. It is a premise many would dispute. Our official land policy is dead set against higher densities. It is decentralist, like official policies in most other countries. The primary thrust of it is to move people outward; reduce densities, loosen up the metropolis, and reconstitute its parts in new enclaves on the fringe.

I do not think it is going to work out this way. Certainly, outward movement will continue, but if our population continues to grow, the best way to accommodate the growth will be by a more concentrated and efficient use of the land within the area. The big "if" is whether or not intensity of use will be coupled with efficiency of use. It may not be. But it can be. Europe is the proof of this. Many of those who ask why we cannot take care of the landscape like Europeans do fail to realize that these landscapes, both urban and rural, accommodate far more people per acre than do ours. The disparity is not due primarily to our averages being weighted by the vast open spaces of the West. Even in our most urban states the metropolitan areas average out to lower densities than their counterparts in Europe—indeed, to some entire European countries.

The case for higher densities cannot rest on a shortage of land. There is none. It is true that top-grade agricultural lands are being overrun by urban expansion, that open space in the right places is increasingly difficult to save. The fact remains, however, that if we wish to go the expansion route, there is room for it. Expand the diameter of a metropolitan area by only a few miles and enough land will be encompassed to take care of a very large population increase. This may be a poor way to do it, but the option exists.

Nor are our cities running into each other. Metropolitan areas are being linked more tightly, but this is not the same thing as collision. Consider, for example, the great belt of urban areas along the Eastern Seaboard from Boston to Norfolk. It is well that we are paying more attention to the continuities of this megalopolis, as Jean Gottman has done so well, but to call it a "strip city," as many are doing, is misleading.

There is no such city, and the proposition can be easily tested. Fly from Boston to Washington and look out the window. Here and there one suburbia flows into another —between Baltimore and Washington, for example—but the cities retain their identities. This is especially apparent at night when the lights beneath simplify the structure so vividly: the brilliantly lit downtowns, the shopping centers, the cloverleafs, the spine of freeways that connect it all. But just as striking is what is dark—the forests of Massachusetts and Connecticut, the pine barrens of New Jersey, the farmlands of the Eastern Shore, the tidewater of Virginia. For many miles along the great urban route you can look down and see only the scattered lights of farms and small towns.

Urbanized sectors in other parts of the country—excepting, always, Los Angeles—show much the same characteristics. They are systems of cities, tied by high-speed rail and road networks, but they have not yet congealed into an undifferentiated mass. There is room outside them for expansion. There is room inside them. Whichever way is best, a measure of choice is still open to us.

The choice is by no means an either-or one, for there are forces working in both directions, and there is only so much we can do by planning and public policy to shape these forces to our liking. But this margin is important. Our government programs for transportation, for new housing and urban development have a great leverage, and a shift of emphasis one way or the other could have a considerable effect on the metropolis of not too many years hence.

Decentralize or concentrate? Most of the prescriptions for the ideal metropolis opt for decentralization. Expansion of the metropolis is to continue, only this time the expansion will be orderly. Instead of a sprawl of subdivisions, new development is to be channeled into planned new communities, with rapid transit linking them and green belts separating them. Some proposals would place the new communities outside the metropolitan areas altogether.

Obviously, the limits of suburbia are going to expand some in any event, and obviously there are going to be new communities. But the main show is not going to be out on the perimeter. Outward expansion looks easiest, but it is the least efficient way of taking care of an increased population. As development moves further outward from the core, returns diminish and costs increase, and at an accelerating rate. Water distribution is an example. If you double the population within a given area, you can service it by enlarging the diameter of the present pipe system; if you try to take care of the population by doubling the area, however, you not only have to enlarge the present pipes, you have to lay down a prodigious amount of new ones, and as they poke out into the low density areas costs become progressively steeper. The new residents may be charged an extra sum to help foot these capital costs, but the rest of the community bears most of it.

The same is true with mass transit and other utilities and services. A disproportionate amount of capital investment is needed to provide urban services for people out in the low density areas out on the periphery, but because of the rate structures that usually apply to these services, the fact is masked that other people have to pay more than they should to make up the difference. The other people are the ones in the high density areas that are easiest and most profitable to serve. We have made utilities, economist Mason Gaffney observes, "an agency for milking the center to feed the border, thus subsidizing decentralization."

Concentration provides efficiency; for the same reason it provides maximum access to what people want. This is what cities are all about. People come together in cities because this is the best way to make the most of opportunities, and the more accessible the core, the more choice of opportunities there are, the more access to skills, specialized services and goods, and to jobs. By subsidizing new freeways and peripheral beltways we can make it easier for people to move about within the outer area, but vigorous centers are not the less vital for this but the more, and a policy for dispersing their functions will fail.

Business and industry talk decentralization but while firms may be dispersing their production units, they have been centralizing their office and managerial operations more than before. As I have noted earlier, the British tried to reverse this trend by doing everything possible to stop commercial growth in London and make it go somewhere else. Despite the constraints, commercial growth expanded mightily, and an office building boom of spectacular proportions took place.

For a while we also entertained notions of a commercial exodus. Right after the war it was widely predicted that corporations would be moving their headquarters to campuslike retreats in the suburbs, and there was much favorable publicity when several firms in New York did so. Executives, it was said, would be able to think more; the office force would be closer to home, and more content; space would cost less; the surroundings would be more pleasant in every way. But the movement never quite came off, and several firms who had moved quietly repatriated. New office buildings went up, and on the highest-cost land in the center of the city. Before long, in what seemed almost a frenzy of centralization, whole blocks of big buildings on Park Avenue were being torn down to put up bigger buildings.

The center of things attracts because it is the center of things. What the decentralists would like to do is to cut down the number of things, or, rather, put them somewhere else. They are for urban renewal, but at much lower density. They want to open up the center, disperse as many of its functions as possible, and reassemble them in subcenters out in the hinterland where, in miniature, will be all the advantages of the city—art, music, commerce, universities, urban excitement—but without the disadvantages.

A dull metropolis it would be. This kind of decentralization would not only be a very inefficient way to accommodate growth, it would go against the grain of all the forces that give a metropolis its vitality. Rather than pursue this ill-conceived provincialism, we must look inward as well as outward, to the strengths of the metropolis, and seek a much more intensive and efficient use of the land already within it.

One way is to raise housing densities—both by putting more people on acres developed for housing and by bringing into use acres now wasted or underused. Densities are, of course, relative. What would be considered a very high density for suburbia—twenty people to the acre—would be low for the core, and densities will probably always tend to diminish as the distance from the city grows. At almost any point, however, there could be some increase in density without a lowering of living standards. In some cases the standards would be higher if there was an increase.

This is particularly true in the city. The decentralists who bewail its insensate concentrations talk as though cities are bad because we have been compressing more and more people into them. But we have not been. The populations of our cities have remained static or have decreased. One of the big problems of the gray areas of the cities, indeed, is that they do not have a sufficiently large or varied population to support an urban concentration of services and stores. Instead of cutting down the densities still further, it would make more sense to raise them.

In the city, English architect Theo Crosby points out, high densities are needed for a high level of amenity. Transportation, for example. "The typical planners' compromise—between 100 and 200 people per acre," says Crosby, "makes the vehicle-pedestrian dilemma insoluble. It is only at reasonably high densities (200–300 people per acre is the minimum) that the car is downgraded to the status of a luxury. At this density you can choose to use a car; you don't have to use it. Such a density also means that the network of public transport can be afforded, for it is only at high densities that rapid-transit systems make economic sense."

Density also has an important bearing on the look and feel of a neighborhood. If it is urban it ought to be urban. Most of our redevelopment projects are too loose in fabric. They would look better, as well as being more economic, if the scale were tightened up. This is true even of one of the best; the Southwest redevelopment area in Washington. Some of the architects involved believe that there would be more life and style to it if they had been able to pull the components closer together.

This does not mean putting everybody up in towers. Unfortunately, the arguments for and against high density are usually presented in terms of towers versus anything else—either spread out or go up in the air.* But this is a false choice. A well-knit pattern of low buildings can house a great many people, and often quite amenably. So, obviously, can towers; on any one acre, the maximum possible. But there are other acres to be counted. When towers are spaced out in rows, as in the conventional urban project, the density figures for the over-all project can be surprisingly low.

The usual redevelopment or public housing project generally houses less people per acre than the neighborhood that was torn down to make way for it. The design formulas call for lots of space, almost to a suburban scale, and a big point is made of how little ground is taken for the buildings themselves. The projects of the New York City Public Housing Authority, for example, cover some 2000 acres, an area almost a seventh the size of Manhattan Island. The Housing Authority proudly

---

* Philosophically, the most influential exponent of low density housing has been Britain's Town and Country Planning Association. It equates high density housing with standard high-rise projects. It detests them, with good reason, and has been berating the authorities for continuing to build them. People do not like living in them as well as in low-rise housing, the Association argues, and they especially miss having private gardens of their own. This is a strong case, but in arguing it the Association gives short shrift to the possibility of designing the more human scale low-rise housing to higher densities. To do so, it warns, would be to court the delusion that "skill can create a new Utopia by cleverer compression." This polarizes the case much too much. Utopia, no, but surely there is a middle ground between high-density towers and low-density garden towns. People who want to build only towers like to have the argument thus polarized. Just goes to prove, they say, that they have no reasonable alternative.

points out that only sixteen percent of the area is used for buildings.

What is gained? Open space, it is said. But the open space is drab and institutional and much of it is forbidden to human trespass. The open space is for the architects, so they can have enough ground to put up towers. But to what end? The design does not pursue its logic. The towers are put up, presumably, for density's sake—to make up for the housing that was not built on the open space. But the net density remains low, and not just by slum standards. In the standard public housing project the number of people per net acre is lower than in many middle class neighborhoods of three and four story houses.

This is an inefficient use of high cost land, and if we are to continue it, we ought to have some strong social reason for doing so. The stock justification is that lower densities mean healthier living, and planners of this persuasion make much of the correlation between the number of people per acre and the rate of crime and disease in slum neighborhoods. There is a correlation. But is it cause and effect? There is a distinction to be made between over-crowding—that is, the too many people per room—and a high number of people per acre. Overcrowding does make for an unhealthy environment; high density may or it may not.

A lot of nonsense is heard these days about the psychological effects of living too close together in cities, or of living in cities at all for that matter. Many of the stock criticisms are quite ancient—filing-cabinet apartments producing filing-cabinet minds, neuroses, tenseness, conformity, and so on. But now the accusations are being made more scientifically. There is a rash of studies underway designed to uncover the bad consequences of overcrowding. This is all very well as far as it goes, but it only goes in one direction. What about undercrowding? The researches would be a lot more objective if they paid as much attention to the possible effects on people of relative isolation and lack of propinquity. Maybe some of those rats they study get lonely too.*

If we study the way people themselves live, we will find strong empirical evidence that they can do quite well in high-density areas. It depends on the area. Some neighborhoods with relatively low densities have high disease and crime rates. Conversely, some neighborhoods with higher densities have low disease and crime rates. Obviously, other factors are the determining ones. (Hong Kong, one of the most densely populated cities in the world, with up to 2800 people per acre, has relatively low disease and crime rates compared to congested areas in the U.S.)

Why is it, furthermore, that so many of our high-density neighborhoods are the most sought after? This is not just a matter of high-rise luxury apartments; in New York some of the tree-lined blocks of four- and five-story brownstones with interior gardens have net densities higher than nearby public housing projects. The latter average about 250 people per acre. Remodeled brown-

---

* One phenomenon they might look into is the way people often jam up in groups when they do not have to. Cocktail parties, for example. People who go to them habitually complain about the crowding, the noise and the smoke. But notice how they behave. They do not like too much room. They bunch together and towards the end of the party they will have themselves all jammed into one corner of an otherwise empty room.

The way people behave in the out-of-doors is not totally dissimilar. In a trenchant study of national parks, Noel Eichorn and Frank Fraser Darling comment on the curious psychology of the camp ground: "To some of us [it is] a quite baffling phenomenon. Mr. Lon Garrison told us of his study in Yosemite in the 1930s when he found that many people apparently like being crowded in camp grounds. At least, when the density of occupation of camp grounds decreased after Labor Day, there was a general movement from the outliers to the center, where the density consequently remained high." (*Man and Nature in the National Parks,* Washington, The Conservation Foundation, 1967.)

stone areas run from about 180 people to as high as 350 people per acre.

Brooklyn Heights is an example. The fine old homes there (which are about 25 feet wide by 50 feet deep, plus a 50-foot garden) have been lovingly rehabilitated into a neighborhood of outstanding charm. But densities are high. For each gross acre (including streets) there are about 13 houses, and, on the average, they provide a total of 65 units. The number of people per unit averages between 3 and 3½ people, giving an over-all density of about 200 people per gross acre. On the basis of land-use efficiency, let alone amenity, this beats many a high rise collective.

Other attractive examples can be found in Washington, Chicago, San Francisco, and many other cities; areas that by orthodox planning standards should be hopelessly congested are among the most pleasant, and sought after, in the city. Too much should not be made of the correlation, but surely something is wrong with a planning policy which calls for density standards so out of whack with the marketplace.

The standards are the legacy of a utopian concept which was never originally intended for the city. It is the garden city ideal: difficult enough to achieve in suburbia, and wholly inapplicable to the city.

In some aspects the original model was more realistic in its specifications than the current standards. Ebenezer Howard's ideal garden city called for somewhere between 70–100 people per acre and this was to be out in the country. For rebuilding of our cities some planning standards call for densities not much greater—about 100 people per acre for ideal neighborhoods, rarely more than 150 people.

To do away with congestion, these plans would do away with concentration. But concentration is the genius of the city, its reason for being. What it needs is not less people, but more, and if this means more density we have no need to feel guilty about it. The ultimate justification for building to higher densities is not that it is more efficient in land costs, but that it can make a better city.

There are now prototypes to prove that this can be so. For years many people had been arguing that the conventional project design, with its towers and malls, ought to be abandoned. In its stead they proposed a flexible approach that would combine high rise and low buildings; such projects would fit existing neighborhoods, would provide economically high densities, and in the form of stepped terraces and enclosed gardens the kind of amenity—and privacy—not found in the lower density tower projects. There was nothing particularly new about the idea—it is essentially a modern adaptation of the residential square—but it was objected to as being too visionary. Even if it was desirable, some housing people said, it would not be possible to get such designs through the mills of the lending institutions and government agencies. But a few did get through the mill—the redevelopment of Washington's Southwest area, for example—and then came a few more. They worked. They were economic. People liked them. Lately even more imaginative approaches have been demonstrated—most notably the design of Montreal's Expo '67 Habitat. I would wager that they are going to work too.

Public housing people are testing new approaches. To the delight of locals, the New York City Housing Authority has commissioned a series of "vest pocket" projects under the Model Cities demonstration program, and it has picked some really good architects to design them. These projects will be small—some will take up only part of a block—and none will look quite like the others. The buildings will be low, mostly of four stories. The ground coverage will be higher than in the conventional tower projects, but though there will be proportionately less open space, it will be put to much more effective use. The open space will be enclosed by the buildings; instead of being dribbled on the streetside, it will be massed in the interior and all of it will be for people.

Because these projects are to so human a scale, some

people have surmised that the densities have necessarily been set too low to make them truly economic. This is not the case. Architect Norval White, who is coordinating the work of the various architects, believes that the *apparent* density will be low—as it is in Brooklyn Heights. But the actual density will be high, averaging around 300 people per acre.

Further out, densities will continue to be relatively low, and on the outer edge of suburbia fairly large lots will probably continue to be the rule for many years to come. Over-all, however, there is bound to be an increase in the number of people housed in a given area, and much of this increase will be concentrated in pockets of high-density housing.

So far, cluster has not been used to increase density, but the efficiency with which it can house more people per acre is so great that inevitably it is going to be used for that purpose. Developers already have this in mind, as local governments are only too aware; their density zoning ordinances, roughly translated, mean no more density. For the moment developers are not pushing too hard to up the allowable quota of houses; they are getting enough in return in construction savings to be content. But this happy coincidence of self-interests is too good to last much longer. The next big drive of the developers will be cluster *and* more houses, and if the population increase continues they are going to win.

Another rich source of suburban controversy will be apartments. Most suburbs do not want them, and at re-zoning hearings the opposition, often the best people in town, will offer statistical proof that apartment people breed too many children, get more out of community taxes than they pay, have little allegiance to the place, and are in general not the element one would want. But the apartments have been going up just the same. Too many people need apartments, and the pressures have been translated into land prices of compelling force. If a plot can be rezoned from one-family residential to garden apartments, the market price per acre vaults immediately, and if the change is to high rise, it can leap as much as $250,000 an acre. The possibility of this profit overspill will prompt other local citizens to argue that apartment people have to live somewhere; breed few children, move to houses when the children are school age, are above average in education and income, and are highly desirable in every respect.

But a zoning variance is almost always necessary. Despite the clear warning of the market place, most suburbs are not anticipating apartments; they have their zoning so set that no new apartments will ever get built without a zoning change. They are playing Canute. There will be changes, just as in the density in density zoning. All in all, suburban zoning boards are in for a rough time.

There are other ways to raise the carrying capacity of our urban land than having more people per acre. We can also increase the number of effective acres, and this can be done without pushing farther out into the country to find them. Within the metropolitan area there is a considerable amount of land that is not used at all, and an appalling amount that is used wastefully.

Parking space is the greatest wastage. Even with our present parking technology, backward as it is, we are allocating much more space for cars than is necessary. A study by the Urban Land Institute of a cross section of shopping centers indicates that from a purely economic point of view the best rule of thumb would be 5.5 spaces per 1000 feet of shopping space. Most shopping centers far exceed this average—an under-use of high-cost land that would be more functional for the environment if it were used for almost any other purpose, including plain grass.

Industry is profligate too. The trend to the one-story, horizontal plant has good reasons behind it. Aesthetically, the new plants are built to a considerably higher standard than most new subdivisions. But they, too, consume a great amount of space, and as with shopping centers more of it is given over to parking than to the primary activity. Industrial parks pool space more efficiently, and they require no more land for buffering or landscaping than one isolated plant. If industrial expansion continues, it would seem inevitable that land costs would induce more of this kind of concentration. But might there not also be something of a reversal in the trend to the horizontal? Within a decade we may be hearing of the revolutionary new concept of a vertical stacking of manufacturing space, with improved materials handling making it possible to have factories four and five stories high.*

Utility rights-of-way should be tightened up too. High tension lines are so unsightly our eye tends to blank them out, and few people realize what a considerable swath they cut through our urban land. This single purpose use of land is unnecessarily wasteful, and as I noted earlier, the rights-of-way can be put to good use as connective and recreational space.

Nor does so much land have to be taken. The most striking thing about a utility map of an area is the duplication of effort by different kinds of utilities. Oil pipelines, water conduits, and electric lines angle this way and that along separate rights-of-way, except, as in the central city, where they have been forced into joint routes. Why could they not be pooled? Several new high voltage transmission lines have been laid down over railroad tracks. The kind of right-of-way that has been greediest of space, the super highway, offers similar potentials. The New York Thruway Authority is now merchandising to utilities the idea of leasing space in a strip along its right-of-way. In Pennsylvania a "utilities corridor" bill has been intro-

---

* Another possibility is a high-rise shopping center. This would concentrate on one acre what now is spread over many. The goods and services would be grouped by category, stacked in floors one above the other, with vertical transportation systems tying in with mass transit lines underground. No cars or parking spaces would be necessary. The entire complex would be enclosed and kept at constant temperature and humidity. It could be termed a department store.

duced which encourages the same kind of pooling along any new highway.

Bridges can be made to do more duty. Instead of putting up massive towers for a new river crossing, utilities can put electric lines, even oil pipelines, on the underside of existing bridges. Most bridges are forbidden to such uses, but where they have been permitted the lines or pipelines have proved compatible. The bridge authority gets revenue it otherwise would not, the utility saves a great deal by not having to build the towers, and the public does not have to look at them.

Such efficiency, to repeat a point, makes for good aesthetics, and in some cases it is the aesthetic argument which has tipped the scales. But the most compelling factor is economic, and that is why with some optimism we can look forward to more of such measures for better land use.

Some kinds of under-use will not be so easily resolved. For planners, the most frustrating open spaces to contemplate are the cemeteries of the city. Together, they take up a large amount of space—in some areas, like Queens in New York—they form the bulk of the urban open space. Many a planner has toyed with the thought of all the good things that could be done with the land were there a relocation effort. Those who are wise have kept the idea to themselves. Title problems are immense, and the whole subject politically explosive.

Reservoir and watershed lands of private and municipal water companies are in many states restricted to any use except the gathering of rain. Pressure for recreational use has been mounting—particularly from sportsmen—and in time it would seem inevitable that these lands will be opened up to multiple use. The delaying action is strong, however, and in one respect it has been quite beneficial. The fact these lands have been unavailable as usable open space has made it easier to get public support for acquisition of other open space.

In the city, perhaps the most exciting potential for gaining extra space is the use of air rights. Railroads are old hands at leasing these out; the New York Central's Park Avenue operation, started in 1913, is still the prime example. For good and financial reasons, railroads have recently been doing a lot more to get their freight yards and tracks decked over with revenue-producing projects. Railroads in the Chicago area have been particularly active, and many of the most striking new buildings there have been going over tracks.

City-owned land has great capabilities too. In New York City, for example, subway freight yards, together with railroad yards, total some 9641 acres. These are probably the dreariest acres to look at in the city, and development over top of them could greatly improve the looks of the city as well as its finances. A few starts have been made. Two new public schools are being built over subway storage yards. Since school buildings are customarily low and flat roofed, in some cases it would make sense to go a step further and lease the air rights over the schools for yet another structure. In a project for one new high school in New York, part of the air rights are to be used for the construction of an apartment tower. The lease payments will pay a substantial portion of the interest on the school construction bonds.

City-owned reservoirs can be decked over too. Philadelphia is now considering the proposal of a developer to build a commercial and shopping complex over a city reservoir. The city's planners and engineers like the idea; in addition to the income, the structure would keep the sun off the water in summer and there would be much less loss through evaporation.

Expressways and streets are going to be exploited more vigorously. Back in 1961 Governor Nelson A. Rockefeller's Committee for Urban Middle Income Housing proposed a large scale program for housing one million persons in New York City in developments using air rights, many of them over streets. At the time, the proposal was deemed much too visionary, but now a number of specific projects along this line are being given serious consideration. One is a "Linear City" that would group schools, low- and middle-income housing, stores, and community facilities of private and public uses over a stretch of expressway.

There are problems, of course, in this kind of construction. An apartment project built several years ago atop the Manhattan approaches to the George Washington Bridge, for example, has run into difficulties because of the great amount of noise and air pollution the high concentration of cars beneath sends up. But the technical challenge is not too difficult. The real problem, as the New York *Times'* Ada Louise Huxtable has pointed out, is governmental. "In the city," she notes, "the municipal pipeline is jammed with simple projects unable to clear the hurdles of requests, reviews and multi-departmental jurisdiction. A proposal of the scope and size of Linear City must cut across all city departments and agencies. A design breakthrough is not enough. An administrative breakthrough is equally necessary."

But ways will be found. There is revenue pressure to find them. Highway departments are an example. Not so many years ago most would have recoiled at the thought of buildings over their rights-of-way. Now they have become very open minded about such projects and in some cases vigorously opportunistic. The New York State Thruway Authority has been circularizing developers with a brochure *Fashion Your Future Out of Thin Air* and lists the acreages in various urban areas that it thinks would be excellent for commercial development. (In response to a query from the City of Yonkers, it said it would make air rights available free of charge for municipal projects; if any federal money became available for municipal purchase of air rights, however, the authority said it would want to be paid.) The Massachusetts Turnpike Authority has leased air space in the Boston area for the construction of a supermarket and is promoting the development of other segments. By all indications, there is going to be a lot more of this kind of double development in all the states, and for all kinds of highways.*

Let me turn from the techniques of compression to the matter of whether or not it is justified. In bespeaking a more intensive use of the land I have been accepting the fact of growth. But is it inevitable? And is it good? A number of ecologists and conservationists think not. They are horrified by the spectre of a growing population devouring the resources we have left. Space is finite, and thus any rate of growth must at some time finally fill up that space. The Malthusians believe we are very close to that time. Unless nature or catastrophe intervenes, they hold, we must find a way to limit the growth ourselves.

They even see a danger in planning measures to make better use of the land. Only a palliative, they say. Writing in *Science* (July 1965) geographer George Macinko puts the case thus: "The operating assumption that a continuing demand for space can be met by ingenuity in allocation of space is untenable for a limited space subject to a continuing demand. Such space allocation is a delaying or rearguard action that slows down the ultimate confrontation. It does not 'solve the problem' and may in the long run have adverse effects. By appearing to be a solution, it temporarily hides one of the most pressing reasons for public concern—the fact that open land is in danger of becoming exceedingly short in supply."

Malthusians argue that planners can no longer make sensible plans unless they face up to the issue of population control, and as a minimum, demonstrate to the public the choices involved. They point out that in almost all of

* Toll road authorities have been in the forefront because they are exempt from many of the restrictions to regular highway projects and they are by nature quite promotion minded. But now the road is open for air rights development on the interstate highways. The Federal Aid Highway Act of 1961 authorized the use of air space above, and below, interstate highways for almost any purpose that would not conflict with the highway.

the alternative regional design plans growth is assumed; in the worst alternative presented, "unplanned growth," the bad word is "unplanned." Why not, critics ask, a "planned no-growth" alternative? The planners could say to people, look, we've shown you different ways we can handle a growing population; now we'd like to show you what a job we could do if the population doesn't grow, or if we find ways to deliberately restrict it. The Malthusians have little doubt that this would be the best of the alternatives.

I wonder. On the face of it, it would seem easier for land planners to cope with growth if there were not any, or, at least, much less. But there is a challenge and response equation involved. When growth pressures were less we wasted land and abused it. And were there respite we might be as bad as ever. We are, of course, still enormously wasteful, but we are beginning to feel guilty enough about it to try and mend our ways a bit. Events have forced us to, and it is quite doubtful if we would be now adopting better land-use measures except for the pressures of growth.

It is a shame so much land had to be sacrificed to force the recognition, but the blight seems a necessary stimulant (it is not by accident that so many of the new approaches have been tried first in California). We have to have our noses rubbed in it. Whether or not, as the Malthusians hope, the discipline leads us to the further step of population control, we are being goaded to a more effective use of space, now, and the process is hardly a palliative.

It is a necessity. Perhaps, in time, people will have far fewer babies than they are having now. They have been cutting down the rate, certainly, and if they continue to our estimates for year 2000 may be well over the mark. For the years immediately ahead, however, we are bound to have a bigger population, and on the basis of the future parents already born, for at least the next twenty years we are going to have to house a lot more people than we have now. This means higher densities and we should do the best job we can to cope with the fact.

21. The Last Landscape

>>

In putting the case for higher density, there is one argument I have not made: that by putting more people on developed land, more land will be left undeveloped, i.e., that we can have more people *and* more open space. It is a tempting proposition, and in theory it could be true. In practice the prospect seems quite unlikely. Let me be consistent: If we are to seek a much more intensive and efficient use of land for development, we should apply an equally rigorous standard to open space.

We are going to have to. Even if the drop in the birth rate continues, we are going to have more people and less space. Vigorous open space programs will help keep a balance, but the pressures for urban land are so intense that it is difficult to foresee how there is going to be more open space in metropolitan areas than there is now. In absolute terms, there is going to be less; in relative terms of space per person, far less.

This may seem a negative way to start off a summary

of the prospects for open space. But these pressures need not mean a poorer environment. True, we might have a better one if we could also save huge swaths and green belts, but until someone shows a practical way to do this we should concentrate on saving land that can be saved now, and this calls for increasing attention to the smaller spaces.

There is a danger in bespeaking the case for the small spaces, for it can be easily misused by people who would be only too happy to have open spaces small and nothing more. Let it be said again, therefore, that if we have to err in our acquisition programs, let it be toward more open space. I criticize the grandiose plans not because they will gain too much open space, but that by being unrealistic they will in the end gain too little.

A good cause does not exempt us from competitive pressures. The dominant trend is toward more intensive land use, and this, not the machinations of speculators, is why land prices are so high. These prices make acquisition tougher, but they are also a discipline; just as they have forced developers toward a more efficient use of their tracts, so should they force planners to get much more out of each acre of open space. Each square foot, indeed.

We must make every piece of space do double and triple duty, and we have all the tools and precedents we need. With ingenuity, we can make the smaller spaces seem larger; we can find ways to link them and to emphasize their continuities; we can make them far more accessible to people, and if not to the foot, at least to the eye. It is the *effect* of open space we are seeking, not just the space, and with this approach a given acreage of open spaces can be knit into a pattern more pleasing, more useful, and seemingly more expansive than a far greater acreage laid out in conventional fashion.

It could be said that my emphasis is on the microenvironment. This scale is all very well for local and neighborhood planning, some might hold, but it is the macroenvironment that should get the emphasis, for it is in these big-picture terms—the structuring of the region—that open space fulfills its highest function.

But can open space restructure the metropolis? More to the point, can planners restructure the metropolis? Those who are now assuming the burden of regional design see structure as the great new challenge and open space as a major tool; by interdicting growth in the wrong places, open space will help channel it to the right places and thereby give form and structure to the region.

I think they expect much too much. Open space can help people perceive the structure; open space cannot reshape it, and it is difficult to understand why planners are fretting so much over the matter anyway. The structure is already set. The topography and the transportation lines are what give structure to the region, and they were laid down a long time ago. They can be modified, expanded, intensified. Except in very exceptional circumstances, however, they cannot really be changed.

Most of the growth in the last fifty years has been a fleshing out of a pattern. The first wave of suburban expansion was channeled along the rail lines—the main line of the Pennsylvania westward of Philadelphia, the New York Central north to Westchester County, the Southern Pacific down the peninsula from San Francisco. Once established, these trends have shown a remarkable persistence, even to the degree of fashionableness of particular tangents. It is also surprising to note on old maps how early suburbia pushed to its present limits (and on old timetables, how little improvement in travel time has occurred since). With the coming of the trolley lines and the automobile there was a gradual filling in of the spaces between the rail corridors. It is still taking place, and it is in these areas that most of the remaining open space opportunities lie.

The postwar highway building program did not change the basic pattern. Circumferential thruways, such as Boston's Route 128, have established new lines of forces within the pattern, and new thruways and rapid transit extensions have accelerated growth of particular areas.

Transportation planners, however, are a conservative lot, and in most cases new rights-of-way are set down to service trends already apparent; indeed, the standard cost-benefit formulas for choosing routes virtually insure it. Transportation follows transportation.

New mass transit systems are not likely to change the pattern either. Since a good bit of government money will be going into them, it is conceivable that an effort will be made to have some mass transit projects deliberately cut against the grain and establish entirely new development corridors. It would take a whale of a subsidy, however; mass transit systems have to carry lots of people, and these are to be found where the railroads and highways have taken them. The Bay Area transit system for San Francisco is a bold effort to curb sprawl by outcompeting the car; it is notable that to do this the rights-of-way are being tied to the high-density centers more or less paralleling the spine of the highway network. Such transit systems will not reshape the structure; they will strengthen it.

So it should be with open-space action. The best way to enhance the structure of the future metropolis is to save open space now for what it will do now. Later there may be new and unforeseen uses for the land, but we cannot put it in escrow and set aside open-space reserves, the function of which can be decided later. We could never hold land very long this way against competing commercial uses, or competing "good" uses, like hospitals, or government installations. To repeat, use it, or lose it.

The use does not have to be recreation, though this is of first importance. In a few cases intensity of use will be low, as with a nature sanctuary. But in almost all cases there should be maximum visual use.

Linkage is the key. Most of the big tracts in our metropolitan areas have already been saved, or they have already been lost. The most pressing need now is to weave together a host of seemingly disparate elements—an experimental farm, a private golf course, a local park, the spaces of a cluster subdivision, the edge of a new freeway right-of-way. If these elements can be linked, each will gain a much greater access, and the sum can make a very effective whole.

The most important elements for linkage already exist. Nature has laid down a regional design of streams and valleys that provide superb natural connectors, and into the very heart of the urban area. Here the priorities are self-evident. Where streamside land has not been secured against development, it should be; where the continuity has been broken, the pieces should be reclaimed wherever it is at all possible.

Next, we should look for the man-made links. We should reclaim abandoned rights-of-way of railroads, unused aqueducts, the wastelands underneath the high tension lines of utility rights-of-way. We should do more to exploit the potential of all kinds of derelict lands—empty lots, the leftovers from public works projects, dumps, sand and gravel pits, and sanitary land fills.

These bits and pieces cannot always be joined into a unified network; some will remain bits and pieces, and they need not be scorned for this. But the more that are secured now, the more opportunity there will be for joining them by filling in the links. These open spaces will cost money: in many cases a great deal of money, but in terms of benefits their costs may be very reasonable.

We should seek the maximum effect from the edges of the open spaces. One great advantage of a linear open-space network is that it has far more perimeter than the same acreage in one large tract. It is the perimeter that people see most often and use most intensively. Laid out well, a relatively narrow strip can create more of a feeling of open space.

The visual aspect of open space is probably the most important, yet most open-space planning is done with too little thought as to how people will see it—people on the ground, or in cars. For this reason open-space acquisition and regional planning need to be tied together with a landscape approach. If we are going to have regional design, let us at least follow good design principles. The design that counts is not the macro-view of the land-use maps. This is for planners. Most people do not see the region that way. Planners should look at the region as people see it, walking and driving. From this perspective, scale becomes much more subtle. Spaces that seem insignificant on the map can be large in the experience of people; by the same token, some of the big spaces on the map may in reality be insignificant for the simple reason that few people ever get to use them or see them.

I put such emphasis on the aesthetics of open space because I believe that of all the benefits this is the most compelling one for people. Usually, it is put farther down the list, and most open-space programs have been justified by their supporters primarily on the tangible benefits of recreation and resource conservation. I think the aesthetics were the main motivating force. It is not how people think about open space so much as how they feel about it that makes them give their support.

For years conservationists have been trying to arouse the public over the destruction of our coastal wetlands. They have stressed the ecological arguments—the importance of wetlands as breeding grounds for fish and shellfish; as wildlife habitats, as regulators of water flow, and so on. Now, at last, the public is voting through programs to save the wetlands. I doubt, however, that it is the ecological arguments that have tipped the scales. The coastal wetlands happen to be one of the principal elements in the scenery of our shore, and there has been enough diking and filling and commercialization to make people realize how much poorer their communities will look if the destruction continues.

We should push the aesthetic case much more forcibly and explicitly than we have been. There has been enough of a shift in public attitudes to warrant the frankness, and the new stress may well mean the critical margin of support in the years ahead. Conservationists have been exercised over man's inhumanity to nature, and thanks be they have been. But people of the urban region are more concerned with the "man" part of the equation; specifically, what's in it for him? Plenty, of course; but the most elemental appeal is the aesthetic, and we should make the most of it.

Thus to my final point. Let's be on with the job as though there were little time left; let's address ourselves to the needs that are pressing, use the tools we have now, and not worry so much over what will be right for A.D. 2000. The coming of the next millennium is still over thirty years away, and while the current attempt to project this future makes for an interesting intellectual exercise, it is also something of an effort to write history ahead of time, and it can be truly diverting.

I have heard some people earnestly debate whether it is right to choose open spaces and plan a landscape on the basis of current tastes. May we not, they ask, be imposing on future generations the values of today—even worse, the *middle class* values of today? Some fear that too much action too soon may freeze us into an obsolescent pattern, and on the very brink of an explosive new era.

It is still not a bad idea to plan with the values we have now. Maybe the new ones will be different, but we don't know what the new ones will be. And do aesthetic values change so very much? There have been many fashions in landscape; the formal Italian school, for example, and the English "natural" approach. But while each was rooted in a particular period and clientele, the best examples are eminently pleasing today. Some styles do date—the more pompous expressions of the City Beautiful movement are an example—but it does seem that if something is really well done for a particular time and place, it tends to remain functional for a long, long time to come.

Vigorous action now will not preclude future choice; it will give more choice. We don't have to divine the future adaptation; if we do a first rate job with the landscape of today, the pattern of spaces will be functional for several generations to come. The people of the year 2000 can take it from there.

So let's be on with it. Over these past years a great tide of public support for open space and natural beauty has been building up, and now it is at flood. How much longer can we count on it? If ever there was a time to press for precipitate, hasty, premature action, this is it.

Our options are expiring. As far as open space is concerned, it doesn't make a great deal of difference when the projected new population reaches target or whether it is going to be housed in green-belted megastructures or linear cities or what. The land that is still to be saved will have to be saved in the next few years. We have no luxury of choice. We must make our commitments now and look to this landscape as the last one. For us, it will be.

Bibliography

CHAPTER 1

CHARLES ABRAMS, *The City is the Frontier*. (New York: Harper & Row, 1965).

Beauty for America, Proceedings of the White House Conference on Natural Beauty. (Washington: U. S. Government Printing Office, 1965).

HANS BLUMENFELD, "The Modern Metropolis." *Scientific American*, September 1965 (published in paperback; New York: Alfred A. Knopf, 1966).

F. FRASER DARLING and JOHN P. MILTON (ed.), *Future Environments of North America*. (Garden City, N.Y.: The Natural History Press, 1966).

H. WENTWORTH ELDREDGE (ed.), *Taming Megalopolis*, 2 vols. (Garden City, N.Y.: Doubleday Anchor Books, 1967).

WILLIAM R. EWALD, JR. (ed.), *Environment for Man—The Next Fifty Years*. First of three volumes sponsored by American Institute of Planners. (Bloomington: Indiana University Press, 1966).

The Editors of *Fortune, The Exploding Metropolis*. (New York: Doubleday Anchor Books, 1958).

JEAN GOTTMANN, *Megalopolis: The Urbanized Northeastern Seaboard of the United States*. (New York: Twentieth Century Fund, 1961).

—— and ROBERT A. HARPER (eds.), *Metropolis on the Move: Geographers Look at Urban Sprawl*. (New York: John Wiley & Sons, 1967).

JANE JACOBS, *The Death and Life of Great American Cities*. (New York: Random House, 1961).

LEWIS MUMFORD, *The City in History*. (New York: Harcourt, Brace and World, 1961).

Outdoor Recreation Resources Review Commission, *Outdoor Recreation for America*. (Washington: U. S. Government Printing Office, 1962).

Regional Plan Association, *Spread City*. (New York, 1962).

JOHN W. REPS, *The Making of Urban America: A History of City Planning in the United States*. (Princeton: Princeton University Press, 1965).

CHRISTOPHER TUNNARD and BORIS PUSHKAREV, *Man Made America: Chaos or Control*. (New Haven: Yale University Press, 1963).

STEWART L. UDALL, *The Quiet Crisis*. (New York: Holt, Rinehart & Winston, 1965).

RAYMOND VERNON, *The Myth and Reality of Our Urban Problems*. (Cambridge: Harvard University Press, 1962).

WILLIAM H. WHYTE, *Open Space Action*. Study Report 15: Outdoor Recreation Resources Review Commission. (Washington: Government Printing Office, 1962).

LOWDON WINGO, JR. (ed.), *Cities and Space: The Future Use of Urban Land*. (Baltimore: Johns Hopkins Press for Resources for the Future, 1963).

CHAPTER 2

Advisory Commission on Intergovernmental Relations. *The Role of the States in Strengthening the Property Tax*, 2 vols. (Washington: U. S. Government Printing Office, 1963).

MARION CLAWSON, "Suburban Development Districts." (*Journal of the American Institute of Planners*, May, 1960).

Metropolitan Communities: A Bibliography Supplement 1958–1964. Compiled by Barbara Hudson and Robert H. McDonald. (Chicago: Public Administration Service, 1967).

ANN LOUISE STRONG. "Factors Affecting Land Tenure in the Urban Fringe." (*Urban Land*, November, 1966).

WILLIAM L. C. WHEATON, "Form and Structure of the Metropolitan Area," in *Environment for Man—The Next Fifty Years*, William R. Ewald, Jr. (ed.). (Bloomington: University of Indiana Press, 1967).

SAMUEL E. WOOD and ALFRED E. HELLER. *California, Going, Going . . .* (Sacramento: California Tomorrow, 1962).

CHAPTER 3

RICHARD F. BABCOCK, *The Zoning Game.* (Madison: University of Wisconsin Press, 1966).

Berman v. Parker, 73 Sup. Ct. 98 (1954).

MARION CLAWSON, "Why Not Sell Zoning and Rezoning? (Legally, that is)" (*Cry California,* Winter 1966–67).

CHARLES HAAR, (ed.), *Law and Land; Anglo-American Planning Practice.* (Cambridge: Harvard University Press, 1964).

Regional Plan Association, *The Race for Open Space: Final Report of the Park, Recreation and Open Space Project.* (New York, 1960).

JOHN W. REPS, "Requiem for Zoning." *Planning 1964.* (Chicago: American Society of Planning Officials, 1964).

ANN LOUISE STRONG, *Open Space for Urban America.* Prepared for Department of Housing and Urban Development. (Washington: U. S. Government Printing Office, 1965).

NORMAN WILLIAMS, JR., *The Structure of Urban Zoning.* (New York: Buttenheim, 1966).

CHAPTER 4

RUSSELL L. BRENNEMAN, *Private Approaches to the Preservation of Open Land.* (Waterford: Conservation and Research Foundation, 1966).

ARTHUR A. DAVIS, "The Uses and Values of Open Space." *A Place to Live: The Yearbook of Agriculture 1963.* (Washington: U. S. Government Printing Office, 1963).

Bureau of Outdoor Recreation, *Recreation Land Price Escalation.* (Washington, 1967).

National Park Service, *Report of the Land Acquisition Policy Task Force.* (Washington, 1965).

Open Space Action Committee, *Stewardship.* (New York, 1965).

SHIRLEY ADELSON SIEGEL, *The Law of Open Space:* legal aspects of acquiring or otherwise preserving open space in the tri-state New York Metropolitan Region. (New York: Regional Plan Association, 1960).

WILLIAM H. WHYTE, *Connecticut's Natural Resources: A Proposal for Action.* (Hartford: Department of Agriculture and Natural Resources, 1962).

NORMAN WILLIAMS, JR., *Land Acquisition for Outdoor Recreation—analysis of selected legal problems*. Study Report 16, Outdoor Recreation Resources Review Commission. (Washington: U. S. Government Printing Office, 1962).

CHAPTER 5

Department of Transportation of Wisconsin, *A Market Study of Properties Covered by Scenic Easements along the Great River Road in Vernon and Pierce Counties*. Special Report No. 5. (Madison, October, 1967).

ALLISON DUNHAM, *Preservation of Open Space Areas: A Study of the Nongovernmental Role*. (Chicago: Welfare Council of Metropolitan Chicago, 1966).

HAROLD C. JORDAHL, JR., "Conservation and Scenic Easements," *Land Economics*. (November, 1963).

JAN KRASNOWIECKI and ANN LOUISE STRONG, "Compensable Regulations: A Means of Controlling Urban Growth Through the Retention of Open Space," *Journal of The American Institute of Planners*. (Washington, May, 1963).

Scenic Easements in Action: Proceedings of Conference December 16–17, 1966. (Madison: University of Wisconsin Law School, 1967).

WILLIAM H. WHYTE, "Open Space and Retroactive Planning," in *Planning 1958*. (Chicago: American Society of Planning Officials, 1958).

—— *Conservation Easements*. (Washington: Urban Land Institute, 1959).

—— "Plan to Save The Vanishing Countryside," *Life*. (August 17, 1959).

HOWARD L. WILLIAMS and W. D. DAVIS, "Effect of Scenic Easements on the Market Value of Real Property," *Appraisal Journal*. (January, 1968).

CHAPTER 6

Council of State Governments, *Farmland Assessment Practices in the United States*. (Chicago, 1966).

PETER W. HOUSE, "Preferential Assessment of Farmland in the Rural-Urban Fringe of Maryland." (Washington: Economic Research Service, U. S. Department of Agriculture, 1961).

JAMES PICKFORD and JOHN SHANNON, "Metropolitan Zoning and Tax Equalization Reforms; Cushioning the Impact of the Divisive and Regressive Property Tax," *Planning Research 1966*. (Washington: American Institute of Planners, 1966).

WILLIAM H. WHYTE, "Tax Techniques on Open Space," *Timber Tax Journal*, Vol. IV, 1967.

ELLIS T. WILLIAMS, *Forest Taxation and the Preservation of Rural Values*. (Washington: Forest Service, U. S. Department of Agriculture, 1967).

CHAPTER 7

American Bar Association, *Junkyards, Geraniums and Jurisprudence: Aesthetics and the Law*. Proceedings of a two day National Institute, June 2–3, 1967, Chicago, Illinois.

LOIS FORER, "Preservation of America's Parklands: The Inadequacy of Existing Law," *New York University Law Review*. (December, 1966).

ROGER TIPPY, "Review of Route Selections for Federal Aid Highway Systems." *University of Montana Law Review*. (Spring, 1966).

SAMUEL E. WOOD and DARYL LEMBKE, *The Federal Threats to the California Landscape*. (Sacramento: California Tomorrow, 1967).

CHAPTER 8

Association of Bay Area Governments, *Preliminary Regional Plan for the San Francisco Bay Region*. (Berkeley, 1966).

Baltimore Regional Planning Council and Maryland State Planning Department, *Metrotowns for the Baltimore Region*. (Baltimore, 1962). *Futures for the Baltimore Region: Alternative Plans and Projection*. (Baltimore, 1965).

Capital Region Planning Agency, *Regional Plan Alternatives*. (Hartford, Connecticut, 1961).

Connecticut Interregional Planning Program, *Connecticut: Choices for Action*. (Hartford, 1967).

CHARLES W. ELIOT, *Land Planning Considerations in the Wash-*

ington Metropolitan Area. Staff study for U. S. Congress. Joint Committee on Washington Metropolitan Problems, 1958.

JACK LESSINGER, "The Case for Scatteration: Some Reflections on the National Capital Region Plan for the Year 2000," *Journal of the American Institute of Planners.* (August, 1962).

Maryland-National Capital Park and Planning Commission. *On Wedges and Corridors: A General Plan for the Maryland-Washington Regional District.* (Silver Spring, Maryland, 1962).

MARTIN MEYERSON, "The Utopian Tradition and the Planning of Cities," *Daedalus.* (Winter, 1960).

National Capital Planning Commission, National Capital Regional Planning Council, *A Policies Plan for the Year 2000.* (Washington, 1961).

Regional Plan Association, *The Region's Growth: A Report of the Second Regional Plan.* (New York, 1967).

JOHN H. RUBEL, "The Aerospace Project Approach Applied to Building New Cities," *Taming Megalopolis,* Vol. II, H. Wentworth Eldredge (ed.). (Garden City: Doubleday Anchor Books, 1967).

"Toward the Year 2000: Work in Progress," *Daedalus.* (Summer, 1967: single subject issue).

CHAPTER 9

J. T. COPPOCK and HUGH C. PRINCE (ed.), *Greater London.* (London: Faber & Faber, 1964).

DONALD FOLEY, *Controlling London's Growth: Planning the Great Wen 1940–1960.* (Berkeley: University of California Press, 1963).

BRANDON HOWELL, "Review of the South East Study," *Town and Country Planning.* (April 1966).

DANIEL R. MANDELKER, *Green Belts and Urban Growth: English Town and Country Planning in Action.* (Madison: University of Wisconsin Press, 1962).

Ministry of Housing and Local Government. *The Green Belts.* (London: H. M. Stationery Office, 1962).

——, *The South East Study 1961–1981.* (London: H. M. Stationery Office, 1964).

GERALD SMART, "Green Belts—Is the Concept out of Date?" *Town and Country Planning*. (October, 1965).

CHAPTER 10

Civic Trust. *A Lea Valley Regional Park*. (London, 1964).
The Hudson: the Report of the Hudson River Valley Commission 1966. (New York, 1966).
Regional Plan Association, *The Lower Hudson*. (New York, 1966).

CHAPTER 11

The Conservation Foundation, *Three Approaches to Environmental Resource Analysis*. Study of the methods developed by G. Angus Hills, Philip H. Lewis, Jr., and Ian L. McHarg. (Washington, 1967).
PHILIP H. LEWIS, JR., "Quality Corridors in Wisconsin." *Landscape Architecture*. (January, 1964).
A Comprehensive Highway Route Selection Method: Applied to I-95 between the Delaware and Raritan Rivers, New Jersey. Prepared by Wallace, McHarg, Roberts, and Todd. 1966.
IAN L. MCHARG, "Where Should Highways Go?" *Landscape Architecture*. (April, 1967).
—— and DAVID A. WALLACE, "Plan for the Valleys *vs.* Spectre of Uncontrolled Growth," *Landscape Architecture*. (April, 1965).

CHAPTER 12

Federal Housing Administration, *Planned Unit Development with a Homes Association*. (Washington: U. S. Government Printing Office, 1963. Revised 1964).
ANTHONY N. B. GARVAN, *Architecture and Town Planning in Colonial Connecticut*. (New Haven: Yale University Press, 1951).
JAN KRASNOWIECKI, *Legal Aspects of Planned Unit Development*. (Washington: Urban Land Institute, 1965).

CARL NORCROSS, *Open Space Communities in the Marketplace.* (Washington: Urban Land Institute, 1966).

SUMNER CHILTON POWELL, *Puritan Village.* (Middletown, Connecticut: Wesleyan University Press, 1963).

Urban Land Institute, *Homes Association Handbook.* (Study directed by Byron R. Hanke, Washington, 1964. Revised 1966).

WILLIAM H. WHYTE, *Cluster Development.* (New York: American Conservation Association, 1964).

CHAPTER 13

EBENEZER HOWARD, *Garden Cities of Tomorrow.* New edition edited by F. J. Osborn with introductory essay by Lewis Mumford. (London: Faber & Faber, 1946).

MARSHALL KAPLAN, "The Roles of the Planner and Developer in the New Community," *Washington University Law Quarterly.* (February, 1965).

—— and EDWARD EICHLER, *The Community Builder.* (Berkeley: University of California Press, 1966).

HOWARD ORLANS, *Utopia Ltd.: The Story of the English New Town of Stevenage.* (New Haven: Yale University Press, 1953).

FREDERIC J. OSBORN, *Greenbelt Cities.* (London: Faber & Faber, 1946).

——, "Housing: Shortage and Standards," *Town and Country Planning.* (April, 1965).

—— and ARNOLD WHITTICK, *The New Towns.* (New York: McGraw-Hill, 1963).

HARVEY S. PERLOFF, "New Town in Town," *Journal of the American Institute of Planners.* (May, 1966).

GOREN SIDENBLAH, "Stockholm: A Planned City," *Scientific American.* (September, 1965).

CLARENCE S. STEIN, *Toward New Towns for America.* (New York: Reinhold, 1957).

ROBERT J. WEAVER, *Dilemmas of Urban America.* (Cambridge: Harvard University Press, 1965).

CHAPTER 14

NORMA EVENSON, *Chandigarh.* (Berkeley: University of California Press, 1966).

DAVID R. GODSCHALK, "Comparative New Community Design," *Journal of the American Institute of Planners.* (November, 1967).

MORTON HOPPENFELD, "A Sketch of the Planning-Building Process for Columbia, Maryland," *Journal of the American Institute of Planners.* (November, 1967).

ROBERT D. KATZ, *Design of the Housing Site—A Critique of American Practice.* (Urbana: University of Illinois, 1966).

DONALD J. OLSEN, *Town Planning in London—the Eighteenth and Nineteenth Centuries.* (New Haven: Yale University Press, 1964).

JOHN SUMMERSON, *Georgian London.* (Baltimore: Penguin Books, 1962).

——, *Heavenly Mansions and other Essays on Architecture.* (New York: W. W. Norton & Co., 1963).

ANTHONY WALMSEY, "Islamabad: Planning the Landscape of Pakistan's Capital," *Landscape Architecture.* (October, 1965).

CHAPTER 16

DONALD APPLEYARD, KEVIN LYNCH, and JOHN R. MYER, *The View from the Road.* (Cambridge: M.I.T. Press, 1964).

PETER BLAKE, *God's Own Junkyard: the planned deterioration of America's landscape.* (New York: Holt, Rinehart & Winston, 1963).

Center for Resource Studies, *The Maine Coast: Prospect and Perspective.* (Brunswick, Maine: Bowdoin College, 1967).

SYLVIA CROWE, *Tomorrow's Landscape.* (London: Architectural Press, 1956).

GYORGY KEPES, *The Education of Vision.* (New York: George Braziller, 1965).

DAVID LOWENTHAL, "The American Scene," *Geographical Review.* (January, 1968).

KEVIN LYNCH, *The Image of the City.* (Cambridge: M.I.T. Press, 1960).

IAN NAIRN, *The American Landscape: A Critical View.* (New York: Random House, 1965).

Citizens' Advisory Committee on Recreation and Natural Beauty, *Community Action for Natural Beauty.* (Washington: U. S. Government Printing Office, 1968).

JOHN ORMSBY SIMONDS, *Landscape Architecture, the Shaping of*

Man's Natural Environment. (New York: F. W. Dodge Corp., 1961).

DOROTHY STROUD, *Capability Brown.* (London: Country Life Press, 1950).

————, *Humphry Repton.* (London: Country Life Press, 1962).

SAMUEL E. WOOD and ALFRED HELLER, *California, Going, Going . . .* (Sacramento: California Tomorrow, 1962).

CHAPTER 17

Assembly Interim Committee on Natural Resources, Planning, and Public Works, Edwin L. Z'berg, Chairman, *Highway and Freeway Planning.* (Sacramento: California Assembly, 1965).

SYLVIA CROWE, *The Landscape of Roads.* (London: Architectural Press, 1960).

PAUL DAVIDSON, JOHN TOMER, and ALLEN WALDMAN, *The Economic Benefits Accruing from the Scenic Enhancement of Highways.* (New Brunswick: Bureau of Economic Research, Rutgers University, 1967).

LAWRENCE HALPRIN, *Freeways.* (New York: Reinhold, 1966).

Highway Design and Operational Practices Related to Highway Safety. (Washington: American Association of State Highway Officials, 1967).

California Transportation Agency, *The Scenic Route: A Guide for the Designation of an Official Scenic Highway.* (Sacramento, 1964).

U. S. Department of Commerce, *A Proposed Program for Scenic Roads and Parkways.* (Washington: U. S. Government Printing Office, 1966).

CHAPTER 18

Grady Clay, "The Woodland Scene: Time for Another Look," *Landscape Architecture.* (October, 1965).

CRAIG JOHNSON, *Practical Operating Procedures for Progressive Rehabilitation of Sand and Gravel Sites.* (Silver Spring, Maryland: National Sand and Gravel Association, 1966).

Landscape Reclamation issue, *Landscape Architecture.* (January, 1966).

Central Planning Office of Vermont, *Vermont Scenery Preservation.* (Montpelier, 1966).

CHAPTER 19

EDMUND N. BACON, *Design of Cities.* (New York: Viking Press, 1967).

California Roadside Council, *More Attractive Communities for California.* (San Francisco, 1961).

Catalog of Federal Programs for Individual and Community Improvement. (Washington: Office of Economic Opportunity, 1967).

GORDON CULLEN, *Townscape.* (New York: Reinhold, 1961).

GARRETT ECKBO, *Urban Landscape Design.* (New York: McGraw-Hill, 1964).

HENRY FAGIN and ROBERT WEINBERG (ed.), *Planning and Community Appearance.* (New York: Regional Plan Association, 1958).

VICTOR GRUEN, *The Heart of Our Cities—The Urban Crisis; Diagnosis and Cure.* (New York: Simon and Schuster, 1964).

MARTIN MEYERSON, with JAQUELINE TYRWHITT, BRIAN FALK, PATRICIA SEKLER, *Face of the Metropolis.* (New York: Random House, 1963).

ROBERT L. MORRIS and S. B. ZISMAN, "The Pedestrian, Downtown, and the Planner," *Journal of the American Institute of Planners.* (August, 1962).

The Threatened City: A Report on the Design of the City of New York by the Mayor's Task Force. (New York, 1966).

The Lower Manhattan Plan. Prepared for the New York City Planning Commission, 1966, by Wallace, McHarg, Roberts and Todd; Whittlesey, Conklin and Rossant.

CHAPTER 20

MICHAEL M. BERNARD, *Airspace in Urban Development.* (Washington: Urban Land Institute, 1963).

THEO CROSBY, *Architecture: City Sense.* (New York: Reinhold, 1965).

PETER HALL, *The World Cities.* (New York: McGraw-Hill, 1966).

LESTER E. KLIMM, "The Empty Areas of the Northeastern U.S.," *Geographical Review,* Vol. XLIV, 1954.

DANA E. LOW, "Air Rights and Urban Expressways," *The Traffic Quarterly.* (October, 1966).

A *Report of the Interdepartmental Task Force on the Delaware Expressway in Philadelphia, Pennsylvania.* (Philadelphia, 1967).

FAIRFIELD OSBORN (ed.), *Our Crowded Planet.* (Garden City, N.Y.: Doubleday, 1962).

Research Group papers on Population Densities in Human Settlements. *Ekistics,* Vol. 22, Number 133. (December, 1966).

ARTHUR T. ROW, *A Reconnaissance of the Tri-State Area.* (New York: New York-New Jersey-Connecticut Tri-State Transportation Committee, 1965).

Parking Requirements for Shopping Centers. (Washington: Urban Land Institute, 1965).

Index